THE GENERATION GAME

DAVID McWILLIAMS

Gill & Macmillan

For Sian

Gill & Macmillan Ltd
Hume Avenue, Park West, Dublin 12
with associated companies throughout the world
www.gillmacmillan.ie

© David McWilliams 2007
978 07171 4224 8

Index compiled by Cover to Cover
Typography design by Make Communication
Print origination by TypeIT, Dublin
Printed and bound in Great Britain by MPG Books Ltd,
Bodmin, Cornwall

This book is typeset in 12pt Minion on 14.5pt.

The paper used in this book comes from the wood pulp
of managed forests. For every tree felled, at least one
tree is planted, thereby renewing natural resources.

A CIP catalogue record for this book is available from
the British Library.

5 4 3 2 1

CONTENTS

ACKNOWLEDGMENTS

I'd like to acknowledge the efforts of my wonderful researchers, Grainne Faller, Eoin Cunningham, Saibh Hooper and Rachel Fahey. They contributed enormously and invaluably to this book. Not only did each bring his/her own unique insights to the analysis, but most importantly, they kept their sense of humour, even when the situation looked desperate.

I am also indebted to Naomi Walker, Pinchas Landau, Amos Rubin, Professor Kevin O'Rourke, Professor Cormac Ó Gráda, John Kelly, Edgar Morgenroth, the Dublin Airport Authority and the gardaí in Dublin Airport, Kevin Kelly, Pat O'Sullivan, Tim O'Connor, Hugh McCutcheon, Clare Ridge, Russell Jones, Kevin Costello, Sean Melly, Gerard O'Neill, Bernard Berger, *Daft.ie*, Patricia Fitzsimons, the Central Statistics Office, Damien Kiberd and Professor Declan Kiberd.

Thanks also to the editors of the *Sunday Business Post*, Cliff Taylor, and of the *Irish Independent*, Gerry O'Regan, for giving me the time off to write the book.

A huge debt goes to Alison Walsh, my editor, who grabbed the book by the scruff of the neck at the eleventh hour. She worked and re-worked the script until it made sense, taking out large chunks of waffle and dropping in brilliant last-minute suggestions. Fergal Tobin and Deirdre Rennison Kunz at Gill & Macmillan also deserve special mention.

As always, Sian is the person that helped most. This book is hers as much as mine. She stayed up late to read every word, query every concept and check every assertion. She was with me when the book was conceived in New York in November 2006 and she was there, checking the final line, when it went to print in August 2007. Without Sian, this book would not have happened.

Croatia, August 2007

PART 1

Falling Down

| TRANSIT NATION 1

Check-in, Dublin Airport, 6.50 a.m.

Tatiana, a Russian from Latvia, has not been into Dublin city yet, although she has worked at the airport for four months. She secured this Bagel Factory job before she had left the airport on her first day in Ireland. She arrived with her cv ready and resolved not to step out of the terminal without a wage. Tatiana worked her first shift after two hours in Ireland, borrowing someone's uniform and stashing her suitcases under the counter. She hasn't stopped working since. Her flat, which she shares with her cousins in Swords, is next door to the Central Statistics Office—the only official people who know she exists. She has been home to Riga twice for one-day visits but has never been to Henry Street. Given that there are five low-cost flights a day from Dublin to the Baltics, it is less hassle and cheaper to go to Latvia than Leixlip.

Twenty yards away, four English forty-something men with shaved heads, wearing outsized combats and teenage trainers, struggle to get their Big Berthas onto the excess-baggage carousel. They're frisking themselves to find their ticket-less stubs which verify that they're on the flight. The lads are chirpy in a still-drunk type of way, heading home following a second-time-round stag weekend in Dublin. The Slovak check-in girl with bad teeth who sleeps four to a box-room in Hazelhatch is in no mood for their jaded *double entendres*.

The recycled air reeks of that sickly combination of Shake 'n' Vac, Alpine air freshener and human flatulence. The shaved heads snigger childishly. Three Polish immigrants in bottle-green double-breasted suits, the type favoured by one-hit wonders and Fianna Fáil councillors in the 1980s, queue in an orderly fashion. They're going home with the month's takings to put a deposit on a house. The Poles still dress up to travel, the way we did twenty years ago.

Beside our gaseous fortysomethings, just beyond the ambitious Slavs, a group of peroxide-haired Geordie hen-night lassies sing Shakira numbers as they display their varicose corned-beef legs. At half-seven in the morning this shows a refreshing, if rather scary, self-confidence. Their 'Kiss Me Quick, I'm Irish' leprechaun hats fail to hide the swollen love-bites.

The big Romanian touts for work at the Kiwi buff-stop shoeshine. Business in Dublin is quiet—the Irish haven't been rich for long enough to indulge in such public displays of master and servant. That'll take decades. Attitudes to shoe-shine services reveal something of the psychology of a country. People who unselfconsciously use shoe-shine boys in public—particularly in foreign airports—tend to come from countries where social democracy never really took off. Today, three Chinese Christmas-toy salesmen with identical glasses, navy suits and severe side-partings are perched on the shoe-shine throne.

Across the hall, last-minute texters work their fingers frantically as guilty, duty-free children's presents are stuffed into counterfeit Prada handbags and large groups of overweight third-generation Irish-Americans with yellow hair, visors and name-badges clutch onto each other, terrified by the foreignness of it all. These 'tour-bus Americans', with a weakness for purple polyester, are like a flock of endangered birds negotiating their way through the make-shift labyrinth.

You can spot the Marian tour pilgrims going to Lourdes: they are the nuns disguised as gender-studies lecturers. They are also the only people in the airport with packed lunches. Beside the self-conscious nuns, a twin-setted and pearled Sloaney fund manager, all expensive blonde highlights and fetish heels, rabbits into her top-of-the-range Motorola camera phone and snaps at the check-in girl, who's on €10 an hour and whose very presence seems to irritate little Miss ISEQ.

Democracy is so foul, she thinks to herself—all these people, horrible. It's hard to imagine her as the student activist she once was, with the megaphone, Sandinista T-shirt and Doc Martens, screaming about students' rights outside the Dáil in the early 1990s. But one of the beauties of our New Ireland is the liberation to reinvent. If you don't like yourself, just make up an avatar. It's *Second Life* for real people.

Local property developers, Ireland's new chieftains, scour the *Financial Times* while simultaneously checking out the tabloids. They are the first tribe to buy both the *Sun* and the *FT*—deviant shopping behaviour which renders redundant the quack science of modern consumer profiling so beloved of advertisers.

Except for the gap-year, credit-card Crusties on their way to Nepal, deep in the shallows of Deepak Chopra, men of all ages and classes devour the Monday-morning sports supplements. Sport is the new news. It bonds us.

Everyone is fielding mobile calls from the office and slurping coffees.

Have you noticed how people in airports appear to be constantly eating and drinking? We ate a quarter-of-a million sandwiches in the airport last year and drank 1.6 million cups of tea. We devoured over a million slices of toast, gulped 1.2 million coffees and close to a million cappuccinos, while we stuffed over half-a-million Danish pastries into our gobs. 672,000 muffins were served by 23 different nationalities as were a similar amount of bottles of Coca-Cola. The airport turns over more than €5 million in food alone. Is it any wonder that Rennie antacids are amongst the bestselling items in the airport shops, along with Taytos?[1]

Some races bring their exiles reminders of home, like books, DVDs and newspapers. Central Americans tend to bring religious imagery from the old country to their emigrant friends. Irish people bring each other crisps.

The more Taytos bought at the airport, the more of us are emigrating. The Taytometer is a more accurate indicator of the state of the economy than anything you'll get from government press releases. Last year, we spent €96,000 in the airport on packets of Tayto crisps.[2] Watch this figure closely in the next few years as the slowdown forces many of us back on the boat again. If the Taytometer rises, you know that things are getting worse here. Looking for a start, boss?

The incongruous Italian tourist in his Bono Stetson looks aghast at the huge watery coffee served up for €3 by Magda the Pole, who left the plum hair dye in too long last night, making her look like an extra from Michael Jackson's 'Thriller'. The two water-drinking developers' wives from Dungarvan—former Avon ladies—are head to toe in Ib Jorgensen. As they glare in the mirror, they practise their Elizabeth Arden pouts, complaining about the delay to New York but it does give them more time at the MAC counter, which is cosmetic heaven.

If anything tells you about the extraordinary excesses of the Irish consumer, and explains why Botox clinics are opening on the Walkinstown Roundabout, it is the Dublin Airport Big MAC Index. The MAC counter at Dublin Airport is tiny. And yet this single small counter is the sixth busiest MAC shop in the world. This includes the likes of Fifth Avenue, Bond Street, rue du Faubourg St Honoré, Milan and Hong Kong. And despite the fact that Dublin airport is only the 50th biggest in the world, the MAC counter is the second busiest of any airport.[3] Irish girls are piling on the slap, no matter what the cost.

The Avon ladies have seven empty bags and return tickets to Woodbury Common from Port Authority. They can't wait for Thursday afternoon in New Jersey; they're tooled up with maps of the shops and strategic meeting points. The shopping planner is meeting them tomorrow morning in Fitzpatrick's Hotel to take them on the Sex and the City Tour before the full-frontal assault on Bloomingdales. After that, cocktails in the Waldorf Astoria beckon with the girls from Nenagh.

This year, it is expected that over 350,000 Irish people will visit New York—the vast majority of these to shop. This figure is increasing by over 30% per year and is up 145% since 2001.[4] The tourism campaign, 'Next Stop NYC', was created last year by New York retailers to capitalise on the booming Irish travel market which is currently—according to the New York Times—'the fastest-growing among New York City's top-ten origin markets'.

The young woman, Castleknock's finest, is, like everything else on that side of the Áras, on her way up, fast. She's off to Barcelona for a weekend with the girls. They are not alone. The short-break market has exploded in Ireland in the past three years along with its hand maiden, chick lit. We spent €560 million on short breaks last year.[5] Of the 22 new routes out of Dublin in the past two years, short-break destinations account for 15 of them.[6]

Dublin airport, like the rest of the country, runs on a combination of exhaustion, excitement and stress. It is straining under the volume of passengers that cheap travel affords, bursting at the seams. This offers us a vision of our metropolitan future, at one time mixed-up, blocked, snarling, angry and ready to ignite, while simultaneously compliant, empathetic, communal, tolerant and patient.

Ireland is on the move, coming, going, rushing—everyone's got somewhere to be, someone to meet and something to do. Everything in our lives is snatched, grabbed and rushed. The clock is on, time is money. The airport is our speeded up, just-in-time, clock-watching life. We are the Transit Nation.

The Last Democracy

Dublin airport is the last place in Ireland where all the social classes mix. It is our melting pot. It's a democratic and class-free environment. If your flight is delayed, don't fly off the handle, sit back, fork out half the price of your Ryanair ticket for a coffee and watch the country. All Irish life is here, from the top dogs to the bottom-feeders. Spend a day here and you'll see New Ireland, warts and all.

Only the extremely poor and the extremely rich avoid the airport. For the rest of us, wedged in the middle, the airport is as close to a commune as we are likely to experience.

The synchronised clackedy-clack of heels announces five Aer Lingus hostesses, all up dos and eyelashes, pulling behind them five identical suitcases on wheels. As they castanet confidently past the security check, you are briefly reminded of a different age. When my mother was young, an air hostess was the swankiest job a girl could have, what with those fitted French-looking uniforms, suggestive caps and *Vanity Fair* pilots with Ray-Ban Aviators and Leonardo diCaprio looks. Now in the era of thirty-minute turnarounds, stag-nights and €1 promotional fares, a career as a prison officer is more prestigious. The collapse of the status of flying and the resulting democratisation of airports has been one of the most dramatic social features of the past twenty years. Once flying was the privilege of the sophisticated few, today it's about as glamorous as Jade Goody. It is mass transport for the mass market.

At the make-shift check-in counter, the soon-to-be-outsourced corporate man on his way down brushes shoulder pads with a cosmetically-enhanced 'nail technician' on her way up. This Enda-Kenny-meets-Kerry-Katona moment could only happen here. These types would never meet each other in real life but at the check-in desk, they are one. Pinched collar meets muffin-top across the queue and just for a split second, they are linked by the last communal activity known to man, queuing up at the airport as the grumpy Czech security man on the minimum wage rifles through their wash-bags. We are all suspects, potential shoe-bombers or moisturiser murderers, tied up and stuck here, gelled together in almost Blitz-type stoicism.

With the increasing hierarchies in the education system, the health system, sports facilities and gentrification (which is a nice expression for the more accurate but Yugoslavian-sounding term 'social cleansing') of huge swathes of our cities, where else can you see the full social mix?

In education, the obsession with school league tables means that parents will pay any price to get their children into the 'better' establishments. This leads to kids from the same social class all going to school together. Sophie never sleeps with Wayne. Abercrombie and Dubes rarely meet hoodie and Nike Air Max, unless they're buying drugs.

It's the same story in the health service. Mr Private VHI Plan E runs a mile from Mrs Public waiting list. Apartheid is the governing philosophy. Meanwhile, multi-storey shopping centres have put paid to the chance social meeting of the classes that used to be commonplace in that greatest of public spaces, the Main Street. Sport, although less so than it was, is also segregated along old tribal lines. Even for spectators, at most big games there is tiered pricing, making sure the *hoi polloi* remain firmly away from the respectable. The rule-of-thumb in Ireland's exploding world of corporate entertainment is that only the poor pay at the turnstiles; the rich get in free.

In contrast with our segregated tribal behaviour, the airport is an exercise in social engineering which would doubtless please James Connolly. The Unicorn meets Abrakebabra, crab timbale and rocket rubs shoulders with chicken nuggets and chips. Lexus queues up with HiAce and croquet chats to soccer, if only to borrow a pen: last-minute name-tag panic knows no class. The airport is as close to forced collectivisation as we have ever come. Everyone's a comrade.

According to the airport authorities, 21 million people—five times the population of the country—will pass through its doors this year. Estimates indicate that over 800,000 Irish people will travel—most by plane—this Christmas.[7] This is an extraordinary figure for a country with a workforce of just 2 million.

More phenomenal is the amount of immigrants coming through the place. In 2005, 143,000 Poles passed through here.[8] Last year, that figure jumped to 580,000.[9] Passengers from the Baltics increased from 147,000 to 340,000 in 2006.[10] At this rate, by 2016, these countries will be empty. As in the Second World War, the Polish Parliament will sit in exile, perhaps in Lucan rather than London.

Aeronomics

A day spent in the major airport of a country gives you a better insight into the true nature of the place than many convoluted political lectures. As a quick rule of thumb on the economic front, you can tell where the country is in the economic cycle by the queues. If there are no queues, there's a recession. When you see orderly queues and strong national airlines, it means that the country is in at least the fourth generation of wealth. Generally speaking, the more people, screaming kids and makeshift check-in desks, the higher and more unstable the growth rate.

As for house prices, which so many people fret over, what can you tell about them from looking around the airport? Well, first, prefabs are a bad sign because they imply that the construction industry is operating at full tilt and builders are throwing up anything. Prefabs anywhere in the airport tell you that we are near the top of the boom cycle because everyone is just making do at the moment, builders are scarce and things are being thrown together with little thought. Prefabricated Portaloos rather than the real deal, implies you should start worrying about the value of houses. Once you see prefab corridors masquerading as fully-fledged terminals, you know it's too late to sell. Cops in prefabs and you know the house party's all over.

You can also be pretty sure that if the place is full of 'cancer-flirters', that personal borrowing is going through the roof and the dodgier end of the market is booming. The cancer-flirter is that person who places post-Christmas pinkness ahead of personal safety. You know the type who comes back to work in the rain on 7 January with third-degree burns, who is described by that great Irish euphemism as having 'got the sun'.

For the economy, thousands of pink tourists in winter, coming back from somewhere their natural skin pigmentation is not used to, is a sure sign that this country is spending more than it earns. If people are reckless enough to fry for a fortnight, despite everything we know about skin cancer, you can be sure that this country isn't too worried about its carbon footprint, has a weakness for interest-only mortgages and that when everything goes pear-shaped, the general population won't care about handing back the keys. These people don't take advice, let alone play by the rules. Repossessions are just around the corner. Liquidators are salivating.

What about the arrivals hall? What can we glean from it? Clusters of foreigners on mobiles still in their dusty work overalls means the country is going through a period of mass blue-collar immigration. Dubious stilettos and back-combed hair is a sure sign that the society is in the second phase of immigration: the family is following two years after the father came to make money. Granny is on the next flight. This is the phase where immigration numbers multiply rapidly. The schools in the commuter belt of this country will be overcrowded, multi-lingual and under-funded.

Looking around, if the shopping areas are better staffed, kitted-out and presented than the loos, the information desks and the car-parks, you know the trade unions are in control of much of the country, that sewage works are delayed and that there is a significant chance that you'll encounter a bewildered man with a 'stop/go' sign managing traffic on the country's main roads.

A day in the life of Dublin airport demands the patience of a saint, the humour of a condemned man and an explorer's sense of direction. A packet of Solpadeine, a compass, an overdraft and some Valium would come in handy too. But remember, you've got to arrive early. Like a good safari, a busy airport is best seen at dawn.

But before we head out to Santry via the clogged M1 and M50 intersection, where HGVs dodge demented Africans in Nissan Micras and salarymen try to break the world land-speed record in their top-of-the-range BMWs—let's look at how it could be. (By the way, we could go through the Port Tunnel, the most expensive piece of infrastructure ever built in Europe, but our government, having gone on about it for years as if Ireland was sending a man to Mars, now wants to keep it a secret. So, at a price of €12 to go three kilometres, they've made it more expensive to drive through than it is to fly with either Ryanair or Aer Lingus to Rome.)

Fantasyland

Imagine you arrive at Fantasy Airport in the back of a clean cab, preferably a new car with well-sprung seats and an unobtrusive driver, who isn't giving you his opinion on Steve Staunton. In Fantasyland, you can choose—there is also high-speed monorail link from the city centre.

You enter the departure lounge. You look up. Immediately, you see a brightly illuminated departures board, not an ad for O'Brien's sandwich bars. Everything in the triple-height, galleried terminal is open and accessible. Breathe in the design. The public art is prominent but discreet. These people don't need to brag. There are no ads for the local boy band anywhere.

It is clean. The queues are orderly and there are more than enough check-in desks, staffed by employees who don't have to buy their own uniforms. The signs are clear and the intercom announcements are comprehensible in five languages. The floor-staff, unlike Dublin airport's insomniacs, look as if they've had a good night's sleep.

In our ideal well-run airport there is soap at the washbasins. The hot-air dryer works and wastepaper baskets are emptied regularly. The place is calm. The ceiling is high and far away. The sky-light is just that, a clear view to the sky letting in light, rather than a steamed-up, filthy, out-size piece of corrugated Perspex. You feel that you are in a transport hub rather than Lidl. There are wireless internet hot-spots with high-speed connections. All is working, coordinated and reassuring.

Countries with fantasy airports also have UNESCO-protected heritage sites, hands-off politicians, good train services and no MRSA. Health magazines sell well and all houses are properly insulated. Local primary schools don't feel the need to fundraise. Builders don't fold overnight and disappear without a trace. These are the types of places that plan ahead, invest in life-long learning and have bi-lingual, pre-school teachers who are also accomplished gymnasts. Heart disease is not common, breast checks are regular and smiling children sing, rather than mumble, the national anthem. Pyjamas are worn in bed, not in Spar.

The people are tolerant and courteous, if a little dull. They rarely own more than one house and education is free. Think Canada with European trams and Japanese bullet trains, where uniformed traffic wardens could grace the pages of *Wallpaper** magazine. These are countries where celebrity is retiring and TV presenters are, well, just TV presenters.

Now, consider Dublin airport—the gateway to the New Ireland. Compare it with the futuristic glass-and-steel cathedrals to taste and design that are Münich airport, Schipol or Charles de Gaulle. Or what about the new Asian airports, built for twice today's capacity in order to prevent over-priced, last-minute, cheap-looking pre-fab jobs in ten years' time?

Can you imagine these places having signs which declare with odd syntax: 'pardon our appearance' as you are funnelled down a two-mile corridor to another cow-shed? These airports, with their high-speed trains linking terminals, ample car parking and real espresso are built to reflect the aspirations of societies that are at ease with themselves, where economic growth is manageable and where immigration is thought through. They are not over-indulging, over-hyped or bursting through their shabby seams. They're also not much fun.

But Dublin airport, in contrast, is Us. It is an A&E ward for slightly healthier people. It is a microcosm of the new, out-of-breath, indigested, lastminute.com Ireland. It is the Calcutta of the skies which waves its contemptuous two fingers at the traveller through its broken masonry and interminable queues, snarling at you with the Ryanair quip, 'What the hell do you expect? You only paid a fiver.'

But on the other hand, if you want to get a good sense of the dynamism and the chaos, the Babel of voices, the gridlock, the sticking-plaster solutions and hope, optimism and expectations that drive our country forward, spend some time here. If you want to see how somehow Ireland powers ahead despite itself, come here. This is Ireland's hall door.

Landing

The Latvian check-in girl has learned how to deal with the complaining Paddies. Just smile and they blow their own tempest out in time. Unlike in Latvia, the Irish never report you to anyone. It's the ones with too much panstick and two-tone hair who are the worst. Airport people call them 'Jiffies'.

The Jiffy gets off the plane from Malaga in late January, with a little skirt on, bright red legs and a boob tube which doesn't so much prop up, as hold in place, a scorched, scarlet cleavage. She's stooped from years of sticking her mouth out and dragging deeply on cigarette butts, giving her the disturbing appearance of a pigeon wearing blusher.

She of the bejewelled incisors is laden down with duty-free Johnny Blue and her pink ghetto-blaster is pumping out an Usher and Rihanna mix. The Jiffy loves R'n'B. When she bends down to grab her 'chrysalised' phone, her sunburned butterfly tattoo appears just above her G. She examines her stick-on nails, and continues to drone on about the contents of her duty-free swag and the fact that a litre of Bacardi only cost €7 in some country called 'Spaint'.

Everything's a 'meal', from breakfast, to tortillas, to steak and chips. And all 'meals in Spaint' were 'whopper'. Her fella, Fran, whose shaved head and neck fused with his torso a few years back, giving him the look of a rhino from the back, is rubbing his bare Johnny Adair arms as he shapes down the stairs. If there was a shaper's catwalk at Dublin Fashion Week, he'd win a prize for the best razorblades-under-the arms swagger.

Jiffies are a year-round attraction. They usually travel in packs of eight or ten minimum with their Ma or other members of the extended family. They get a 'd'apartment' which they trash. They used to be localised in Spain but now they're just as likely to be on packages to Koh Samui.

Like the Jiffies, most of the Irish have bitten the travel bug and the average person you see at the airport will leave the country six times every year.[11] We are now the best travellers in the world. We are global gypsies who are in and out of the country on holidays or business, on the move, trading, spending and spoofing, keeping the entire show on the road.

The Jiffy cranes her neck out of the plane door, looks up at the grey overcast Dublin drizzle. She's overweight, under-dressed and over-accessorised. She glances at her mate Colette who can hardly walk as the back of her knees are scalded. In unison, like synchronised swimmers, both grab their exposed thighs, rub their nipples, grimace and screech—'Jaysus Its Fuckin' Freezing, Yeah'— J.I.F.F.Y.

The Jiffy is home.

Darkness Falls

By nine o'clock, the Jiffy is glued to a double-bill of *Coronation Street* and shouting to Fran to turn down the sound of the football on his plasma in the next room or she'll burst him.

Around this time, the airport changes and another aspect of modern Ireland takes over. In the arrivals hall, they are beginning to congregate. It looks like a scene from *Gorky Park*. Slavs of all sorts assemble to meet friends and then disappear to the remotest parts of the country in a Vilnius-registered Audi Quattro—the favoured car of Lithuanians. It was declared extinct here in 1996, only to reappear last year.

Sometime in the evening, the arrivals section turns into a holding pen for East Europeans. You notice the crew cuts and fake Ducati biker jackets in various garish shades of orange and yellow with misspelled motor oil ads emblazoned across the back. They look like bouncers, big bullet heads on them, broad shoulders and Soviet-Special-Forces handshakes. Revealing that our culture is rubbing off on someone, they've a disturbing fondness for sovereign rings and Champion Sports clothes.

The girls are mostly Slavic-pretty, long limbed, with high cheekbones, sallow-skinned and green-eyed. They are the closest to thing to a supermodel Mulhuddart has ever seen. Behold the next TV3 weather girl. It's amazing how the lads all look a few shillings short and the girls could have stepped out of the pages of Italian *Vogue*. There is a disturbing amount of stonewashed denim and a few trademark Slovakian mullet-and-moustache combinations. Meet our future.

Céad Míle Fáilte

'Fearful pigs face death as water rises.'

The notice board in the immigration office reveals that the gardaí can laugh at themselves. The headline has been cut out of one of the tabloids and pasted on the board over the usual notices for mileage-allowance changes, overtime rates and for-sale ads for second-hand Opel Omegas. There is also the picture of probably the worst passport impersonator they've seen yet—a Chinese man trying to blag his way in on Slovak papers. The most conspicuous notices are for translation services, the mobile numbers of immigrant polyglots putting their superior education to use. When they are not serving kebabs to drunks who can hardly speak English, they are translating three languages simultaneously.

The whiteboard is the one to watch. This reminds gardaí coming on the morning shift that there are people to be deported tomorrow and where these transients are sleeping tonight. This evening there are two Sri Lankans in Santry Station, one in Arbour Hill and a Ukrainian in Malahide.

Ironically, the first image a would-be immigrant sees in Dublin airport is walls adorned with pictures of destitute Irish emigrants looking starved, emaciated and beaten as they disembark from famine ships in New York. We've come full circle. Our immigrants are building Ireland in the same way as we built America.

The immigration gardaí are a bit apprehensive tonight. In the last few months the big problem has been Romanians. Lads they threw out last year are now coming back, goading their former tormentors with impunity of an EU passport. In the first three months of 2007, 10,000 Romanians arrived in this country.[12] The government has introduced the policy of allowing Bulgarians and Romanians to travel here freely, but they are not allowed to work without a permit. So the gardaí at immigration is asked to police the unpoliceable, by a State that doesn't know what it wants, but knows what it doesn't want— if you know what I mean.

That's not surprising, of course, because Ireland's immigration policy is made in London. Because of the border with the North, which we don't want to turn into an Iron Curtain, we can't have a different immigration policy to Britain's. Well, we could, but we couldn't be bothered. So, when the British government in 2003 said that it would open its doors to all the accession countries, Ireland followed suit. And, in 2006, when they decided not to allow Bulgarians and the Romanians to work without a permit, we followed them again.

Our interest rates are determined in Frankfurt and our immigration policy in London. In the new world of globalisation, when house prices and immigration are two significant challenges, we have given away the only two policies that might give us some control over either. It's no wonder people are confused. We have no policy at all other than, 'it'll be grand'.

Back at Pier B, the gardaí have recruited a couple of Romanian translators, but even though they know that the vast majority of Romanians are coming to work in the black market, there's nothing they can do. The inspector drags his hands through his hair as he resignedly explains how the gardaí are called 'girlie cops' by macho Ukrainian smugglers, who fully expect to get a proper hiding when caught. Within minutes, they lose all respect for the gardaí when they are read their rights and given access to a doctor and a lawyer.

The Amsterdam flight touches down at 10 p.m. As expected, it's full of Brazilians who, as if on cue, all tell the immigration officers that they are here to see our castles. This is a sign to the cops that they will be on the next plane to the UK once they get their Irish tourist stamp. As for the Irish castles, no-one knows where that comes from. The Brazilians are mainly using Ireland as a way into the UK, where there's a community of over half a million.

And that is one of the patterns of immigration—people go where their mates are. The amount of Poles coming to Ireland is determined by the size of the Polish community here as well as the wage differential between here and Poland. The pull of the existing emigrant community was evident in Irish emigration patterns to the US between 1850 and 1920, when we were the largest ethnic minority in the US, ahead of the Germans who also left in their millions.

The immigration officers' hatches are cramped, strewn with empty coffee cups, GAA-National-League supplements and rulebooks and guidelines.

A couple is asked to step aside and they are shown into one of the two holding rooms just beside the immigration hatches. That's a return ticket to Santry Garda station for them tonight, by the looks of things.

Human nature doesn't change and they are only trying to do what we did in the 1980s. Many of us remember lying through our teeth to get into the US. In the summer of 1986, I wedged my illegal body behind four Hondurans and a couple of white South Africans, full-time, no-going-back immigrants both. The South Africans were waved on after a grilling, but the Hondurans were given the full treatment. By the time I faced Lieutenant Mahoney of the US immigration service, my accent was somewhere between Tom Cruise in *Far and Away* and Pat Shortt of D'Unbelievables. Mahoney, probably because he wanted to, believed my unbelievable auntie-in-Yonkers yarn. Once on American soil, I disappeared into the kitchens of Manhattan.

Our immigrants are at the same game. The only difference is that they are faced by men who've been on the other side of the glass. Our gardaí are probably the only immigration officers in the world who have themselves experienced being illegal somewhere. Two of the lads on duty had spoofed their way into Logan Airport in the dark 80s, so their sympathies were with the desperate people they faced.

At 12.10 a.m. a Filipina girl, very well dressed and nervous, is stopped. She looks petrified. This is the human face of globalisation. She is nearly in tears and you can see her trying to keep it together. Try to imagine what's going through her head. Think about how much it took to get this far. Freedom is just a yard away, yet it's miles. Anyone with a conscience would claim her as his wife just to get her across the line.

She licks her lips. She looks away from the glass. Her nerves leave her mouth parched. Who is she thinking about? Her mother, her brother, husband or boyfriend? Who is waiting for her at the far side? Who is willing her through customs? Her phone beeps with an anxious incoming text.

The garda asks her to stand back against the wall where there is a life-size ruler. He checks her height, asks her for another paper, her letter and invitation. He phones someone. Will she incriminate her friends who are waiting at arrivals for her? Might the gardaí use her as bait? She's not too sure. She can't hear. It's all happening too quickly. The rest of the queue is staring at her, irritated. There's nothing more impatient than a bunch of Poles who three years ago were in the same predicament as the Filipina but now feel an entitlement. They examine their fake Rolexes, shaking their heads. Eaten bread is easily forgotten.

Then she hears it. It's faint at first. Is someone talking to her? No, it's metallic. It's the click of the visa stamp pressing down on her passport bearing the official seal of Ireland, engraving the smudged ink with the harp. It's a chance of a new life, giving her a new lease, she is in. She cries. All this trauma to change the bedpans of frail Irish geriatrics whose own families, for whatever reason, can't look after them.

The next batch is four Baltic flights and one from Brussels. As the Balts stream in, you can sense the rents in Tyrrellstown rising. It's like watching the entire staff of a large Centra on the move. The gardaí catch a cup of tea. The boss's 'Eye of the Tiger' ringtone goes—it's the missus asking him to bring back a curry.

The investigative team arrives. He's half-*Miami Vice*, half-*Garda Patrol*, kitted out in full GAA-club chic: beige suit, brown soft shoes and green tie. You couldn't make it up. Her hair matches his suit. They work together—good cop, bad cop. They're working on a Moldovan prostitution ring. They've also been tracking a Nigerian fraudster gang for weeks now, but Don Johnson claims that the Nigerians are harder to crack than any other criminals. All police work is based on local intelligence and the Nigerians don't grass up their own—even with the threat of deportation hanging over them. Most others will sing like canaries when they're threatened with expulsion—not the Nigerians.

There's a Japanese passport alert just in from our man in Paris. The gardaí have a network around Europe, watching, noting and passing intelligence back and forth. They work closely with other cops but given the sheer numbers of people arriving, they only catch a fraction of the action. The smugglers know this. They know the odds are stacked in their favour. It's a game of cat and mouse, with human pawns.

At any one time, there are 30 million Chinese people on the move around the world.[13] Picking on rich Japanese is common. Chinese smugglers steal Japanese passports from expensive hotels on the continent. They then line up their stable of would-be illegal migrants and examine everyone for similarities. If one of the Chinese can pass for the Japanese in the picture they will cut her hair and change her clothes accordingly. They work on the assumption that we can't tell the difference between Chinese and Japanese, in the same way as they couldn't tell the difference between an Irish person and a Latvian.

The stewardess announces the incoming Brussels flight. The passengers queue up with the confidence of western Europeans which, counter-intuitively, means looking at their shoes, slightly guiltily. One young woman is different. She constantly changes queue at the faintest sign of a hold-up. She is well dressed. Her papers are in order. Something is not quite right. Her palms are sweating. She looks like the

French woman in the photo: everything matches. The officer checks again. She's wearing a long dress. He asks her to inch closer. 'Please turn around, Miss.' He asks her to stand against the life-size ruler. She's the right height, but quite tall for a West African at five foot eight. She looks around nervously and tries to regain her composure by flicking her hair and examining her impressively varnished nails. She plays with her earrings. She's trying to flirt without making eye-contact.

He points to her ankles. She doesn't move and pretends not to understand. He motions again and asks her to lift up her dress. She begins to shake and speaks French to anyone who will listen. But human nature is cowardly. When the quarry is being chased it is vaguely interesting, when the game is up and the prey cornered, no-one has the stomach to watch.

Underneath her long skirt is a pair of customised eight-inch heels. The poor girl is practically crippled. She bursts into tears. She is Congolese, fourteen years old, in a strange country and has probably been pimped here on false, stolen documents. She is nowhere near the height of the person she is supposed to be. She's about five foot and she stands there sobbing, frightened and alone. The woman who, three minutes ago was checking her nail varnish, is now a distraught child. The middle-aged gardaí see their own daughters in front of them. Someone in the queue is drafted in to translate.

———

Dublin airport is our Ellis Island. These people are our huddled masses. This is what the new world order means, and Ireland is on the front line.

Chapter 2 ⌒
| VERTIGO

Dream On

Have you noticed the respect you get in estate agents lately? It feels good. You are important again. Your money has value and you have a certain stature that a buyer hasn't had in a while. It is a sign of things to come.

Last year you were treated with haughty contempt by the pretty girl with beige hair, pencil skirt and French-manicured gel nails. Today, Ms Pencil Skirt fawns over you as if you were a precious commodity. Well, you are a buyer and there aren't many of you around. She flicks her hair and breathlessly raves about the generous proportions of the seven-hundred-square-foot, honey-coloured starter homes.

They all have curved drives, you know.

A bend in the drive, no matter how small, gives the impression (to whom, one wonders) that there is a broad sweep in front of an impressive home. Or so she learned on her weekend auctioneering crash course. Last year, this was a selling point. Last year, she simply opened up the plans, sat back and took deposits. This year, she's been up to all sorts of tricks: installing water features, rockeries, black bamboo, anything to make the 87 unsold homes move. The developer, who used to spend all day in his helicopter, is on the phone constantly.

She's trying her best. They even gave away two houses on FM104 as part of an all-out marketing campaign. But nothing's moving. She's convinced the offer of a free kitchen will work. The kitchen suppliers are only too glad to give the stuff away at a discount. Their stores are full of Shaker units. Last summer young parents were crawling all over the place; today there isn't a jogging stroller in sight.

The banks have been very helpful in putting together a soft financing option for the first 500 buyers. (They would do that; their share price depends on it.) But it's still dead, even with the developer's offer to pay the first year's mortgage. The only rent is coming from Department of Social Welfare clients, but if she's honest, Ms Pencil Skirt knows that the sight of unemployed Africans has never done much for sales.

Now, I'm not racist or anything, but you know what I mean?

She clicks her false nails off her IKEA flat-pack desk. Ms Pencil Skirt has a small ladder in her tights that no amount of nail varnish can arrest.

The ladder is like confidence in the housing market in Dublin 15, the fastest growing suburb in the country.[1] No amount of schmoozing can obscure the fact that there are too many 'for sale' signs up, houses are languishing on the market for months and the supply coming online is enormous. Prices are falling, landlords are panicking and although she can't see it, there's more at stake than the repossession of Ms Pencil Skirt's cream convertible VW Beetle called Babes. Where have all the buyers gone?

Drive out to any of our new suburbs, the ones that we've thrown up in the past two or three years, and you get a feeling that something is not quite right. Yes, we have built 310,000 new houses since 2004 and yes, 122,000 of these are empty,[2] without tenants and generating no rent, but it is not just the economic numbers that are not adding up, something else doesn't quite fit.

———

Wedged in the crook of the Dublin-Meath border, where the last of the Dublin Mountains gives way to the flat lands of North Leinster, the new villages of Dublin 15 are the face of New Ireland. These are places of removal vans, foreign-registered Honda Civics, kitchen showrooms and overcrowded multi-lingual pre-fab schools. But these places, homes to thousands of us, are presented as an experiment in nostalgia. If you think you've just walked on to the set of *Fair City*, you are not alone. You are surrounded by old-looking new stuff. Everything is mock something or other. A sanitised version of the past is on sale, the dream of a life less ordinary up for grabs. We are stepping back in time to a pastoral Ireland, where milk bottles were left out, doors were left unlocked and children were left alone to fly kites.

But if you feel that you are hurtling forward, propelled along by the new forces of globalisation, why the overriding obsession with the past? What is it about the word 'village'? Sign after sign on the endless maze of ring roads points to the so-called 'village centre' as if by calling it a village, you imbue it with a whiff of history.

But we all know that there is no village here. We know that a village is something that evolves over time, centuries in many cases. We understand that a village has a soul and the soul is the people, the dead generations giving the place a distinct flavour, almost a smell which is spiced by rivalries, tall tales, jealousies, loves, losses and rural legends, all of which go to make up the story of the place. A church helps too. What makes a village different from a shopping centre is history. We know all this; yet, we are prepared to accept the preposterous conceit that there is a village centre in Ongar, Dublin 15, when there is manifestly not. It was built two years ago.

Ongar is a fabrication, as much as *Fair City*, *Glenroe* and *Coronation Street* are fabrications. Dublin 15 is now dotted with these 'instant villages'. Much in the same way as the estates have incongruous names such as 'The Boulevard', the instant villages aim to create the illusion of 'established communities'.

We are all culpable. Jump in a cab and ask to go to Ongar Village and the taxi-driver will nod with the same familiarity as if you said Ballymore Eustace. He might even ask, 'Is it the village you want or one of the estates?'

So we are playing a big game of Let's Pretend. Let's pretend we don't live in a new estate built in the past three years, where we have no idea who is living beside us. Let's pretend that we don't commute. Let's pretend that we actually live in a peaceful village, not a concrete jungle with speed bumps. Let's pretend that this is where our grandfathers came from, where we chased in the fields as kids, picked blackberries, made tree huts, played conkers and ate homemade brown bread baked by neighbours. Let's recreate Arcadia west of Clonsilla.

The reason for this nostalgia trip is that Ireland is moving forwards but looking backwards.

———

It begins with the developer, who creates a myth. He sets aside an acre or two of retail space within the vast complex and calls it a 'village'. The planners are in on the joke. The village will then grow backwards. First, the retail space is marketed to retailers just like the ground floor of any new shopping centre. An anchor tenant, such as Dunnes Stores, will be secured and this will act as a honeypot to lure other retailers, like Spar or Centra. The roads on the surrounding estates will be designed to funnel people into the shopping complex. This will create profit-maximising footfall and is the new-development equivalent of one way escalators in Liffey Valley shopping centre.

Once the anchor retail tenant is in, the developer will get on with the ludicrous business of creating the instant village to encase the twee shopping centre. In the next month or so, a makey-uppey village will rise out of nowhere. Here, modern Ireland is grafting on the idea of community to make shopping centres more palatable for planners. Everyone is scrambling for a bit of community these days.

Let's see, what else do we need to create a community? A school? That would be far too much hassle and it doesn't pay the rent. Let's start with a fake clock tower and a village green. What else do we need? Maybe a set of Victorian railings going nowhere in particular, fencing off nothing in particular and a wrought-iron pretend water pump? A village green with an ornamental 1960s' P&T telephone box, some overflowing hanging baskets and two new Edwardian-style benches might do the trick. The focus group told the developer that's what people liked, a sit-com-set village made them feel permanent, rooted and at home rather than what they were, transient, floating, in flux.

The developers are selling an illusion. Everything, except the plasma screen in each home, is retro.

In no time, the developer has succeeded in passing off a field in Meath as an early-20th-century market town like Kenmare. The new village resembles where you came from. It is a tranquil, complex market town with local characters, solid shopkeepers, village gossips and idiot savants. If people want nostalgia, we'll give it to them. We want to go backwards to go forward. Glenroe is our destiny.

Why now? Why the nostalgia bonanza? Possibly because we are afraid of the future. When people are on the move, uprooted and dislocated, we yearn for some ideal vision of the past, a romantic fantasy of a place secure from the nastiness, chaos and anxiety of modern life. We don't want to be just number 176 in a suburb of over four thousand new houses and apartments; we want to be a member of a community and a neighbourhood. Don't worry about the fact that the pace of change in your job, your relationship and your family is knocking you off course, why not just pop down to the village for a pint of milk, the newspaper or just a quick chat to catch up on the gossip? It is all so familiar, even if the shop assistants are Poles bussed in at dawn from Blessington.

The instant villages are, in fact, the bizarre creation of a graphic designer who lives in a loft and would not be seen dead in D15. He has a shaved head, sculpted facial hair and wide-rimmed Bono glasses. He sits behind an Apple Mac in Grand Canal Basin, working in an open-plan office with an *à la carte* urban-planning graphics package made in China. Just about as far from a real Irish village as you can get.

But he understands that the sales pitch of the new village appeals to something very deep in us, the need to belong. In modern Ireland this wanting to belong is made all the more acute because we have just come through one of the most dislocating cultural spin cycles in our history. We have been tossed around by financial and social upheaval. We are clutching at straws. What happened? How did we get here? Where are we going?

Turn on the radio today and you will hear countless chat shows about the old days and why things were better. These are being hosted and contributed to by people old enough to remember the old days. This is middle-aged radio, for middle-aged people. But nonetheless, it reveals the obsession with nostalgia. When things are moving forward at such a dramatic pace, there is a yearning to slow things down, to go back to an idealised, slow life before TV dinners and YouTube. There is a great urge to escape the modern world and to revert to a mythical cocoon of grainy early-Technicolour home videos of children in short pants, stable families and stay-at-home mothers with beehive hairdos.

These Let's Pretend villages are simply digitally re-mastered versions of the original—repackaged, re-sold and hyped up.

Today, we are in Ongar Village, one of the biggest developments in West Dublin, named bizzarely after an Essex commuter town. As well as a fake water pump, there are two shops, three crèches, the ubiquitous Curves gym, a Domino's Pizza, an off-licence (but no pub), a Paddy Power bookmakers, three hairdressers and seven estate agents. Yes, seven. This is the set of *Ryan's Daughter* where John Mills is a mortgage broker. But nothing's selling, the market is going the wrong way.

Ms Pencil Skirt gazes out the window across the village green, past the black traffic warden standing by the ad for Dunnes Stores. She's dreaming of her cute texter, living for the weekend. She applies more nail varnish to the ladder in her tights, wondering how she's going to shift these 87 apartments without dropping the price. From wistful to wishful thinking. Her tights stick to her waxed legs.

Don't Look Down

Clumsy self-delusion and hoping for the best are two of our national characteristics. We can deceive ourselves about anything: we deny that we have a housing addiction, despite the fact that 83 cent of every euro borrowed last year went into property or construction-related investment.[3] We have all chased the housing dragon for years— anything that looks like a comedown is to be denied at all costs. No-one wants national cold turkey.

But by joining the dots, it is clear that we are past the tipping point. We are at the top of the economic cycle. Don't look down. It's a long way to the ground.

Ireland is in trouble. The Irish dream of mass home ownership at any price is set to crash into the global reality of enormous economic change, at a time when the gravitational pull of interest rates is irresistible. This implosion will alter the country in three profound ways.

First, the financial miracle of the last five years is likely to be exposed as nothing more than a monumental overdraft secured on dramatically overvalued property. When payback time comes, young working families, the backbone of society, will be hardest hit. They are the ones with the most debts and the least wealth. They are the ones with the insecure income made more fragile by the twin forces of globalisation and the disappearance of the 'job-for-life' culture. They are also the people most in competition with the new wild card in the Irish pack: immigrants.

When the economy is going well, all these conflicting drags can be easily ignored. But when the cycle turns, it's a different story. The cycle is turning and this will lead to a demographic war, not so much between the haves and have nots, the rich and the poor, the Left and the Right but between the young and old. The Irish property boom has greatly enriched the middle-aged at the expense of the young. The dividing line is when you bought property: if you bought last century, you are cushioned, if you are just on the ladder in the past few years, you are exposed.

Second, as a result of this new economic reality, the country will feel wounded, let down and deflated. Domestic politics could be set for a period of severe turbulence. In the run-up to the 100th anniversary of the 1916 Rising, the political pendulum will swing. Yet again, Ireland will have to reinvent itself. Everything that we take for granted has been structured in the context of an economic boom, with ample revenue and enough cash to smooth over the rough edges. When this changes, all bets are off. Hard choices will have to be made, new challenges faced and novel directions taken.

Third, the social forces unleashed by an economic downturn, caused by a falling housing market and enormous debts, will be so powerful that the direction of the country for the next ten years is at stake. A battle for the heart and soul of the nation is likely to play out as it has done in other countries that have come through a similar experience. Everything will be questioned. Will we try to close ourselves off? Will Ireland choose nationalism over globalisation, interventionism over laissez-faire, regulation over deregulation, Hibernianism over cosmopolitanism? What are the likely implications for immigration, the EU, freedom and tolerance? Is there another way—an Irish solution to an Irish problem, combining the best of Irishness with the best of globalisation?

To make clear decisions, we have to stop pretending that nothing is wrong. We need to accept that Ongar and all the other 'villages' in Dublin 15 are about as real as *Fair City*; accept that nostalgia won't protect us from the future and that one of the least densely populated countries in Europe[4] can't sustain the highest house prices in Europe[5] indefinitely. We won't progress until we accept that the property obsession is a monster that is cannibalising us, and far from being good for the economy, the property boom is making us feeble. It is elbowing out proper business and sucking in all the resources of the economy. It is our greatest weakness, not our greatest strength.

It is creating a dangerous demographic divide in our society which is pricing thousands of young people out of a future and lumbering thousands of others with ludicrously large debts which will affect their quality of life and that of their children for a generation. This is socially divisive but more than that, it is a betrayal of the expectations of a generation. Since time immemorial, societies have been based on the idea that the old and middle-aged pass wealth on to the young. In Ireland, the young, via the property market, are passing wealth up to the middle-aged. The worker bees are supporting the drones.

The first part of this book will focus on this demographic divide. There are three generations competing for the fruits of the boom. The first generation is the middle-aged 'Jagger' generation who have been dramatically—and in many cases, unexpectedly—enriched over the past few years. They have most to lose from a change in the status quo and, as such, will try to keep the party going for as long as possible. The second generation, coming just behind the Jaggers, are the 'Bono Boomers', Ireland's first 'permalescent' (permanently adolescent) generation. While not sitting quite as pretty as the Jaggers, they are doing quite nicely, thank you. The third generation, the 'Jugglers', is made up of the worker bees, the unintended victims of ludicrous house prices, massive debts, underfunded pensions and potential negative equity. They are told they've never had it so good, but, in fact, they are pinned to their collars. Up until now, this generational divide has been disguised by the effervescence of the housing boom. Now that the housing market is faltering, the generation gap will be exposed, leading to serious social and political consequences.

The crux of the dilemma for Ireland is that we find ourselves in a Catch-22 situation. Domestically, and for local political reasons, everything will be done to prevent the housing market from falling. However, internationally, the Irish economy will not regain competitiveness unless house prices fall so that the economy may recover and society rebalance itself. Hesitancy at this stage will be an act of economic sabotage which delays the inevitable. Difficult as it is to appreciate now, in the longer term, a house price slump will allow us to blow the froth off the economy and come through the far side much fitter and more open to the opportunities that the brave new globalised world affords us.

———

That's the challenge. The next five years will be crucial.

Chapter 3 ～
| THE JAGGER GENERATION

The Winner Takes All

Billy Bunker has just picked up his corporate hospitality tickets for the gig of the century: the Rolling Stones' Bigger Bang Tour concert at Slane. Ironically, he didn't go the last time, 25 years ago. Now, however, courtesy of *www.corporate.ie*, he can get a weekend hospitality ticket for the Stones and bring clients. The *Irish Times* has produced a four-page supplement on it. This will be the Ryder Cup with music. It will be the day out for the gilded generation, the people who run the country.

When you examine where the reins of power are held, you see that when you strip back the spin and hype suggesting that it's the young who have all the opportunities in the New Ireland, there's always a middle-aged man with his finger on the button. We are ruled by an evergreen generation, like their idol, Mick Jagger. They are all well into their 50s, but never want to get old. They are good fun, and will always be the last people at the party. They were Ireland's first teenagers and are not going to let it go now.

No music shop can do without them. They are the ones who buy all the CDs, those Cream back-catalogues, top-of-the-range iPods, corporate boxes as well as Mini Coopers. They were the people who made *Reeling in the Years* one of the bestselling CDs ever. They know the words to 'An Dearg Doon', make the annual pilgrimage to the Vibe for Philo and consider nuclear power to be the spawn of the devil, while holding up France (Europe's biggest user of nuclear power) as the cradle of Republican civilisation.

The Jagger Generation is not a bad generation: you can't pin genocide, ethnic cleansing or the Magdalene laundries on them. The charge against them is that they have financial serendipity on their side—an ally most of us would welcome with open arms. They were on the right side of the property boom and have been enriched beyond their wildest dreams. They are reasonably good citizens with a weakness for tax-relief car parks, pension scare-mongering, the *Late Late*, digitally remastered Van Morrison CDs and Marianne Faithful memories.

The Jaggers were born between 1945 and 1960 when the country was in trouble. Many of their older brothers and sisters emigrated in the great flight of the 1950s when the entire Irish Republic project was being questioned, even by the original revolutionaries who created it in the first place. Close to half a million people left our country between 1945 and 1960.[1] Those who stayed found themselves in a denuded country, on the cusp of social change.

Most of our enlightened laws have been made by and for the Jaggers. They are tolerant. The Jaggers supported the EEC, they fought for the separation of Church and State and kept the place afloat in the late 1970s and early 1980s.

They were Ireland's first hippies and Ireland's revolutionary generation. They made Carnsore our Woodstock, drove Citroen 2CVs with 'Atomic Power, *Nein Danke*' stickers, picketed the British Embassy, marched at Wood Quay, took condom trains and manned the 1970s' barricades. Those who weren't so public about their politics, privately wrestled with their own conscience and went on anti-tax marches. Together, the Jaggers dragged Ireland, screaming and kicking, into the modern age.

They did all this while also breeding like rabbits. They had big families early, who they educated well. In fact, the tempo at which they bred was quite impressive in the first years of their marriages as the population of suburban semi-detached estates of the 1970s attest. Their marriage boom climaxed in a crescendo in 1973, when there were more weddings in Ireland than in any year before or since.[2]

Many of these marriages are now fracturing as the gelling agent of children has loosened and the empty nest is echoing hollow. Early retirement is allowing many of the mothers, who've never looked better, to flog it all, split the house proceeds and head off for Marbella and winter golf. There are now considerably more divorces per head amongst Ireland's Jaggers who were brought up in Catholic Ireland than amongst the younger commuters who were brought up in secular Ireland.[3]

All in all, the Jaggers are just older versions of the rest of us except for the fact that, now they are in power, they have abandoned the idealism that defined them and have replaced it with pragmatism. And that means holding on to what they have. Because they only make up 14%[4] of the population, the Jaggers' stake in society is hugely disproportionate and their wealth has been bolstered by the housing market, the very asset that is an anvil around the neck of the commuting generation, the Jugglers.

The Jaggers have inherited the very country they should now be bequeathing. What's more, they are going to be around for a long time and have no intention of passing the baton, so we'd all better get used to them. Whether it's a phantom swing with Tiger at the K-club, or 'My Generation' with the WHO at Marley Park, the Jaggers are in the driving seat, in top gear.

From the corporate sector to the media, from heads of academic departments to senior civil service and many of our TDs, the entire Irish establishment comes from this Jagger Generation. In the years ahead, the political battleground in Ireland will not be between Left and Right, Catholic and Protestant, urban and rural Ireland, but it will be between the asset-rich, well-off Jagger Generation and the rest, particularly the younger, cash-strapped, heavily indebted Juggler Generation about 20 years behind them, who keep the whole show on the road.

The Jaggers were at Slane in their thousands on 18 August, air-guitaring along with Keith to 'Sympathy for the Devil', while checking their Blackberries. Like Jagger, they led the revolution, railed against the system and threatened to overthrow the power, but today they are the power. In the same way as former rebels, the Rolling Stones, play like court jesters at Bill Gates' 50th, the Jagger Generation has joined up, opting-in rather than dropping out. Whether they are Lexus-driving, chino-wearing golf obsessives or lentil-eating, yoga-driven high-end spa devotees, they are bound together by their age and their taste in music. They were all at Slane. They still can't get no satisfaction.

When their parents were their age they were tucked up in bed, but not these lads. They're partying harder in their 50s than they did in their 20s. So long as the ticker holds out, there's no inconsistency here. Although a cynic might say that inconsistencies are the Jagger Generation's calling card.

Many vote Green but take more polluting short-break flights than anyone else. They speak the language of Labour, yet have holiday homes in Connemara. They support the Rossport Five, yet invest their pension funds in American multinationals. They argue for better public hospitals, yet are fully paid up VHI Plan-E members, en route to the Beacon Clinic. They rail publicly against the price of houses for first-time buyers but are actually the largest bunch of investors in the country, cannibalising the first-time buyers. They want more motorways, but vote for lower taxes; they were the first generation to benefit from free education, yet send their kids to private fee-paying schools. They are all united behind the Luas, particularly the Sandyford line.

As they now control the 'commanding heights' (an expression they were fond of when they were young) of the media, it was easy for them to take over the airwaves for days to mourn George Best and Charlie Haughey, while the rest of the country went to work. In fact, despite claiming to hate the tabloids, Rupert Murdoch and Michael O'Leary, they turned Best into the Britney Spears of sport—a tabloid freak, an accident waiting to happen, and then mourned his passing with crocodile tears as if it were somehow unexpected. On the other hand, they vilified Haughey privately when he was alive, afraid to confront him for fear it might affect a friend's Aosdána application. When he died, they eulogised him publicly as a genius rather than a thief. The death of Haughey was a Jagger-fest of monumental proportions. The radio and television were full of gab-fests about Haughey. But it wasn't about Haughey; it was about the Jaggers, their youth, their lives and their memories. Most people under forty never had the chance to vote in a Haughey election.

As for Michael O'Leary, they all love to hate him in public—they are the ones you'll hear complain loudest at the carousel about Ryanair's excessive golf-club charges—but they are also the ones at the front on the maiden flight to Pula with their chequebooks open, hoping to be 'first in' in the latest Ryanair-inspired, cheap-flight-enabled property bonanza.

You will hear them over a pint in O'Dowd's in Roundstone or over lunch in Fallon & Byrne, still arguing about Lennon versus McCartney, Haughey versus FitzGerald, Church versus State, Roe versus Wade, balsamic versus tarragon, focaccia versus ficelle and spin versus substance.

They are the sultans of spin: they make it up as they go along, history is reinvented, victories appropriated, core-positions dropped and the future is inherited now, not in the afterlife. This is the generation that went from civil rights to property rights, from burning the British Embassy down to talking the British housing market up, from revolution to risotto, from Long Kesh to Long Beach.

———

How did the generation that was going to change other people's lives, end up buying other people's lifestyles, more worried about grinding coffee than grinding poverty?

Before we answer this, let's examine the Jagger Generation, Ireland's new ruling class, more closely.

There's nothing new about the middle-aged running the country or the middle-aged constructing it in its own likeness. Jaggers all over the world are at the same carry-on. This is what happens in social democracies. A few years ago, while interviewing the old English socialist, Tony Benn, on the issue of ageing, he turned to me and said, 'Young man, the old and the young have one thing in common: they are both bullied by the middle-aged.'

But what is interesting in the Irish case is just how dominant the middle-aged Jaggers are, how few of them there are in comparison with the rest of society, how much richer they are than anyone else and how oblivious they are to the fact that they are now at the epicentre of power. Nothing happens in Ireland without them, no laws are passed which might affect them negatively and the country has been turned into a middle-aged playground. Most interesting of all is that they think they are still young and as a result, they are the only generation to have pissed off both their parents and their children. Now that's some achievement.

The Jaggers fall into two broad camps. Only recently have these tribes realised that they have more in common than they thought. Listen to the paper-reviewing panels on Marian Finucane's RTE Radio 1 show on Sunday morning if you doubt that. In an extremely good programme, with the most naturally talented radio broadcaster this country has probably ever produced, there is a nice consensus, driven more by age than ideology. The Jagger fusion has happened.

But it wasn't always like this. Back when they were young and angry during the set-piece battles of the 1970s, both camps were implacable enemies with very different views of what Ireland should be. As they've got older and more similar, they have realised that they have much more in common with each other than with anyone else in society. Power is not only a great aphrodisiac, it focuses the mind. Every generation has its price and in the end, the great arguments of the two opposing camps of Jaggers who came of age in the 1970s, were ultimately settled by money.

The Redundant Radicals

The first Jagger tribe is the Redundant Radicals, who realise that their bluff was called in 1989 when the Berlin Wall fell and who have been desperately groping around for a new identity ever since. Finally, like the Labour Party and Sinn Féin, they've thrown in the towel and succumbed to the allure of tax cuts. It's hard to sustain a world of capital-against-labour when most workers are capitalists and when the main unions in the country do not represent endangered hod-carriers, but pampered public-sector workers. Also, international workers' solidarity is hard to maintain when the main threat to the living standards of what remains of the Irish industrial working class is not the boss, but hungry workers from Poland who are prepared to work for the minimum wage because they live three-to-a-room in investment properties owned by the Jagger Generation.

Along the way, the Radicals lost Marx but found Joyce, dropped *Das Kapital* and picked up *Ulysses*. Truth be known, they have probably read neither; but that hasn't stopped them from turning Bloomsday into their very own May Day, complete with a communist weakness for uniforms and role playing, an absolutist and unwavering devotion to the sacred text and a Soviet-style obsession with minute detail and reinterpretation. They are disciples, after all. Ironically, despite anti-clericalism being their unifying thread, hating, as they do, all things religious, they retain a fondness for sacrament and ritual and dietary exclusiveness as they munch their way through piss-smelling kidneys at eight in the morning, head to toe in ceremonial Edwardian costume. But it's all good fun in that first-edition, 'in crowd' type of way.

Redundant Radicals are prominent in the media, politics and academia, which might possibly explain why the former two are often lagging indictors of social trends, why much of the media misread the last election and why Irish universities do not figure in international league tables.

From such elevated safe-ground, the Redundant Radicals can launch broadsides against fictitious class enemies while continuing to live in Victorian Ranelagh. They can also rail about developers exploiting immigrant labour, while they extend their second houses in the West using bewildered Latvian lads just two weeks in the country. Even they have realised that bashing the Church is a blood sport. They still read *Hot Press* and are behind the new obsession with public awareness campaigns. So, instead of hard, unambiguous legislation to police bad behaviour, we have soft, woolly public awareness campaigns like Age Action Week, Dental Awareness Week, Racism Awareness Week, International Women at Work Day, and Be Nice to Dad Day. What next? Be Nice to Pet Rabbits Day? Take your pick. They accept that the tribunals are a waste of time (apart from their left-wing college mates at the Bar who set out to change the world and ended up changing the Volvo).

The Redundant Radicals have had to migrate to the corners of the protest movement not because they were unsuccessful, but because everything they campaigned for, they got. They won the war because they were right but they are too self-absorbed to realise that they've won. They still want to be taken seriously, but have ponytails. In many ways, modern Ireland is the place they dreamt of in 1969, only richer and more decadent.

Because they defined themselves as rebels, giving the two liberated fingers to authority, many have been unwilling to set out rules, regulations and discipline for their children. The vacuum vacated by the Church has not been filled by anything, except Doors back-catalogues and serial inoffensiveness. This has blurred the lines of parenting, leading to the bizarre and generationally confusing outcome of children who are more conservative than their parents. Children have to rebel against something so they rebel against the rebels. But the Radicals can't see this; they don't realise that they are the power.

Like Sting and the Police, the Radicals just can't stay out of the limelight, so they reform and tour, playing, talking and writing for their generation—the very people who've always loved them and share all their views anyway. Hopefully, now that they have money, no-one will notice that they are in favour of lower capital gains tax.

The Corporate Boxers

The second group of Jaggers are the Corporate Boxers. They are responsible for the success of Fianna Fáil Lite under Bertie Ahern, the corporate boxes at Croke Park and the Mercedes virus on our roads. The Corporate Boxer loves a Merc. This is the only constant in a rapidly changing Ireland. Give the Boxer a few quid and the first thing he'll buy is the Merc.

They also have a weakness for Louis Copeland for him, Louise Kennedy for her, golf for both, home cinemas and, in recent years, as well as the beloved GAA, the Munster rugby is the focus of their affections. Some might still go to Mass unless they're on a short break (which is about half the year at their place on the Algarve). Their prominence also signals the final chapter of the complete rural take-over of suburban Ireland, most clearly evidenced by the explosion in popularity of hurling in traditionally slíotar-free zones like Dun Laoghaire.

If the Redundant Radicals are made up of urban sophisticates and self-loathing culchies, the Corporate Boxers are White Boys and Ribbonmen with university degrees.

Apart from Bill Haley's gigs in the Theatre Royal which kicked off the rock 'n' roll years, the most interesting social development at the time was how small farmers—De Valera's foot-soldiers—adapted to the changing Ireland of the 1960s much better than the urban working class. Amazingly, in 1950, after 30 years of independence, Ireland was more dependent on agriculture than it had been in 1870. This startling figure is either a damning indictment of De Valera's dingbat economics or evidence of how successful this rural fundamentalist movement was.

The Corporate Boxers might have gone from Angel's Delight and a pint of milk to angel-hair pasta and a glass of Sancerre, but they still have dirt under their fingernails. They came from the last small farmers in Western Europe and the way they worked the system was impressive.

The small-scale farming structure emerged as the system in rural Ireland as a result of the great social transformation that followed the end of the landlord oligarchy in the final decades of the 19th century. These small farmers experienced a significant increase in their living standards up to the late 1920s. From 1870 to 1930, the economic system was based on one son getting the farm and the rest emigrating. If they couldn't emigrate, they tried to find a job in the towns or in Dublin or hung around—landless and single.

In the 1930s this system broke down. America closed its doors to migrants in the early 1930s, and De Valera's perverted economy collapsed, meaning there wasn't a sniff of a job away from the farm and there was only England left to absorb indigent Irishmen. Between 1950 and 1960, half a million of us emigrated to the country which the mullahs who ran our Banana Republic told us was the Great Satan.

The small farmers, or more accurately, their Irish Mammies, saw this dead-end coming. They realised that the game was up and that the only way out for the sons who didn't get the farm was either emigration or the public service. The rallying cry of Irish mammies went up: 'Sure, where would you be without your education?' A new class was born which took full advantage of the free secondary education introduced in the mid 1960s.

An ESRI paper written by Damian F. Hannan and Patrick Commins in 1994 entitled, 'The Significance of Small-Scale Landholders in Ireland's Socio-Economic Transformation', found that the single most important determinant of a county's educational achievement in the 1960s and 1970s was the number of small farmers.[5] This is quite extraordinary and unique to this country. De Valera's foot soldiers were on the march, camán in one hand, Latin for Today in the other.

Compared to their urban, working-class counterparts, 30% more children of small farmers did the Leaving Cert and 50% more went on to third-level education in the 1960s.[6] They turned into the teacher aristocracy, bringing with them to Dublin a love of the GAA, squeeze boxes and Farah slacks. Their success in education catapulted them into the public service in great numbers when the government started handing out civil service jobs like miraculous medals in the 1970s.

Back then, they drank cans of Harp in cold bedsits in Rathmines around a Superser. They were on first-name terms with the inspectors at Busaras and for a few years, they'd go home every weekend with stories of gamey Protestant nurses from the Adelaide who smoked Mores, talked about sex and listened to Joni Mitchell. Now, the Corporate Boxers are the best paid public servants in Europe and, if they haven't opted for early retirement, are earning on average 46% more than their mates in the private sector.[7] They engineered this through shams like benchmarking and social partnership which saw them having the same success in wresting cash out of the State as their great-grandfathers had in prising land away from the landlords.

Many put on the good suit, kissed ass and found their way into banking, insurance and other white-collar jobs, much to their mammies' delight. All those 'big jobs' up in Dublin played havoc with the social hierarchy at the front of Mass on a Sunday. They went from no-collar to white-collar within five years.

But that's not all. The Corporate Boxers had an ace up their sleeves. The same forces that propelled them into education also left them with an inheritance. This inheritance of farming land has been re-valued by the housing boom and the land frenzy, with the result that the Corporate Boxers have been enormously enriched.

While many thousands left the land, they did not sell it. Today only 6% of the workforce works on the land, yet a quarter of all households still own land.[8] One of the hangovers from the past in Ireland is a reticence to sell land. No-one wants to be landless again. So if there is land in a family it gets handed down long after the last sons have stopped taking an interest in farming. Only 1% of Irish farming land changes hands each year.[9]

This peasant mentality was reinforced by the EU which has gradually made 'welfare mothers' out of farmers who increasingly, like teenage mothers in their pyjamas and slippers, are totally dependent on State handouts. The farmers have willingly, without pride, turned themselves into the rural equivalent of a work-shy underclass.

This State subsidy had enormous ramifications for the rural Jaggers.

It allowed them to hold on to the land in the 1980s and early 1990s, leaving it fallow at no cost. As the price of land soared in the mid-1990s, the sons and daughters of the soil have been sitting on goldmines. They have been selling sites ever since. If you could have planned an agrarian revolution, you couldn't have done it better. This was a Marxist revolution without the bloodshed and today, these same children of small farmers run large parts of the country.

As Hannan and Commins conclude: 'not only have the smallholders as a class succeeded in retaining their property and relative income position, but they have also succeeded in capturing a significant proportion of local off-farm employment. They have been more effective than working-class families in utilising the education system to gain access to off-farm opportunities for their children.'[10]

The success of the Corporate Boxers, due to their enormously re-valued property portfolios, explains the provincial chic phenomenon we've seen recently. It is behind the explosion of French restaurants with misspelt names, organic food shops, Botox parties, Versace handbags and Manolo Blahnik shoes in places like Thurles, Roscommon Town and Abbeyleix—places you'd have spotted tumbleweed in ten years ago.

Radical Boxers and Corporate Revolutionaries

Ireland is now a country run by a motley rainbow coalition of Radical Revolutionaries, who are the power but don't realise it, and Corporate Boxers, who can't quite believe their luck.

The broad Jagger church realised that they had more in common than not and more importantly, they had more to lose, so they came together. The Corporate Boxers, always conservative economically and socially, dropped their aversion to divorce, sex before marriage, homosexuality and Protestants. The Redundant Radicals, always liberal socially and left-wing economically, dropped their dislike of low taxes, 20% capital gains, privatisation, multinationals and toll-bridges.

So we now have a fusion of Radical Boxers and Corporate Revolutionaries. In the 2007 election campaign Pat and Enda snuggled up to each other, each adopted the other's stance in a desperate bid for power. Enda became Pat and Pat became Enda, giving us a strange hybrid: Enda Rabbitte and well, what can I say, Pat Kenny. But neither of these hybrids could out-Jagger the über-Jagger himself, Bertie Ahern.

The fusion is a marriage of convenience. The old conservatives have become liberal and the old liberals have become conservative. Like many marriages forged through common interest rather than love, it has durability. They met through those most convincing of matchmakers—money, age and power.

These disparate forces, mortal enemies in the early 1970s—the era of the Beatles, Dusty Springfield, Horslips, Mao's *Little Red Book*, civil rights, the liberal agenda, hot knives, the Dandelion Market, Carnsore Point, Bob Marley at Dalymount, summers in London, the Magic Bus—are now fused together by off-plan sites, off-site weekends, friends in high places, nods and winks, county managers they were in school with, access roads, property syndicates, equity release and private-school fundraisers.

The Jaggers devote entire radio shows to Bob Dylan's lyrics and then wonder why the demographic reach of their radio station is stuck at 50 plus. They reminisce in an embarrassing way, desperately trying to be seen as rebels while they agonise over where to get the best sushi, porcini mushrooms and rye bread. The formerly GAA-hating Radical Revolutionaries marvel at the passion of Croke Park, while the GAA-mad Corporate Boxers rhapsodise about its design. Ruairi Quinn and Pat Spillane have become one.

————

While money and power have served to ease historical animosities, a third factor gels the Jaggers together and that is a narcissistic fear of growing old. They are Ireland's first teenagers, a Peter Pan generation that has no intention of leaving the stage and BUPA, the Blackrock Clinic and Botox will see to the rest.

The Jaggers are our biggest spenders and, as you'd expect from a generation that is petrified of wrinkles, they spend fortunes on cosmetics, fillers and health supplements as well as the run-of-the-mill Irish diet of booze. They keep thesaurus-plundering, unkempt foodies in business, while they're fêted by charlatan wine experts over expensive lunches in Peploe's.

Ireland's gilded generation have never had it so good, and they are spending like there's no tomorrow. People in their 50s are not saving in Ireland. This is unprecedented in the western world, where the 50s is the decade in which most people save most money. In contrast, our Jaggers are richer than they have ever been, on the right side of the generation gap in Ireland, and they are splashing out.

The Market Gardeners

It's hard to hear the cracks in the housing market when you are on the flat of your back, listening to the simulated sound of rushing water, getting your toes massaged by a Filipina. You are in the new nirvana of Ireland's Jagger Generation, the spa.

The spa is the Jaggers' revenge on the electric immersion, which terrorised every Irish household on a Saturday evening and led to ferocious rows about who'd be first in the bathroom. Back then, there was only one bathroom. Now, if anything signals our reversal of fortune, it is hot water, lots and lots of hot water, always on, never rationed, roasting hot water. Think about the amount of time an immersion takes to heat a steam bath and then lie back, let your pores open and luxuriate in our new status. We are rich, we are worthy, we have hot water and to show the rest of the world just how rich we are, we are going to build spas, lots and lots of spas. In fact, we have turned into a nation of spas. This is where Botox Betty comes, with her tanorexic daughter, to recharge, reinvigorate and eat steamed broccoli.

Spa obsessives have a water fixation and can neither get enough water into them, nor enough water around them. You'll see them surgically attached to a bottle of Riverrock ('water you wear'), while bubbling away in a sea-salt bath, before they plunge into a freezing imitation-Finnish lake. Neo-spa women have a pathological fear of dry things; nothing freaks them out like dry skin, dry hair, dry lips, dry cuticles and dry you know what. Hair masks and sock salve are *de rigueur*. They'll be growing gills next.

The spa obsession is one of the many signs that the Jaggers have fashioned a new Tír na nÓg in Ireland. From boutique hotels, to spa retreats, bespoke therapies, colonic irrigation, Botox, massage rooms, veteran's football, third apartments, corrective eye surgery, five-star restaurants, weekend city breaks, digitally re-mastered Horslips CDs, classic cars, Darina Allen, 50th birthday parties, hill walking in Santiago, the Shannon cruise, tax-break holiday homes in Kerry, non-contributory defined-benefit pension, early retirement, the

Ice Bar, Louise Kennedy, the Police reunion, interior design and *Questions and Answers*, the whole country is a Jagger playground.

The spa is a religious place, full of ceremony and learned behaviour, like Lourdes for lapsed Catholics. It is not a place to worry about such materialistic concerns as unsold apartments, bad tenants and the mounting credit card bill. It is a place for denial, a dream world where our spiritual side can be respected. As Mass attendance plummeted, spa devotion exploded. This is big business for a generation that needs to be rewarded for existing.

A smiling receptionist with unfeasibly clear eyes and shiny-apple skin welcomes you to Ciúnas in hushed tones, barely whispering. This is a peaceful place. This is a retreat. It is Lough Derg for people with Neff kitchens and no financial worries.

This new-age sanctuary is run by a dreamy middle-aged couple, with unfeasibly tight tummy muscles, who know how to heighten your senses while lightening your wallet. Most of these people have had quasi-religious epiphanies where they have seen the light, mended their ways and changed their lives. They tell you about this event again and again as if they were the only people in the world to have had this privilege.

The husband is a down-sizing property speculator who saw the light while walking the Great Wall of China the day after he put half of Anglo-Irish Bank into a deal in Shanghai. She—the Goddess—used to be a corporate witch, breaking balls in mergers and acquisitions. Now she's terrorising local farmers while she makes plant-based treatment products using local ingredients. Both look disturbingly like Evangelicals.

Botox Betty isn't concerned about the falling housing market. She bought three apartments before 2000 and she's part of a new tribe. She is a market gardener. In the market for gardens, she has cashed in her chips. The young man from Lisney with the unprepossessing stammer gushed that she was sitting on a goldmine and the back garden was worth millions. As the children were gone and her husband had traded her in for a set of golf clubs sometime in the late 1990s—and she'd never been a gardener, unlike their nice Protestant neighbours the Wilsons, she decided, why not? Her husband, Billy Bunker, wouldn't care as long as he was on the greens.

Botox Betty is not alone. The market gardeners are a growing sub tribe of Jaggers in the suburbs. Look around you, all over the country, developers are buying up bits of back gardens, buying pairs of old suburban houses, knocking them down and putting up apartment blocks. It's an odd thing but the Jaggers, the generation who complain loudest that Ireland has lost its soul and its sense of community, are the first to sell up blocks of four 1970s houses for apartments, cashing in on the boom and thereby destroying the very communities they harp on about in the first place.

In fact, in a complete turnaround from Famine times when the poorer you were the more likely you were to sub-divide your land, in early-21st-century Ireland the tables have turned. Today, the richer you are, the more likely you will be to sub-divide your garden. If you don't believe me, just look at the patchwork that is Shrewsbury Road, Ireland's most exclusive piece of real estate. Years ago, this was a stately road with long avenues and acres of garden. These days, our oligarchs are buying up houses for fortunes to knock them down and build two or three seven-bathroomed McMansions in their place. Now everyone's at it. Greed is contagious and everyone wants to be a market gardener.

Every spare piece of land in the suburbs is being hoovered up. This land-grab is extending to golf courses, tennis clubs and football grounds. No decent-sized garden is safe. Large 1970s suburban gardens with side entrances are gold. They are creating instant millionaires all around the country.

These are people, like Botox Betty who, having raised their kids, mollycoddled their husbands and offered themselves up on the very Irish altar of the family, are now flogging the back garden, trousering the shekels and making a break for themselves.

Goddess wraps Botox Betty in a pre-heated, insulated duvet, the type of thing you see dehydrated housewives with jelly legs wearing after a mini-marathon. She leads her, almost but not quite touching, into the inner sanctum.

Come with us, quietly into the labyrinth. Everything is Oriental including the cedar bath with orange peel. Asia is the theme in this part of the retreat. Across the hushed corridor, you leave the Orient and enter the lush rainforest. Further on, through the 'Bluebell Walk', you reach the Enchanted Celtic Copse, resplendent with moss and lichen treatments.

This whistle-stop tour around the world is half-Lonely Planet, half-

Disneyland: Lonely Planet because the sanctuary replicates those parts of the world that feature in the *Irish Times*, places where the local language and culture are under threat; Disney because it is all fantasy.

To our modern-day Irish spa devotee, wrapped in a heavyweight 100% cotton towel which was made by child labourers in Pakistan, nothing could be more plebeian, materialistic and vulgar than Disneyland. Yet Ciúnas offers the same delusion to people with wormeries.

The entire experience in Ciúnas is designed to make you to feel that you are a different person. You can feel the smouldering row at the sales target meeting recede as you inhale the odours of the sea salt, olive oil and oregano body scrub. The door opens quietly, you are vaguely aware of someone else in the room over the faint orchestral Thai music. Goddess arrives and smiles at you beatifically, the St Teresa of spas. After the body scrub, the Abhyanga massage is performed by two angelic therapists using warm sesame oil. You are dozing off, silently content, devising ways of shafting that prick from client account management.

In time, Goddess offers you a deep stomach massage should you 'want to get waste moving'. Nice thought, love. You are in a haze now, dreamily acquiescing to every treatment. Someone is measuring your skin's elasticity, which like every treatment at Ciúnas is marketed as one part 22nd century, one part prehistoric. Everything must have a link to some ancient tradition. In one fell swoop, our Celtic ancestors turn from warlike warriors to mud-wrapped sissies. Bet you didn't know that, as well as throwing rocks from Antrim over to Scotland, Finn McCool was a great man for the minimalist treatment room and that St Kevin's bed up in Glendalough was an early version of the hardwood yoga mat.

At least this is what Goddess is inferring when she makes the heroic leap from her €500-a-night piece of interior-decorated fantasy to our historic past. But in early-21st-century Ireland, fuse a bit of old Irish legend with New Irish prices, throw in a smattering of Oriental exoticism with modern-day professionalism, and finally convince someone that this will allow her to find peace and look five years younger, and you're in.

_____

What all this shows us is that they who should be leading the country, taking charge and preparing us for the years ahead, couldn't be bothered. They're too busy divorcing, playing golf in the Algarve, getting their feet exfoliated and buying up half of Marbella to care. The Jaggers are enjoying their unexpected windfall. As the generation who runs the place, these people should be mature enough to shoulder their responsibilities, but instead, they are reliving their youth recklessly. And who can blame them, no-one told them it would be so good. Go on, have another gin.

But the very forces that presented them with a windfall and drove our economy forward, are now changing. In the past ten years, few other countries have milked globalisation as much as Ireland. We have played the game dextrously and with great stealth. But complacency is the greatest enemy of success. We are in danger of believing our own hype and more importantly, the emergence of China, India and mass immigration will change the rules.

Chapter 4

THE PERFECT STORM

Coming around Omey Island in a blaze of July sunlight, Connemara opens up before you. Looking past the Sky Road, double-spired Clifden and beyond to the Maumturks, it is hard to imagine a more beautiful and peaceful place. That is, of course, until the Atlantic weather turns. If you have ever been caught in a small boat when the seas change, when summer turns to winter in a matter of minutes, when the winds pick up and the ocean swells and when the power of nature envelops you, you will realise that these are forces to be reckoned with.

Forces building in the global economy, which link Ireland with the rest of the world, will converge and impact on Ireland in much the same way.

When Ireland was isolated, we could ignore international economic turbulence. We were spectators, now we are players. Today, we can borrow where we like, buy houses where the sun shines, employ Polish plumbers and waitresses, reinvent ourselves on *myspace.com*, travel for half nothing, watch news as it breaks, log on, blog on, buy stuff from China, get instructions for our lap-tops made in Limerick from help-lines in India, read what we like and see what we like; we are fused with the rest of the globe.

Like the small boat, we are independent yet exposed, plugged in yet cut off, we are part of a community, yet on our own. Ireland is part of everything yet part of nothing. Our economy is the most globalised in Europe; we are the poster-boys of the new world order which means we milk the plaudits while glancing nervously over our shoulders. We are winning, yet have no control. We are running flat out to stand still, buying to discard, eating to lose weight, getting more rest to pack more in.

The Irish have been playing this game for years, adapting, getting by, hoodwinking, accommodating and most significantly, surviving and thriving. We rarely feel foreign anywhere for long. Unlike most nations, the world is not an alien place for us. We were global citizens when many others were isolating themselves. Despite thinking of ourselves as a traditional society up until recently, we are a thoroughly modern people. If modernity is being urban, literate, mobile, flexible, accommodating, impulsive, nimble, rootless and comfortable abroad, then the Irish are one of the great modern tribes. It's not for nothing that we are a global brand. It is because we are everywhere, we are a wandering tribe and that makes us well-placed to get the best out of a borderless world. But the tribe is facing problems back at base.

In *A Perfect Storm*, Sebastian Junger described a 'perfect storm' which hit Nova Scotia on Hallowe'en 1991. A perfect storm occurs when several weather fronts, which individually would be bad enough, converge to wreak havoc. The weather fronts build far out to sea, violently gaining momentum, heading for the coast. Their simultaneous convergence causes the forces of nature to whip up a most violent tempest. This occurs very rarely, but when it does, the results are devastating. The damage depends on where exactly they make landfall. If the perfect storm hits a vulnerable area, which is weakened by a lack of preparation and taken totally unawares (or, like New Orleans, a place which ignored the warning signs that were well flagged), the carnage will be widespread.

The global economy works in a similar way. Far-off events which appear unrelated can have unforeseen and potentially cataclysmic consequences. Most economies can deal with problems individually, but if they all come at the same time, we are in trouble. For all but the very largest economies, there are two separate challenges: events over which you have no control and those which are in your control. Unfortunately, in the past few years, we have chosen to absolve ourselves of domestic responsibility which means our economy is in no shape to weather the coming storm.

The Echo Chamber

For the past 15 years Ireland has profited enormously from two positive global factors over which we had no control.

First, the Berlin Wall came down which had unforeseen consequences, all positive for Ireland. The ten-year German recession which followed gave us low interest rates and the single currency made the monetary link with Germany permanent. By opening up its border to the East, within 15 years, a deep pool of cheap immigrant labour (such as Tatiana in Dublin airport) would be available for Ireland. By reverberating around the world, this event allowed China to open up quicker than even Deng Xiaoping had planned, giving us cheap consumer goods and relatively low world inflation, thanks to Chinese workers working for $1 a day.

That one day, 9 November 1989—another 9/11 as noted by Tom Friedman in his 2006 book, *The World is Flat*—would change the face of modern Ireland and be the rallying call for thousands of us to return home. At the time, most people believed that the main beneficiaries of the fall of the Berlin Wall would be the lands to the east of Berlin. In fact, it was the European country furthest to the west of Potsdamer Platz that reaped Mikhail Gorbachev's harvest.

The second global factor was the end of the Cold War which prompted American multinationals to see the world as one large market, compelling them to seek a bridgehead into Europe: and we provided that platform, tax breaks and all. This reversed the centuries'- old flow of Irish labour to the us; now American capital came flooding the other way.

The Big Picture

This is not new. International events have always impacted on Ireland and trade has been a constant locomotive for change. For example, last year there was a fascinating discovery in a bog in County Cavan. Two poor devils were exhumed, having been slaughtered over 2,000 years ago in a ritualistic killing. Archaeologists believe that they were killed to satisfy a local pagan god. They were perfectly preserved. One was like an ancient Paul O'Connell, the other Peter Stringer—in stature at least.

The tall one had manicured nails; the small one, hair gel. Traces of the gel came from pine resin in southern France, suggesting that there was a decent trade between Ireland and France in beauty products in the time before Christ.

This discovery shows that trade has always been cosmopolitan. Trade wants to be international. People want to buy and sell stuff to each other. Our vain, Iron-Age 'Gel Boy' was doing what people have been doing for years: trading with outsiders to buy things he couldn't get at home. I wonder what he sold in return for his firm-hold gel— humans, hides or maybe cattle? This human drive to trade and be curious about the outside world is what keeps economies going and sometimes the more frivolous the product—like ancient hair gel or modern-day Botox—the more interesting the trading arrangement.

——

Ireland has done extremely well from trade. Our recent economic history could be seen as two contrasting sides of an economic experiment and can be divided into two broad periods of roughly equal duration. From 1922 to the mid 1960s, we cut ourselves off from the rest of the world. This is bizarre from today's vantage point, but at the time it wasn't all that weird. Most of the world did something similar. The world economy went into a tailspin of war, protectionism and militarism. Ireland, being a small country, lost more than most.

From the mid 1960s to today, we opened up, with almost miraculous results. The big fear in the years ahead is that in the event of a crisis, an angry population might blame outside forces and could move to cut ourselves off again or, more likely, that we would support a drift towards early 20th-century-style protectionism, possibly led by the US as it reacts to the competitive challenge of China and India.

The world is changing and Ireland will change with it. There is a once-in-a-century transformation playing itself out in front of our eyes and because Ireland is amongst the most globalised nations on earth, this tectonic shift will have an amplified impact here.

There are two major factors at play. First, the centre of economic gravity is shifting from the Atlantic to the South China Sea. In the future, jobs will migrate to Asia at a rate not seen since the USA began to flex its economic muscles at the end of the 19th century, when millions of people and jobs migrated from Europe to the US.

It is not clear whether this will occur peacefully or without incident. In the run-up to the 2008 US election, increasingly we are hearing protectionist and isolationist murmurs, taking the form of China-bashing. It is impossible to open an American newspaper without reading scare stories about the threat of China and how China is flooding the US market with everything from laptops to Lightning McQueen toy sets. The protectionist streak will also lead some American politicians to question the wisdom of all the tax foregone to places like Ireland. We sometimes forget that there is a lot of populist anger in the US directed at American companies which avoid tax by funnelling large amounts of tax dollars through places like Leixlip. (Imagine the reaction here if AIB were funnelling large amounts of euro through the British Virgin Islands and the resulting shortfall in tax revenues for St Vincent's Hospital was being met through extra income tax.) At the moment, this is an outside risk, but history suggests that wholesale shifts in opinion cannot be ruled out, particularly as the mood in the US today is one of 'bring the boys home', 'pull up the drawbridge', 'leave these foreigners to sort out their own mess'. A threatened America anywhere in the world is not in Ireland's interest. We have benefited enormously from Pax Americana.

The second big change is a demographic one. This silent revolution will dramatically change the traditional economic dynamic of the globe. It is arguably a more extraordinary development than the rapid rise of China and India. Europe, for so long the dynamic hub of world invention, creativity and dynamism, is dying. Large parts of the EU today and the likely new members in the years ahead are inhabited by nations that seem intent on breeding themselves out of existence. The latest *Eurostat* population projections predict population declines in 13 of the current European Union member states, particularly in Eastern Europe, over the next 40 years. In addition, the bigger states which are likely to be either in the EU's sights or major trading partners, are also dying. For example, by 2050, Ukraine's population will be 43% smaller than it is today. The corresponding figure for Bulgaria is 34%, Latvia 27%, Lithuania 25%, Romania 23%, Russia 22%, Moldova 21%, Croatia 19% and Poland, the country we are milking for labour, will see its population fall by 17%. This is Malthusian economics without the Famine.

Such self-inflicted euthanasia is unprecedented and the implications for Ireland are immense because these countries are our new partners. Old countries don't grow: they demand much more social welfare transfers and act as a drag on the economic growth of the entire region. In the past few years, Germany has been getting old, but at least it is rich. The central European countries have no savings of their own which implies that they will want our cash when the time comes. Also, older countries such as these which have little or no trade are more likely to be protectionist when faced with a resurgent India or Indonesia. Ireland has no interest in being part of such a grouping. Yet we have hitched our wagon to these nations that don't want to live.

These transformations will not happen overnight but gradually: it will become evident that geographically, we are in the wrong part of the world. Up to now, Atlantic Ireland's position, between America and Europe, placed us at the crossroads of the world's two great powers. We were in a pivotal position on the modern equivalent of the Silk Road. This no longer holds. Our world is tilting on its axis and we have to tilt with it.

Seaworthy?

So Ireland is facing a perfect storm, with economic tempests building. Up to now, we have convinced ourselves that our little boat is seaworthy enough to navigate these waters. But is it? Is the economy quite as resilient as we think? Unfortunately, while we have been cruising along in the past five years, no-one has thought to carry out basic maintenance on our boat. Now, when faced with changing conditions, the boat that we all thought was unsinkable, is brittle. Let's look at five of the weak points.

Housing

Most worrying, the very thing which we thought made us strong is making us weak: the core of our problem is the housing market which is sucking the life out of the economy.

According to an international survey, in 2006,[1] the typical middle-class home in Dublin cost nine times more than the same class of house in Houston, Texas, three times more than in Amsterdam, twice the cost of Sydney and almost twice the price of Tokyo. This is suicidal for a trading economy. It's hardly surprising, therefore, in a country that is supposed to be competitive, that house prices are now falling. Land and house prices are part of the overall cost of doing business in a country. Sometimes, with all the back-slapping about the economy here, that fundamental fact is overlooked.

Property cycles occur in every society, where either deregulation or outside forces allow cash to cascade into the economy. Prices soar as cheap money seeps into every pore. In our case, when we joined EMU and deregulated the banking system, we created the environment for a property boom of monumental proportions. Certain well-known Dublin banks are now little more than out-of-control hedge funds leveraging themselves and clients into property. When the market finally gives up, these outfits tend to go belly-up. At the very least their share prices will fall so much as to make their net asset value negligible. Remember, that three of the world's top five banks were Japanese at the height of Japan's late-1980s' property bubble. Today, two of those are no more, one of the chief executives did time for fraud and Japanese banks don't figure in the top ten. History shows us the inconvenient truth about banks and property cycles.

The problem is one of confidence. The Irish housing market left economics behind a few years ago and was sustained by the hot air of cheap credit. This situation has now changed, but unfortunately, the builders who saw this coming went into overdrive in an effort to get everything finished before the pyramid scheme was exposed. Now we are facing huge supply and a buyer's strike: people are saying, why should we part with money now when, if we wait a little while, prices might fall further? This hesitancy kills a market; just as house price increases became a self-fulfilling prophecy, on the way down the same is the case. Once the mystique of rising house prices evaporates, confidence dissipates and the market turns.

The problem for the financial system is that due to the narrowness of its business model, so much of its profits are dependent on the housing market and, as two thirds of Irish construction activity is housing-related, the knock-on effects are enormous. The banks are at the centre of an interrelated financial web which includes the government, estate agents, developers and the media, which has shamelessly cheer-led the romp. 40 pages of advertising speaks louder than editorials.

This is all bad news for the new 'Green and Greener' government because the housing market is at the centre of a financial web which links all elements of the economy. 17% of all direct tax revenue comes from property[2] and, although estimates vary, about one euro in every three of all tax is wrapped up in construction. Let's just do a bit of sixth-class maths at this stage. The lads at *www.finfacts.ie* (a brilliant website for all things financial and economic) did a calculation based on a comment by the then Minister for Finance back in 2004 when he stated that about 28% of the average cost of a new house is made up of taxes and levies collected by the State. These comprise VAT of 13.5%, development levies, site stamp duty, along with PAYE and PSRI from the workers building the houses.

Given that there were 93,419 houses and apartments completed last year, up more than 15% on 2005,[3] a back-of-a-brown-envelope calculation reveals that 28% of 93,419 multiplied by an average price of €300,000, is over €7.8 billion. That's a big budget deficit if construction activity were to fall to EU-average levels, which are about half of current Irish output. Add to this the €3 billion from stamp duty from the sale of second-hand property and it is easy to see how tied to the property market our national budget position is.

The first area to feel the pinch has been housing starts. New housing starts fell by 18% in January 2007,[4] while, according to the CSO, planning permissions for new houses plunged by over 21% in the fourth quarter of 2006. All across the country we are seeing the signs of indigestion as the population tries to come to terms with what is happening. Auctions, those voyeuristic little rituals, for so long the bellwether for the market and the subject of dinner-party conversations, are not quite as titillating as they once were. In fact, they are alarming for the propertied classes. The property pages are getting thinner, many trophy houses are now being advertised with the euphemistic 'new price' and the country is in danger of becoming a big Carrick on Shannon.

A town which has been haemorrhaging people for years, Carrick on Shannon looks like a hub of activity these days, with cafés overlooking the river and the formerly strict parochial hall (opened in 1887 to mark the visit to Ireland of Queen Victoria) now offering 'martabak minced lamb curry flavoured with galangal sauce' served by Malaysian waitresses.

On either side of the Shannon, new developments have sprung up. Yet even though in the past seven years Leitrim's population has grown for the first time since the Famine, there is something not quite right. The new buildings are empty. Behind the façades, there is no-one in these apartments. The for-sale signs promise out-of-town business centres, but there are no businesses. One in five houses in Leitrim is empty and most of these are new.[5] This is what happens when you have tax breaks supporting an industry that doesn't need any support at all. In fact, the last thing the construction industry needs when it is operating flat out is tax breaks, but that's what we have. So builders, already panicked by softening demand, find themselves backed up against the arbitrary deadline of a closing tax loophole. If a Martian economist were to land here, he'd laugh and then cry.

Leitrim is just the most extreme example of what has been happening all over the country in the past few years. Drive through any town and you will see them—the ghost estates, developments large or small which have popped up on the edges of villages, past the Mace and before the statue of the Blessed Virgin Mary and the GAA club. Names like Coille Mór, Gurteen Beag or Blackberry Lawns are bestowed on ghost estates with no-one in them, built by Polish labourers who sleep on site in HiAce vans.

A ludicrous 59% of all residential building in Ireland today has been bought either for speculation or for holiday-home investment with equity released from a first home. These 'investments' are the Achilles heel of the market. The 2006 census collectors found that one in six Irish houses was empty.[6] This compares with one in 31 in so-called property-obsessed Britain! Such over-hang is ruinous for a market going through a period of self-doubt.

The housing market is afflicted by a simple problem: prices need to fall for there to be any incentive to buy. And in a sure sign that the market is in trouble, rents—for so long dormant in a market where everyone wanted to buy—have started to rise for the first time in three years as people wait and rent instead of rush and buy.

However, all areas will not be affected similarly. The history of property cycles tells us that outlying areas are worst affected where there is an overhang of supply. The best way to check whether that affects you is to go to *www.daft.ie*, the property website, and it will show you what percentage of houses are not selling in each different area. Lucan's looking much stretched at the moment.

The major problem with property is its sheer size. Property's fingerprints are everywhere in Ireland and it has grown exponentially over the past decade. For example, in May 1998, there were 126,100 employed in the construction sector. The number had risen to 262,700 by May 2006 and increased further to 275,000 by September 2006.[7] Worse still, property has elbowed out all other investment as we are sucked into its vortex: no-one can escape. In March 2007, *www.finfacts.ie* reported that venture capital investment in Irish business, at €192 million, amounted to a mere 2.4% of the €8 billion Irish investors ploughed into overseas commercial property in 2006.[8] This is plainly nonsensical when the yields on property are falling. Things will only get worse before they get better. Construction accounts for a staggering 23% of our total GDP.[9] The average in the rest of Europe is 12%.[10] Given that our GDP is close to €160 billion, to bring it into line with the rest of Europe requires an adjustment of 11% which is over €16 billion. That's a lot of cash. It's a case of 'better not look down' at this altitude.

Because we are in EMU we can't appreciate how bad the situation actually is. But that's not the real problem; the issue is how it plays out. Many argue that EMU gives us a cushion. It's only a cushion if interest rates are falling which they are not. The question is whether we want shock therapy or a prolonged convalescence.

As a result of EMU we won't have a crash like the UK in the early 1990s where the market dropped out of bed and then the country almost ran out of money, having to keep interest rates at 15% to prevent the currency from collapsing. The same thing happened in Sweden and Finland around the same time. But we'll get something worse. Instead of a crash, bang, wallop which is painful but over quickly, we will get something akin to a slow puncture, which is experienced over a longer period, but is ultimately more debilitating. The market will simply expire on its feet as people postpone buying in the expectation that prices will continue to fall. This type of enduring, relatively shallow, slump tends to occur in American states, such as the Massachusetts

Miracle of Mike Dukakis which subsided into the late-1980s' and early-1990s' New-England property quagmire, in turn nearly burying Bank of Ireland via its subsidiary, the Bank of New Hampshire.

Exports

In the makey-uppey world of textbook economics, the painless solution to an economy weighed down by property is to just export your way out of trouble. All successful Tiger economies thrive on exports. The country that exports, grows in a balanced way. Can't we just export our way out of the problem? It's not that easy, because you can't export the houses that we are using all our cash to build.

What about doing what they are currently doing in Spain and Portugal—just get foreigners to buy our houses from us? We did that in the 1970s when our house prices were bargain basement and the Dutch and the Germans bought here for a song. They moved into a countryside which accorded with their image of what Ireland was, rustic, rural, slow and idyllic. But this Craggy Island Ireland doesn't exist anymore and anyway, if it did, property prices have been pushed through the roof by bumptious first-generation barristers who affect the Irish RM when in fact they are the Irish RC.

Pedantic old Gunter isn't going to ride over the hill on his mountain bike to rescue us this time.

So what will take the place of all the houses, top-of-the-range kitchens and bathrooms that are keeping retail sales so high and throwing off so much cash for the State? Well, traditionally, if you can't sell your gear at home, you sell abroad. But here's the snag: 93% of all our exports come from the multinational sector[11] and, despite the fact that the past five years have been the best for world economic growth in two decades, Irish exports have been stagnant. The great Irish export boom is over. Also, while we've been busy buying second and third homes, we haven't noticed that we are still a manufacturing outpost of corporate America, and all that high-value-added stuff, like research and development or marketing and advertising, is being done in America.

The only reason the Americans are here is the tax breaks, allied to a well-functioning service economy to give them good outsourced accountants and lawyers if they need them. It helps that their bored wives can watch *Oprah* without needing cable and their children can get a decent education at half the price without being corralled into a Preppy finishing school. Good golf helps too, as does the English language and the fact that Ireland is probably the only European country where the ordinary people are actually pro-American. In the years ahead, we've got to package this offering, because we can't, and nor do we want to, compete with Asia on price. An industrial policy based on falling wages and living standards makes little sense.

But the major problem with the export economy is that because of the prohibitive cost of Irish labour, everything that is done here is highly capital intensive. That's why the productivity figures from the multinational companies based here are so extraordinary: the 93% of all our exports are produced by the 100,000 people who work in the multinationals.[12] What, you might ask, are the other two million people in the workforce doing all the time? So, even if we were to expand exports, which at this stage looks unlikely, this sector could only absorb a fraction of the tens of thousands likely to be laid off in construction, estate agents, banks, restaurants, bars, architecture, media and design firms in the next few years.

What the export story tells us in a nutshell is that the rest of the world will not tolerate being ripped off by the Paddies; we can only rip each other off at our current wages and prices. In short, Ireland needs to get back to being good value and to do this, we will have to endure falling wages in the years ahead. This deflation makes a bad situation even worse because, over the past few years, all of us have decided to dispense with our critical faculties when it comes to questioning our own propaganda. We're like the bloody Moonies.

Debts

We've talked ourselves into believing that we are seeing an economic miracle in Ireland. This is not true. We are seeing the normal immediate effects of a large overdraft. The nation is on a borrowing binge and we are getting into further debt faster than any other nation[13] in the world.

This year, total Irish private-sector debt will rise to over €250 billion or 180% of GDP.[14] This figure is rising by 30% per year.[15] It is not inconceivable that our debts this year alone will rise by €80 billion or close to half of our total income. This is financial delinquency on a monumental scale.

Nine-tenths of this borrowing is going into the property monster. As this sector generates neither innovation nor enhanced skill-driven jobs for graduates and because it is not exposed to external competition, construction investment actually makes us more insular when the rest of the world is becoming more global.

What are we going to do when we have to pay back all this cash? Already 35-year mortgages are normal because people can't afford to pay off their enormous mortgages over the traditional period of 20 years. This is the thin edge of the wedge. We have condemned ourselves to generations of debt. And what have we done with all this cash? We still do not have a motorway between our two main cities! A horrible feeling begins to sink in that we might have blown it.

The enormous debts are the problem. Economic history teaches us that countries which find themselves in a debtor's cul-de-sac tend to print lots of money to get out of it. This has the effect of creating inflation and this helps people reduce their debt. If inflation is running at 20% per year, it won't be long before your debts get inflated away.

Look at what the us is doing at the moment. The more money it borrows, the more money it prints. As it prints money, the dollar falls in value. Because all their debts are denominated in dollars, the cost to the us electorate of paying for its Grand Cherokee falls too. The Americans have asked the rest of the world to put its faith in the greenback by lending the Americans money and receiving dollar-denominated ious. If the dollar falls by 10% this year, it means that the lenders lose, the borrowers gain.

Now look at this from the Irish perspective: we are borrowing euro and because of emu we cannot print money here. This means that, unlike in previous eras when house prices rose such as the 1970s, we can't inflate away our debts. This has significant implications for the burden of debt. For example, if you were to take an Irish person who bought a house in the early 1970s, by the late 1970s, double-digit inflation would have reduced the cost of that mortgage dramatically. This can't happen now.

We can't inflate our way out of debt because our debt is in euro and we can't control how many euro are printed. In short, we will have to pay it back the hard way. This is the big internal conundrum. How will we pay for all the Mercs, black granite kitchens on the never-never or the 'buy now, pay later' plasma screens and tongue-and-groove flooring which went on the credit card at 18% APR?

Immigration

Now given these housing-debt dilemmas, what will happen to the newest and least understood phenomenon in Irish society— immigration? Immigration is the hand-maiden of economic success and countries need to establish a policy. One in ten of our population is now foreign-born[16] and this figure rises to 13% of the workforce. So, as the economy grows, societies need to prepare themselves for an influx of thousands of foreigners. In Ireland, the extra demand created by the property boom, both directly and indirectly, has led to a massive influx of migrants, who in turn, put more upward pressure on house prices.

This is particularly relevant for Ireland as we are now part of another unique experiment. No other political project has ever entertained the free movement of labour from countries where the average annual wage is €4,000 and there is no social welfare system to speak of, to countries where the average annual wage is €40,000 and the social welfare system is open-ended. Child benefit alone in Ireland is worth more than the average wage in Lithuania.[17] This is creating the biggest peacetime population movement Europe has ever seen with hundreds of thousands of East Europeans on the move. Ireland is now receiving more immigrants per head than any other country in the world.[18]

Like the predicted 'soft landing' in the property market which no-one has ever experienced before, we have replaced a proper discussion of immigration with platitudes and wishful thinking.

On the one hand, the right-wing view, best exemplified by IBEC, is that the only issue revolves around absorbing more and more immigrants to satisfy the appetite of the economy. This view believes that mass immigration is kosher so long as it serves to keep the price of labour low. This framework was first adopted by German business circles when, in the early 1970s, Germany ran out of its own people. There weren't enough Germans left to do all the jobs they were creating. Fearing inflation coming from excessive wage claims as the labour market tightened, Germany opened its door to two million Turks. Integrating this community has taken Germany many tortuous years. The main problem with the business view is that you might import 'workers' but what you actually get is 'people'.

If the Right have a workers-not-people view, the Left, on the other hand, have what can be best described as a 'United Colours of Benetton' approach, where discussion of the wisdom of mass immigration is characterised by sanctimony. The right-on, soft-Left view appears to be that it is our role to take in as many colours, creeds and peoples as possible and it is up to us to adapt to them. This approach leads to silly censorship where any questioning of the appropriate level of immigration is immediately slapped down with accusations of racism. Such Orwellian double-think strangles debate.

This default position seems to have been formed in some 1970s' prism when Ireland was homogenous and all things foreign were seen as progressive simply because they were foreign. There was a time when the intelligentsia, in a repudiation of what went before, seemed to conclude that the more open you were to foreign influence, the more enlightened you were. Now, this festival-of-world-music approach to immigration has led to a dialogue of the deaf.

For example, on a 2006 radio show, the then Minister for Arts, Sport and Tourism, John O'Donoghue, made the point that Bord Fáilte had received negative feedback from many visitors to the country, complaining that they met no Irish people working in hotels and restaurants. He mused that this was a legitimate cause for concern. The interviewer, on a flagship radio programme, automatically suggested that he didn't want foreigners here, which is not what he had said at all. The discussion degenerated into infantile babble about racism, equality and the dignity of immigrants, rather than a response to a legitimate dilemma.

The problem with the public debate on immigration is that it is articulated by people—journalists, academics and politicians—whose livelihood is not threatened by immigrants. In contrast, the people at the coal face are given the cold shoulder.

We need to get a handle on this question because one of the big imponderables is whether the immigrants, in the event of a slowdown, will stay or go home. If they stay, a monumental struggle will ensue between blue-collar Irish workers and the immigrants who are likely to do the jobs cheaper than the Irish. Many of the Polish and Lithuanian lads live six or seven to a house, as we did in the US in the 1980s, and they'll do anything to keep their costs down. The Irish workers—in many cases our younger brothers and sisters—have much higher expectations of what life can deliver and as such, they can't afford psychologically to compete with some of the immigrants.

On the other hand, if the immigrants leave, house prices will fall farther as it is the immigrants who are keeping the rental market buoyant. So we have to ask ourselves whether we want the cost of deflation to be borne by young Irish workers or middle-aged Irish landlords.

Copycats

Another dilemma for the Irish economy is how to deal with the fact that the world has learned our tricks; countries will simply copy us and our tax rates—particularly the 10% tax rate. Already Estonia and Poland have introduced similar tax breaks. Up until recently, we were the only European country that could actually afford to introduce a low corporation tax. We didn't have any corporations, so we raised no tax from them in the first place. We had nothing to forego. We had no domestic capital, so how could we create it? We did the only thing open to us, we made it cheap to use capital in our jurisdiction by giving corporations a tax holiday. Britain, France and Germany, with large corporate sectors and, importantly, ideological Left/Right politics, could never have introduced this. Either the revenue these countries would have lost would be too great, or this corporate-friendly move would have widened the ideological chasm between Left and Right. Ireland had an open goal and we hit the back of the net.

Now, the situation is different. Anyone who has visited many former communist countries can see that they have dreadful tax compliance. People work in the black market, pay as little tax as possible and the governments have a dilemma: how do they pay for their aging populations? The only thing they can do is to levy taxes on consumption, through indirect taxes (of essentials like gas, water, electricity and so on). Just like Ireland in the 1970s, they have so few companies, so giving the foreigners a low tax rate is no skin off their nose. The upshot for Ireland is that we face enormous threats from the copycat economies of the East, whose workers are one tenth of our price. This gradual hollowing-out of the labour-intensive parts of our export industry will continue in the years ahead.

———

But no country has had to deal with global change, a domestic property slump, possible debt deflation and mass immigration at the same time. Worse still, we appear to be blind to these forces, content, like the little boat off Omey Island, to bob about on the apparently calm sea, oblivious to the stormclouds gathering out in the bay.

Chapter 5 ～

| BOTOX NATION

Soft Day, Thank God

On Tuesday 19 September 2006, the nation was holding its breath. The worst storm in years was about to upset the most over-hyped jamboree in the sporting calendar—the Ryder Cup. The country was bombarded by one of the most expensive sports advertising campaigns ever launched. This was a Jagger Generation Jamboree and given their spending power, advertisers were salivating. Our appetite was whetted by the fact that practically every billboard in the country was telling us that this golf tournament was going to be, wait for it, epic. Now 'epic' is the Sphinx and the Coliseum; it is Aphrodite, Helen of Troy, Priam, Ajax and Dionysus. When we think epic, we think of ancient history, heroes, civilisations, pathos, hubris and tragedy. Whatever the K Club is, it's not the Acropolis.

The gods of the New Ireland were panicked but not even Michael, Denis, Dermot and JP, back in the country for a quick break, could stop the hurricane that was thundering its way across the Atlantic. Never have so many masters of the universe sought second opinions on something as trivial as the weather.

That same morning, the *Mayo News* carried a horrifying story. Although the HSE was keen to keep it quiet, an immigrant had been rushed from Westport and was in intensive care at Mayo General Hospital, having been infected with one of the most dangerous toxins known to man. In a matter of hours he would be dead. The toxin was everywhere. An alien bacterium was lodged in his intestine, secreting large amounts of a deadly poison into his muscles. It would lead to total paralysis as gradually the oesophagus would stop working and the patient would suffocate.

When they were told that he'd eaten something that his mother had sent from Poland, at first the medics in Castlebar thought he had food poisoning. The symptoms were straightforward. The doctors figured it would pass. But then he started seizing up in front of them in A&E as drunks with broken arms complained about not being seen.

They ran tests. The lab technician wasn't sure at first. Then she tested again. It was botulism—a toxin so unusual that the hospital pharmacy had no anti-toxin. In a general hospital in a country that is one of the world's largest single producers of pharmaceutical drugs,[1] a young man would die because of a lack of medicine.

He was infected with the most poisonous naturally occurring toxin in the world. *Clostridium botulinum* is the bacteria that produces the toxin botulinum which causes botulism. It kills within a matter of hours. By now this strong 24-year-old Polish lad who was playing football only two days earlier was dying. And his own mother had poisoned him.

The ambulance left Castlebar and headed back to Westport. The driver was confused. There was no hospital in Westport. It was one of the nurses who had the idea: when she heard he had botulism, she thought of Botox and the factory up the road in Westport.

———

Welcome to Westport—a wrinkle free-zone, twinned with Bree Van de Kamp's forehead. Here, in this small, beautiful, upmarket town, the neurosis of millions of women has been eased. In the shadow of the mountain where St Patrick banished the snakes, a new miracle-maker banishes lines and frowns. This is where Joan Rivers will go when she dies.

Botox, the world's fastest growing drug,[2] is made from miniscule amounts of the botulinum toxin and Westport is the Botox capital of the world. A discreet pharmaceutical building just off the Dublin Road, surrounded by trees, houses the Allergan factory which manufactures the world's most loved cosmetic treatment. 800 people are employed in Westport and the factory's turnover is over $1 billion a year.

Allergan generates about €80 million in taxes for the area and it's quite ironic that the roads and public services used by the Rossport Five with their anti-big-business protest 20 miles away are paid for by taxes from an American multinational trading in the shallow world of cosmetic enhancement. That's globalisation for you.

Botox is the biggest employer in the town and, unlike Mayo General Hospital, there is plenty of the botulinum anti-toxin in Westport. The factory in Westport has expanded to keep up with global demand. It is now operating at full tilt, twenty-four hours a day, seven days a week, three hundred and sixty-five days a year, to keep millions of women frownless.

Luckily for our critically ill immigrant and his distraught mother, the anti-toxin worked quickly and he was treated in the Allergan factory before being transferred back to Castlebar. He was discharged in two days, dazed and a little confused but in good health. Had he not lived beside a Botox factory, he probably would have died.

This story seems to sum up some of the contradictions of modern Ireland which make the place both dynamic and infuriating in equal measure. The immigrant, who keeps the domestic economy moving, is saved by the multinational that employs half of Westport and keeps the external side of the economy motoring, while the hospital in the county that produces all the world's Botox, did not have the anti-toxin for botulism. Meanwhile, half of the country is glued to the over-hyped Ryder Cup, the rights of which have been sold to Rupert Murdoch's Sky Sports.

Welcome to Ireland 2007, the Botox Nation, where everything is for sale, everyone has their price and nothing is quite what it seems.

Chemically Enhanced

Every time you turn on *Desperate Housewives* and marvel at Wisteria Lane's smooth faces, pert boobs, lineless mouths and full lips, thank the Lord for middle-aged Americans' neurotic fear of growing old, because it pays for your child's classroom. The cosmetic industry is one of

Ireland's biggest sources of tax revenue. Every time you hear Bree, Lynette, Gabrielle and Susan marvel at the great sex they are having with someone's ex-husband and how the stamina of this hammer-man is truly amazing, count your blessings too because the Viagra that this stud is popping pays for our A&E wards.

Shameful as it is, Ireland is at the centre of an industry which is based on making Americans look and feel younger. We are a new age Tir na nÓg—a mythical country that produces the elixir of life for another country that is afraid to grow old.

Today, there are 78 million baby boomers in the US who make up the huge population bulge which occurred there between 1946 and 1964. These people run the United States. The first of the boomers were 60 in 2006, including Presidents George Bush and Bill Clinton, and other famous 60-year-olds who passed that milestone recently are Donald Trump, Dolly Parton and the oldest boxer still fighting, Sylvester Stallone. Close to 8,000 American baby boomers are turning 60 every day and they make up over one third of the population in the traditionally Irish states of the North-East.[3]

The youngest of the boomers—the Desperate Housewives—are in their early 40s. As they get older, they are obsessed with feeling and looking younger. They live with a pathological fear of crow's feet and are enhanced by huge amounts of pharmaceutical drugs, cosmetics and pills and potions of every sort. They are also Ireland's biggest customers. Without them, the Botox nation has no pharmaceutical industry—the biggest exporter in the country.[4] Without the pharmaceutical industry, more than half our high-tech exports would disappear. Our pharmaceutical industry is the fastest growing in the country and amongst the most efficient in the world.[5] We have a vested interest in the baby boomers' neurosis about getting old: the young high-tech graduate workforce of Ireland is being kept in clover by the neurotic, wealthy baby boomers of America.

And it's not just the Desperate Housewives. Six of the world's top ten blockbuster drugs are made in Ireland, including the number-one bestselling drug in the world, Lipitor, which is made by Pfizer in Ringaskiddy. Last year the sales of Lipitor world wide topped $13 billion, dwarfing Pfizer's better known Viagra which sold $4 billion.[6] Viagra was originally developed to increase blood circulation to the heart to help prevent heart attacks in children. After an adult trial in

Wales, the impressive side effect became obvious and we haven't looked back since. It's turning up in the most interesting places: you can buy handfuls outside rugby matches off the same aul' wans who sell cans of Fanta and Twixes out of prams. That's the free market in operation. The boss of Pfizer in Ringaskiddy told me that apparently there was a roaring trade in Viagra at Puck Fair last year—which gives a new meaning to the expression 'horny old goat'.

Pfizer is the biggest pharmaceutical company in the world with ten per cent of a $500-billion market. The company invested $1 billion here in 2001. It costs $50 million a year to maintain it. The Ringaskiddy plant is a 24/7 operation where the staff work two days and two nights a week. 40 million tablets of Viagra are produced here per year. The active ingredients for dick-swelling come in the front door and the Viagra goes out the back door, straight out to the docks for export, mainly to the US.

Of the top three drugs sold on the Internet, Ireland makes two of them: Viagra and Sibutramine. Sibutramine is produced in Sligo—the surfing capital of Ireland. Just down the road from Strandhill, a cross between Hawaii and Bray, with surfers battling bumper cars for dominance of the seafront, the Abbott factory churns out millions of pills for the world's Desperate Dieters. This drug is marketed as Reductil and is the world's most popular slimming drug. It works by inhibiting the signal from the brain which tells us we are hungry, suppressing the appetite and prompting rapid weight loss. Over 8 million women[7] are currently using it, making it, after Prozac, the most popular Internet drug.[8]

And we produce all sorts of other age-inhibitors such as Preparation H—a haemorrhoid cream used by women to get rid of the bags under their eyes as well as the big one, collagen fillers for the lips. From flaming sphincters to flaming lips.

Inamed, a division of Allergan based in Arklow, is porn-star heaven. If you want anything enhanced, enlarged, made firmer or simply overblown, this is your place. From Jordan's and Pamela Anderson's pumped-up pairs to Courtney Love's or Melanie Griffith's trout pouts, it's all made here in a discreet plant just outside the town. A 2003 press statement made the gushing announcement that 'this new investment will establish the Irish operation as the global centre of excellence for silicone breast implants'.[9] So that's what we mean by the knowledge economy. In the same year, Arklow advertised itself as being at the forefront of new research into a fascinating boob-job product called the 'soft touch implant'. This was trumpeted as something special. I would have thought 'soft touch' a prerequisite. Can you imagine a woman saying, 'It's OK, I'll have the rock hard ones please'?

Another product made in Arklow is the anti-obesity Lap-Band, a bag that you swallow and once inside your stomach, a saline solution is dripped into it by a catheter. The bag swells and fools you into thinking you are full.

So it is easy to see that Ireland's exports are dependent on the limp willies, flabby boobs, thinning lips, laughter lines and crumpled foreheads of America's 78 million insecure baby boomers. As we also produce some of the world's most commonly prescribed anti-depressants, we have an interest in keeping the baby boomers in a state of heightened physical and emotional anxiety.

Ireland hosts 13 of the top 15 drug companies in the world. Their operations are substantial. In total there are 83 facilities, usually on hills outside major towns, employing more than 17,000 people. The IDA's strategy of following the British garrison policy of concentrating foreign factories like garrisons all around the country, means that most parts of the island are implicated in the output of the Botox Nation. When you look for this industry, it's hard to find. The factories seem so innocuous. They all look camouflaged as if we are embarrassed and trying to hide something. When you look closer, they are everywhere.

In Baldoyle, you can have Fluoxetine or Prozac, an antidepressant commonly used for those with eating disorders (which might be the result of you taking our own Reductil from Sligo to lose weight in the first place). Or from the home of Puck Fair and counterfeit Viagra, Killorglin, we can sort you with Affix, a bulimia disorder drug for a condition that might have been prompted by an addiction to NoviSlim, a fat-burning drug made in Waterford. And if the bag is still out of order from this cocktail, we can fix you up with Arthrotec, a gastric ulcer treatment made in Cork. If you're losing sleep over Arklow's boob job, we'll recommend the sedative Diazepam from Clonmel for insomnia. If you are worried about your performance but fancy something more robust than Viagra those nice people in Little Island can give you Caverject to be injected straight into your old man. This list goes on. Whatever you want, whatever your addiction, Ireland can make it for you.

For a country that fancies itself as a good global citizen, always ready to lecture others on morality, foreign policy and the like, we trade some nasty gear, drugs you'd hope your children would never dabble in. When we hear government ministers speaking of the premature sexualisation of our tweenagers and the shallowness of the cosmetic culture that has infected the nation, take a trip out to the countryside and have a look at the stuff we produce. We're up to our necks in it.

Financial Botox

In the same way as Botox makes a 40-year-old woman feel younger, we apply the same logic to our economy. So, while there are lots of wrinkles and problems deeper down, we have obscured them by borrowing other people's money to maintain a flashy lifestyle that we can't afford and don't merit. But on the outside you'd never tell. Easy credit is the financial equivalent of a Botox injection—so Ireland is the Botox Nation in more ways than one. With credit, we can play Let's Pretend We are Rich. Credit, like Botox, is playing tricks on us.

We mix up basic economic ideas, make them interchangeable, use them here, abuse them there. Ultimately, no-one knows what they are talking about. For example, one striking aspect of today's discussions on economics in Ireland is that we confuse income with wealth. A wealthy person can have little income and a person on a big wage can have little wealth. We all understand this basic idea when it comes to our neighbours, but seem to have a difficulty with it when it comes to our country.

But the disparity explains why, when you travel to countries like Germany and you see the trains, roads, hospitals, schools, playgrounds, clinics, municipal playing fields, swimming pools and infrastructure generally, it is hard to reconcile the view that, as politicians sometimes suggest, we are 'the envy of Europe,' or that, 'Ireland is richer than Germany'. If this is the case, why do they not also have crowded A&E wards and creaking 1930s' hospitals crawling with MRSA?

It is because the infrastructure in Germany is a sign of its wealth, not its income. This wealth has been built up over years and stems from the fact that Germany accounts for 10% of all world exports, while having less than 1.2% of the world's population. Just look around your house to see how many of your big-ticket items are made in Germany. The Germans have wealth, built on innovation, creativity and a smart workforce. They are not the power they were in the 1970s and 1980s, but they are still Europe's dynamo. They are understated. Contrast this with your daily experience in Ireland.

The Stop-Go Man

We all know him. The stop-go man emerges out of the rain and the mist like a haunted, gender-confused lollipop lady. The first thing you see is the swivelling 'stop/go' sign as it's about to come through your windscreen, no signs, no warning. It announces what is termed 'major road-works'.

On the drive back from the Botox factory in Mayo, three different stop-go men ambushed this unsuspecting driver. The second one just outside Longford was a gem. The lad had a woolly cap pulled down over his ears as he slowly turned the sign to 'stop'. When he was sure that the cars were stopping, he jammed the sign in the ditch like a pitchfork and walked across to the other ditch, which on this inter-county highway, was a distance of about 15 feet—wide enough for two Honda 50s and a bike. He sat down and slowly, purposefully pulled a packet of Tayto out of his pocket. He grabbed a can of Coke from the other and proceeded to eat and drink, looking at the traffic jam that was building up. With one arm, Mr Stop-Go half-heartedly waved on the on-coming traffic. His phone rang. He had a brief chat and then back to his snack. At this stage, on one of the ten busiest roads in the country on a Friday afternoon, the phone rang again. He was pouring the last of the Taytos into his mouth with the precision of a skilled machinist, flattening the bag twice before attempting the exercise. 87 cars had passed. The second call was from his opposite number about half a mile up the road. Time to switch the sign. 'Go'.

The queue of top-of-the-range cars made for *autobahns* proceeded slowly, drivers craning their necks to marvel at the amazing engineering feat which must have been ahead. These 'works' amounted to nothing more than a couple of JCBs and five immigrant fellas in a hole, watched by a few of our own, who were smoking butts. This was not a roadwork, but a patchwork community employment scheme which knocks off at 5 p.m.

The stop-go man is the difference between Ireland and Germany—

the difference between income and wealth. Both he and the fancy German cars which we have bought with German credit in the first place, are evidence of the gulf between private credit and consumption and public investment. We in the Botox Nation are the Flash Harrys or the *nouveaux riches* of Europe. That's not to say that, over the next twenty years, private income won't turn to national wealth, but at the moment it is all income.

This is the Irish dilemma. Not only is the credit fooling us, it is, in fact, accelerating our degeneration. In the great flirting game that is globalisation, where every country tries to make itself attractive for business, the dance floor is getting crowded. Ireland used to be the cutest girl at the bar, bumping and grinding, keeping the corporate boys keen. Now, the floor is filling up with new hotties with better bodies, flirting outrageously, grabbing attention and promising all sorts of exotic delights. Think Shakira versus Madonna. The middle-aged woman can't compete with the new competition, so she turns to cosmetics. But when the lights go on, we can see the smudged mascara and the lines where the Botox is wearing off.

But instead of accepting reality, we are all in denial. We deny that there is a problem in the housing market and deny that we are living on borrowed time. So we tell lies. But this is not new. Nations big and small have been deluding themselves for years even when they didn't realise it. Equally, there are always those who have an interest in upholding the myth that the emperor has no clothes.

Khruschev's Shoe and Johnny Giles' Boots

Forty-five years ago, Nikita Khrushchev, premier of the Soviet Union, took off his shoe and banged on the table at the UN General Assembly, boasting to the astounded dignitaries, 'We will bury you'.

He was talking about economics.

Khrushchev was convinced, as was much of the rest of the world, that the Soviet Union would overtake the US and the West in general. This confidence was based on the fact that, in the 1950s, the USSR had notched up double-digit growth rates and looked invincible. The economy was roaring, it had just put the first man in orbit and its lackeys were gaining ground in Africa, Asia and Latin America. Just like Ireland has its interested parties who are intent on spinning positive stories, the Soviets had their spin-doctors. The myth of Soviet power was propagated by an unlikely fusion of the McCarthyite, square-jawed, cropped-haired, anti-Soviet analysts in the CIA on the one hand, and the Gitanes-smoking, inveterately anti-American, left-wing intellectuals in Europe on the other. Both these implacable enemies had a common interest in making the Soviets look strong and, in so doing, hoodwinking the people. For the CIA, the more suburban Americans held end-of-the-world, post-nuclear-fallout drills, headed for the woods and stocked up on tinned corned beef, the better. And what more evocative image of an evil empire could you get than doddery old men lining up to salute shiny new missiles at Red Square on May Day? The CIA milked the Soviets for all it could, to such an extent that the CIA ended up believing its own lies.

For the European Left, the more the Soviets appeared to have found economic nirvana (even if it was calculated by counting tractors in Ukraine), the more credible their adolescent pamphleteering. Thus a bizarre Cold-War hydra, half-John Paul Sartre, half-J. Edgar Hoover, inflated the myth of Soviet economic power in yet another example of the Russians playing smoke-and-mirrors with gullible foreigners.

In the end, the Empire came crashing down and the most compelling and non-ideological explanation is that the Soviet Union simply ran out of steam. It was exhausted. It was all an illusion.

In the 1950s and 1960s, millions of petrified peasants, women and German prisoners of war were forced to work in industry. Resistance was futile. They had seen the elimination of the Kulaks for the crime of being small farmers. They had experienced fathers being spied on by sons. They had famine, invasion, forced collectivisation and the gulag. The last thing they were going to do was stand up for themselves. When the Party mobilised you, you mobilised, pronto.

Given the mass flight from the land, the Russians had more cheap workers than almost any other country and the 'big lie' allowed the Soviets to grind these miserable misfortunates into the machine under the dubious banner of virtue as the fruits of this slave-labour were lauded, not for the selfish benefit of greedy capitalists, but for the greater good of the punch-drunk Soviet people themselves.

Anyone who visited the Soviet Union in the mid- to late-1980s would have seen crowds at the exotically named Palace of Science, milling and shoving to get a glimpse of a car that looked little more than a souped-up Talbot Sunbeam with go-faster stripes. To them, this was the height of consumer technology. The reason, of course, was that the Soviet Union didn't do consumer goods. Every last rouble was ploughed into huge investments in hard industries like warheads, combine harvesters and leaky submarines. This explains why in 1988 a pair of Levi 501s bought two prostitutes, five litres of vodka, a dozen fur hats and three original CCCP football shirts, not to mention the Kalashnikov and fistful of enriched uranium.

In economic terms, all these muscles and kopecks applied at the same time pushed the growth rate up. As Solzhenitsyn commented succinctly, the Soviet industrial miracle was built on 'fart power' (and he should have known having spent nearly a decade in a gulag). This just about sums it up. If you have one machine and thousands of expendable peasants, enemies of the people and suspect ethnics working twelve hours a day, whether digging coal, smelting iron or smashing rocks, you can produce quite a lot. In contrast, if, like the degenerate West, you have a few more machines and one hundred workers with four weeks' paid holidays, medical insurance and employment tribunals, it's no surprise that in the short-term you have less economic growth. But at least your workers come home after a hard day at the factory.

The Soviet growth rates of the 1960s were propelled more by brawn than brains and when Russia started to run out of peasants, the growth rate started to fall. Because it had neither the capital nor the money to reinvest, it could not build sophisticated machines to make the peasant workers more efficient.

By the mid-1980s, 20 years after Khrushchev's antics, the Soviet empire was falling apart. The demise would have come quicker had it not been for the oil-boom of the 1970s which temporarily enhanced the coffers of a bankrupt State.

The growth rates had been an illusion based on mobilising huge unused resources into the economy. The achievements were impressive. People were housed and educated in great numbers, schools were built, streets were lit and hospitals were staffed. But so, too, were the costs and what the productivity numbers reveal, is that there was far more perspiration than inspiration and the seeds of the Soviet collapse were evident way before the actual event.

Paul Krugman, the *New York Times* columnist and Princeton economist, made similar arguments in 1994 to suggest that the growth of the Asian Tigers might not actually be that miraculous. He was vilified, particularly by the vested interests—investors, bankers, property speculators and governments—all of whom had much to lose were light shone on this inconvenient truth. Krugman was proved right when the Asian markets crashed ten years ago.

Nikita Ahern?

When we are trying to establish, over all the noise and rancour, whether the Botox Nation is experiencing an economic miracle or facing an abyss, it's a good idea to look at the numbers. Is there a cautionary lesson for us or have we found a way to beat the economic cycle indefinitely? At first instance, the numbers help us to understand why we sometimes get carried away with ourselves, talking about miracles, new paradigms and the like. In contrast to the 'new' theories, there is usually a perfectly logical old explanation for economic developments.

For example, in Ireland we are experiencing something like the superannuated version of Khrushchev's illusion. Whereas Khrushchev was fooled by the masses, we are fooled by the money. Whereas Khrushchev forced thousands of people into the system, we have opened our doors to thousands of immigrants from the East. Whereas Khrushchev over-invested every kopeck he had in heavy industry that he couldn't use properly, we over-invest all our own money and millions of other people's money in houses that we don't need.

Basically, what we have here is what could be termed a 'Lidl Boom', best seen in the car parks of Lidls and Aldis all over the country as immigrants pour into the country. Although they are coming out of choice, the effect on the optics of growth is the same as Kruschev's mobilised masses. It pushes up headline growth but masks the underlying position.

Most crucially, Irish productivity is falling, in spite of all the cash we are throwing at the engine. The only areas where jobs are being created are in the public sector and the construction industry, both low-productivity areas. We are throwing more and more resources at the economy to achieve the same growth rates. This is what Johnny Giles talks about. Giles, as well as having a weakness for yellow ties, has a fondness for the term 'honesty of effort'. When Giles is finding fault with a team, invariably he refers to this idea. If one crucial player isn't 'getting stuck in' or is, to use the vernacular, 'hiding', the team will suffer. Now, let's look at the economy through the eyes of Johnny Giles. A country where productivity is rising is getting the best out of itself, is using its resources to the full, and is playing above itself. If the team is playing 'with honesty of effort', it can afford luxury players like Ronaldo.

Similarly, a country with rising productivity, can afford more debts, more pay rises, more expensive houses, weekends in spa hotels and a new 07 Merc. If not, we're living on borrowed time. We know that if a company pays its workers more than they are producing, the company will ultimately go bust. So if the country's wages are rising without the productivity, it, too, will have financial problems. In Ireland, the gap between productivity and wages has been papered over by borrowing as people live beyond their means. This can't go on forever. If Johnny Giles was an economist, he'd have pointed this out to Bill O'Herlihy years ago.

But what do we care? We feel rich, look younger and have bitten the bug. Last year 20,000 of us used Botox but another 86,000 used other fillers to plump ourselves up, and the market is rising here at 28% per year.[10] The most likely candidates for the treatment are not the older Jagger Generation, but women in their early 40s. This is the generation just behind the Jaggers: let's have a look at those of the expressionless foreheads—more winners in the great Irish Generation Game.

Chapter 6

THE BONO BOOMERS

The Pussycat Moms

What's more disturbing, fortysomething mothers doing melodramatic late-night renditions of 'Total Eclipse of the Heart' or the same Pussycat Moms in tummy-sucking control pants simulating a pole dance while screeching the words to 'Hot Like Me'? Or what about the balding fathers with pairs of designer sunglasses skin-grafted onto the top of their pates, leaping around to 'Smells like Teen Spirit'?

Yes, you've recognised where you are. You are at an Irish 40th birthday party, the rite-of-passage for the second major group in the Irish Generation Game. Just behind the Jaggers, they are not quite as rich and powerful as the older ones but nowhere near as stretched as the younger commuting first-time buyers. They are the half-a-million people born in the 1960s, a decade that was opened by the birth of one Paul Hewson. They are the Bono Boomers, the generation who straddle the generation gap: too old to be hip and too young to be old.

The Bono Boomers are Ireland's Permalescents: When you look for them, you'll see them everywhere, flicking through CD collections in Tower Records, reciting the words of 'Down in the Tube Station at Midnight' and going to Stiff Little Fingers reunion gigs.

In the past few years, the nation has become host to the most extraordinary combination of late-onset hedonism, age-denial and decadence. The 40th has replaced all other parties as the coming-of-age of Ireland's never-get-old, Dorian Gray generation. Once you hit 40, it's time to go mental. Forget the fact that you have kids, a mortgage and a bad knee, this is your night. It's your debs, 21st and leaving do all rolled into one. It's time to scream a 'Message to you, Rudy', 'London's Calling' and 'She Sells Sanctuary' all at once. It's no time for music snobbery or discernment. It's your 40th so for one night 'A Whole Lotta Rosie' and 'Sweet Child of Mine' can share the dance floor with 'Born Slippy' and 'Loaded'. Skinny dance music meets Big Hair, Paul Weller follows Paul Oakenfold and 'Teenage Kicks' is on every play list. Remember, the Bono Boomers were Ireland's first punks. You'll get no Genesis or Van Morrison here. The memories come flooding back. The air guitars are out.

Everything is fuelled by unfeasible amounts of booze and marching powder. Cubicles are mysteriously full of heterosexual middle-aged male couples for long periods.

Ahead of the big night, the Pussycat Moms haven't eaten for weeks. One or two have the tell-tale permanently surprised look of what is neatly described as 'work'. It's a great expression, isn't it? She's had 'work done'. It sounds almost passive as if she didn't instigate it, as if she didn't look in the mirror one day and say, 'I want to look different, I don't like myself nor do I like what I might turn into, so I'm going to pay someone to inject me with botulism which will paralyse half my head and give me fewer lines than my daughter.'

'Work done' sounds more as if the Pussycat Mom has being compelled to do something, like getting a new kitchen—another great Pussycat Mom pastime. Show me a Pussycat Mom content with her kitchen, who doesn't suffer from regular bouts of kitchen-envy, and I'll show you one who's looking forward to the menopause.

Because they are starving, the cocktails go to the Pussycat Moms' heads quickly. This means lots of visits to the loo to reapply their pouty Lip Venom. The toothbrush in their handbag isn't for teeth; it's to scrub their lips before they apply their plumping lipstick for that intentional, full-mouthed, always-willing-and-open message. But after four Cosmopolitans the wannabe Angelina Jolie can look more like a smudged cross between Beatrice Dahl and a boxer.

The party kicks into gear, and some latent homosexual tendencies come out in the Disco Dads as the bemused 20-year-old DJ cranks up the late-1970s disco inferno soundtrack. Decorum is left at the door. People who fancied each other 20 years ago, and have kept the flame well hidden, flirt outrageously. This is dangerous territory—made more treacherous by the smoking ban which offers ample scope for legitimately slipping outside for a while. There is history and former lovers, now happily married with children, eye each other up with the friskiness of teenagers. It's all so obvious but this is the generation that refuses to grow up and this is their night.

When my Dad was 40, he was a proper man, a real grown-up who seemed remote, mature and respected. You could trust him with your life. You wouldn't see him hammered, leaping around to 'Smiley Happy People' at two in the morning, doing his best Michael Stipe wriggle pretending to sing into a megaphone.

But then again he's not a Bono Boomer. The Bono Boomers were born in the 1960s and came of age in the late 1970s and mid 1980s. They were born in a very different Ireland. They were raised in a country that was about to change, but which, up until the late 1960s still had the feel of a place in a time-warp. For example, the population of the country was still falling in 1964. In that year 2,000 babies were born to women with over ten children. This is now almost unheard of. In the early 1960s, 20% of babies were born at home. This is now down to 1 or 2% today.[1] The men who had fought in the Rising were still in power, but things were opening up. The economic disaster that was the 1950s, when 500,000 emigrated, demanded a change of plan and this came with T.K. Whitaker's Programme for Economic Expansion, which was unveiled just before Bono was born.

The Bono Boomers were made for export, finding themselves in New York and London as if it was as natural as settling in Cork or Galway. They are amongst the most globalised of the Irish tribe. Over 250,000 Irish people left this country in the 1980s, the 'lost decade'. But, unlike other emigrants, they are much more likely to have come home in the past ten years, and they now make up the lion's share of the 200,000 or so Irish migrants who came back.[2]

The majority were on the side of tolerance during the great Liberal/Conservative debate in the 1980s but most were either too young or too preoccupied with unemployment to play an active role. They might deny it now, but they had mullets and pixie boots.

Unlike people ten years older, who had the cushion of public sector jobs in the relatively affluent 1970s, the Bono Boomers of all backgrounds are much more likely to have drawn the dole. They were also the most educated emigrants ever to leave the country. One in four Irish people with university degrees emigrated from 1986-1990. Only one in twenty of those who left school before their Junior Cert left in that period.[3] The vast majority of the undocumented Irish stranded in the US are Bono Boomers.

They were the first generation of Irish emigrants to turn their backs on the shillelaghism of the Irish ghettos in London or New York. In fact, they might have been the first generation of self-loathing Irishmen, sickened by the hypocrisy of home and angry that all their learning couldn't get them a job in McDonalds in Dublin. They queued overnight outside the American Embassy for visas and had to endure the ignominy of having to kow-tow to a rude US Marine at the gates of a consulate in their own country. They were the famous smiling faces of the IDA's Young European campaign in the 1980s, aimed at attracting foreign investment based on our educated workforce. Yet when we looked a bit closer, it was revealed that all the Young Europeans featured in the advertising poster, who were supposed to be waiting here to give American multinationals a big corporate *cead mile fáilte* had actually left the country. The Bono Boomers did ANCO courses, wore Lord Anthony parkas and given that half were working in Germany, filled the Necker Stadium to see Ray Houghton lob a header over Peter Shilton that seemed to take half an hour to hit the back of the net.

The Bono Boomer tribe spread out beyond the traditional outposts of England and America. With 'made for export' stamped on their heads from a young age, they didn't need Brian Lenihan to tell them that we all couldn't live on this small island; many thousands couldn't wait to get out anyway, if only to get away from Lenihan and his cronies.

And then in the mid- to late-1990s, the Bono Boomers answered the call and returned in their thousands. They've been coming back at a rate of about 15,000 per year since. Many still feel like outsiders, questioning constantly whether they did the right thing.

Today they are the great phalanx of Irish parents with children in their early teens or younger. Most were just on the right side of the property boom and, unlike the younger workers, they aren't threatened with negative equity or foreclosure.

Freed of severe financial concerns, the Pussycat Moms can focus on the finer things in life. Their personal manifesto is driven by virtue. Virtuous eating, virtuous parenting, virtuous views. As Permalescents they want to live both in the world of grown-ups and in the world of adolescents. So they want to look like their children and they feign hippy-dippy, childlike nonchalance toward responsibilities and competition, but at the same time, they want their children to behave like adults, aware that the world is a nasty place, aware of the great race for perfection and constantly striving for better results.

But such apparent contradictions define the Pussycat Moms. They have a social conscience as big as the Sahara but aren't above a bit of tax-dodging when the opportunity arises. They think Left but vote Right, they like to hob-nob yet be down with the kids. They know their balsamic from their cider vinegar, their fennel from their dill and they are Ireland's first orthorexics.

Orthorexia

Orthorexia is a maniacal obsession with eating righteously.[4] Food takes on a moral characteristic for the Orthorexic. She who eats most righteously is not only healthy but is principled, immutable and serenely above the fray. Orthorexia is now a rampant condition amongst the Bono Boomers. You can easily spot a Pussycat Mom who is suffering from an acute form of Orthorexia Nervosa. The Orthorexic will come into your kitchen with her children whose names can be from any ancient civilisation she chooses, as long as they pre-date Christ by a few hundred years. So Lir, Zachary and Doric bound into the house dressed head to toe in Petit Bateau. The first thing the Orthorexic does is go to your fridge for a 'glass of water', but really, she is performing an orthorexic audit. In her head, she has an orthorexic scorecard, where any foodie *faux pas* can be noted and every organic raw vegetable and piece of raw fish given points. She is lightning quick, calculating, taking away, multiplying, like an off-course bookie's runner. She wants her friend to fail. That's the key. To feel good, the Orthorexic must feel uniquely virtuous. Sacrifice is strength. She spots a packet of Galtee rashers and something inside her perks up. Nitrates!

The Orthorexic's world is full of myths about the dangers of refined carbohydrates and additives. She insists she is not on a diet or image-conscious in any way, yet, despite her twiggy figure, she sucks her tummy in constantly.

This week the Orthorexic is collecting for the 400-mile trek she's doing in Artic Siberia in aid of blind immigrant labourers' children. The 'In aid ofs' are a particularly virulent subset of the Orthorexic. Everything the Inaidov does is aimed at telling you just how virtuous and uniquely sensitive an individual she is. Truth is, she couldn't care less about immigrants so long as they keep the price of laundry down but walking for them puts her, not them, in the spotlight for all the right reasons.

The Orthorexic looks down her nose at the rest of the Pussycat Moms with their bottles of Gavi and pasta at the Wednesday-night book club. At the queue in Liston's delicatessen in Camden Street she swoons over the fresh asparagus tips. (The humble asparagus tip has seen a dramatic elevation to almost deity status in the New Ireland. The Grange development in Stillorgan used to advertise what it described as 'gracious living' in a 'bijoux', 'bespoke' five-hundred-apartment warren, with a picture of an asparagus spear on a fork! Now you know it: asparagus people are gracious types, sophisticated, multi-lingual, extras from the 21st-century Irish version of the Martini ad. *Asparagusez-vous?*)

While she might starve her body and pretend to be free-spirited and chilled, the Orthorexic is neurotic about her children. The starving Pussycat Mom stuffs her children's brains with every single grind and opportunity they can get. She enrols them secretly for the 'gifted child' course in DCU each summer pretending to everyone that they are going to soccer camp. That is until, shock horror, little Doric wins first place in Junior Mastermind.

God knows how it happened, we always thought he was so average!

Bullshit. The poor child has been hot-housed for years. Competition is everything and winners are number one. There's no place for number two.

The Head Start
The Pussycat Mom wants the best for her kids and knows how to get it. She didn't leave the workforce and her pay-packet to be a bad parent.

The stakes are high and she knows it. Her fridge door—in her 'fabulous' kitchen extension—is a magnetic altar to her children's full schedule and achievements. They are, after all, traditional Irish mammies, who have swapped the housecoat for Prada, the Sacred Heart for a Graham Knuttel print and the Mellow Birds for Illy espresso.

Politically, Pussycat Moms are tolerant and liberal without being left-wing or agitating. They are the first generation of Irish women to fully benefit from the culture wars of the 1980s and most are old enough to have taken teenage sides in these battles. The vast majority voted for divorce and lower taxes in the 1990s. In company, they are probably smarter than their salary-man husbands but don't feel the need to show it too often. Many have decided, for the next decade at least, to express themselves through their children—which is a tall order for the child. But thousands of our over-tested kids are in the same boat.

In the years ahead, if trends in other countries are repeated, the Pussycat Moms will initiate divorces in large numbers when their children leave the nest. A quick glance at today's lonely hearts' ads suggests that this is already happening. Late divorces are a western phenomenon and are a function of prolonged health, independent attitudes, boredom and of course an active market in second-time-around lovers!

The Pussycat Mom wears the trousers. She takes all the major decisions in the house from what car is bought to where they will go on holidays and what schools the children will go to.

However, like Cinderella, they are capable of making the most dramatic metamorphoses when they have to. They can switch from the glamorous, suggestive, coke-snorting yet Orthorexic Pussycat Mom to the straightlaced, no-nonsense, early morning creature that is the Hoverer.

The Hovercraft

The school run is a great place to observe the inconsistencies of the Bono Boomers, who talk the language of community but will do anything to make their own children stand out. And that starts with dropping the precious ones to school rather than letting them get the bus or walk. The number of Irish women commuting by car has rocketed over the past fifteen years, much more significantly than men during the same period. In 1993, 34% of women drove to work; by 2006 that figure had jumped to 58%.[5] Women are less likely to walk, bike, get the bus, train or work from home than they were fifteen years ago. This is the age of the hovercraft.

The hovercraft pulls up to the school gates, taking up more space than the school bus which is about to be phased out due to lack of demand. The blind-spot information system bleeps as she backs up as close as possible to the gate, so Lir doesn't have to walk too far. The hovercraft is a top-of-the-range, fourth-generation, fuel-efficient Volvo which retails at €128,000. It takes the best brains a heavily subsidised social-democratic education system can buy to drive a machine that will kill any person it hits, but will not harm the environment—kind of an extreme version of being carbon neutral. Also, by buying Swedish, she extends her ethical shopping reach. They have such an enlightened refugee policy.

She's early. At least fifteen minutes before assembly. She negotiates Lir out of the booster-seat, which wouldn't have looked out of place on Apollo Twelve. In fact, Neil Armstrong probably hurtled to the moon strapped into something much more flimsy. Then again, it is the law.

The Bono Boomers are the most mollycoddled generation, no longer trusted by the State to look after their own children. As if these parents, who know everything there is to know about child safety, need to be threatened with penalty points to persuade them to protect their own children, the most cherished ever.

The Hoverer checks Lir's lunch box again for cheesy sticks just in case that ghastly stone-washed Polish tart has slipped one in again. The Hoverer found one on Tuesday, congealed against the organic raisins and crust-less wholegrain cucumber sandwiches. But there it was, processed, full of monosodium glutamate, dye and E numbers. Oh, the shame of it—packaged products by Glanbia—how pebbledash!

If she had half a chance she'd fire Justyna, the Polish nanny. Poles have not learned that we Irish never say what we mean. In fact, on many occasions we say exactly the opposite. Nor can they iron. Plus their weakness for Knorr soup, green eye-shadow and plum hair dye has to be deeply suspect. But at least they're cheap, don't eat with their mouths open and they baby-sit. So when Justyna, all pert twenty-four-year-old, 32 D and size 8, suggested that the Hoverer get a light perm or when she demanded to know why the kitchen was painted white or, horror of horrors, when she mused aloud as to why the Hoverer had more grey hair on the left than the right, she was lucky not to be out on her overly-pierced Slavic ear.

Today is a play-date with little Saoirse, so the house has to be perfect. A play-date is to hoverers what a viewing is to an auctioneer. It's a chance to advertise your lifestyle, your accomplishments and your perfect family. It's a subtle reminder to all the other Pussycat Moms that you are the standard. By midday there'll be the smell of freshly baking bread and the children's wooden toys, hand carved in Transylvania which she picked up while working *pro bono* for that orphan charity, will be on display. There'll be no sign of Barbie or evidence of the pliant, ever-willing baby-sitter that is the Disney/Pixar DVD double-box set.

Ireland has been turned upside-down. Protestants are calling their children Fiach and living in semi-ds and Catholics are baking scones and insisting on period furniture only. Home-made is now a sign of wealth, not poverty.

The mums, including one or two serial hoverers, congregate at the school gate expectantly. They have so much to say and so little time to say it. They are giddy. Where to start? The sums, the tables, the spelling; or will she broach the subject of the special needs child, who Lord knows, needs help, but not at the expense of little Lir. I mean they didn't rediscover religion and join the parents' association to have him being kept back by a half-wit, did they? After all, the Hoverer had organised the black-tie charity gala ball which raised over thirty thousand for the all-weather pitch.

The teachers look out at them from the safety of the embattled building. No-one told them in training college that the biggest menace of the day would be a 40-year-old, highly educated, pushy mother with too much time on her hands. They were trained to deal with children of all abilities but their mothers are a different kettle of fish altogether.

The main phalanx of hoverers will move at significant pace, rushing the door, designer children flailing behind them. One or two will fan out across the classroom, pretending to dawdle over the children's homework. While the rest of the parents will drop and run, giving a hug, a wave and out into the commute, the Hoverer loiters around the arts and crafts table feigning to rearrange something. She will use any excuse to stay in the classroom as long as possible, checking the child's school bag that she packed only ten minutes ago.

The teacher knows the Hoverer is there. She can feel her enquiring, impatient eyes staring at the back of her head. She can almost smell her menthol mouthwash. She sees her examining recent artwork on the wall to see where Lir's is and how it compares to all the other little Picassos.

Then she pounces. The teacher is pinned against the wall in her own classroom. The Hoverer has an unusual way of addressing the teacher: she looks at her from the side, with a sceptical eyebrow raised. The whole episode resembles a stalker and her prey as if, knowing that she'll have to slaughter her victim, the Hoverer doesn't quite want to make eye-contact first. Her chin comes to rest somewhere close to her left shoulder, eyes now looking upward, Princess Diana-like—half-coquette, half-killer.

The trapped teacher is caught in the hypnotic gaze of the Hoverer and begins to get nervous. Equally, she's aware of the mayhem just over the Hoverer's shoulder, as thirty-one five-year-olds run wild.

'Yes, I'm aware Lir lost his sweets at Big Break.'
'My child doesn't lie, Miss Watson.'
'Maybe he was upset about not being able to go to football.'
'My child does not play football, Miss Watson.'
'But Conor's a lovely child.'
'I'm not disputing that. I'd just prefer Lir not to sit beside him.'

The bell rings. The Hoverer backs off. Victory secure, territory marked out.

She flashes the teacher her expensive brite-smile beam as if to say, that will be all for today. You are dismissed. She climbs back into the hovercraft, puts her MBTs to the floor and off she goes to align her chakras at the one-world yoga shala before tonight's 40th. Back in her hermetically sealed chariot, she feels safe in the knowledge that she is on the right side of the property market. She bought before 1996 and is part of the 'I'm alright Jack' tribe, who are likely to be insulated when the property market tumbles and the great Irish Generation Game is exposed.

Chapter 7

THE HITCHHIKER'S GUIDE TO THE ECONOMY

Timing is Everything

Where have all the hitch-hikers gone? Sometime in the past ten years they vanished from our roads. The place used to be full of them, lads with rucksacks and sleeping bags or Janis-Joplin lookalike girls with homemade signs to Cork, Limerick or Dublin. Hitching was a rite of passage. It went together with badly rolled joints, sexual fantasies of busty housewives picking you up outside Clifden, Féile, the Fender Stratocaster and California. The N11 was our Ventura Highway, with rain and Fiat Mirafioris.

Along with the Yami 125, vinyl record collections, the Holy Hour and Lisdoonvarna, the hitcher was a recognisable part of the Irish landscape. Then, overnight, like Marietta biscuits and butter, they were gone. If you drive out the Naas Road today, you might see one or two forlorn figures, and they're usually Irish-speaking Germans. Not so long ago, the side of the road was thronged with all sorts, thumbing.

Mass car ownership has seen off the hitcher. Ireland is now one of the most car-dependent countries on earth—a consequence of money, atrocious planning and woeful public transport. Whereas in the past, no teenagers had a car or access to a car, today one in five of all provisional licences is held by a person under the age of 19.[1] Given that the legal minimum driving age is 17, that's an extraordinary statistic. Another factor which has driven a nail in the coffin of the hitcher is the mobile phone. The phone has 'locked in' the driver. Although technically illegal, the phone allows us to talk to who we want, when we want, and the proliferation of radio programmes aimed at car drivers means that the car becomes a totally self-contained area.

Many of us feel that when we slam the door, we are in a private place. People do things in cars that they would never do in a pub, like pick their nose or ears, scratch furiously, use the steering wheel as an imaginary snare drum, sing uproariously at traffic lights, smack their children, threaten their babies, eat their breakfast with their mouths open. The car becomes our own private, yet very public other life. We are cut off from reality with a large do-not-disturb sign around our necks. The car is a place we go to. It is not simply a method of transport. We customise it to our liking, with coffee-cup holders and TV screens for the kids. For many, the car is the only time we get to be on our own, away from the clinging, clutching interrupting reality of daily life. As a result, it means that the hitcher, rather than being pleasant company to break the journey, becomes an annoying intruder who might shatter the inner sanctum.

Judging from car sales, provisional licence applications and mobile phone adoption, 1996 seems to be the year the hitcher began to disappear from our hard shoulders.

It is also the year the housing market started to accelerate. Since then the housing market has risen by 350%.[2] Sometime around the late 1990s, the main engine of the Irish economy began to shift from production, productivity and exports, towards the bubble economy we see now, characterised by consumption and the construction leviathan which dwarfs all other sectors, sucks in capital and spews out uninhabited houses.

1996 was about the time we turned into a nation of debt junkies. Initially, we dabbled, smoking rather than injecting, a car loan here, a holiday loan there. Soon it became problematic. We denied it. We claimed we could handle it. We hid it from our friends and families but soon we needed more and more gear just to stay together. The debt began to take us over. Everything was mortgaged, leveraged, borrowed against. Soon existing overdrafts were turned into term-loans and these were in turn rolled up into jumbo-loans with longer terms. We are now a nation of lifestyle addicts, debt junkies hopelessly hooked on the latest fad.

This debt addiction is most evident in the housing market which has created the most divisive demographic divide in the western world and will have long-term sociological and political ramifications.

Accidental Millionaires

Ireland can be divided into two tribes: those who hitched and those who didn't. Although a thing of the past, the economic rollercoaster of the last ten years has meant that the Hitcher will emerge as the clear winner from the Roaring Noughties.

In the late 1990s, as the economy was mutating, the generation who hitched began to pull away in wealth terms from the younger ones. Every time house prices rose by 5%, the Hitchers—those who knew their PLO from their ELO in the mid 1970s—who owned houses got wealthier; the younger ones who didn't, became poorer. The generation who hitched might not have been able to afford a car when they were teenagers but by the time they had reached 50, they were the richest Irish people ever.

The Hitchers are the Jaggers and the Bono Boomers. How did they go from hitchers to riches, from thumbing and bumming to investing and owning, from rent control to rent reviews? The answer is simple really: they were in the right place at the right time. They are Ireland's Accidental Millionaires.

Just Shuffling the Pack

Let's look at the housing-market bubble as a generational struggle between the young and the middle-aged. Let's see who have been enriched and who have been indebted and, more importantly, now that the market is falling, who will lose most and who will be cushioned.

History tells us that asset-price booms—like the great Irish housing boom—do not make societies rich in the aggregate. This is one of the great myths of the past few years in Ireland. Booms simply redistribute wealth from one group in the society to another.

Take as an example what is probably the most ludicrous boom ever: the Tulip Boom, which happened in Amsterdam in the 17th century. Like all booms, the boom in tulips was preceded by a dramatic positive change in the economic fortunes of Holland. The almost century-long wars with Spain were concluded due, in the main, to Spanish weakness after its thirst for South American gold left it impoverished and economically bed-ridden. (This is an interesting warning sign for us. Spain plundered all the gold of Latin America and soon, it got so used to spending this easy credit, that it forgot how to make stuff. Spain didn't worry as it could pay for everything with Indian gold but when the gold ran out, Spain found herself so economically enfeebled that she went into a long decline and isolation. While not so dramatic, our spending of other people's money and our resulting surge in imports, is leaving Ireland similarly weakened. Easy credit can lull you into a false sense of security as many interest-only mortgage holders are realising.)

The Netherlands also began profiting enormously from trading in the Dutch East Indies, the stock market rose and the end of the Thirty Years' War in Europe ushered in a recovery in export markets for Dutch textiles. So, a bit like Ireland in the mid-1990s, a number of positive economic and political forces came together simultaneously to create the platform for a boom. Amsterdam enjoyed a huge building boom and the canals we stroll around today were part of this construction boom.

The other thing the Dutch went mad for were the tulips, first introduced by the Turks. The name comes from the Turkish *tulipan*, which means turban.[3] In an already flower-mad country (the Dutch have been supreme horticulturalists for years), tulips were seen as the top of the tree. They were exotic, the preserve of the very rich and they soon became items that the middle classes coveted not unlike Hermès handbags today. In the same way as Brown Thomas has waiting lists for the latest 'it' bag, it wasn't long before the new rich of Amsterdam started outbidding each other for the prized tulip.

In the winter of 1636, the price of tulip bulbs started to rise dramatically. Those who were in the market at the start sold on for fantastical profits. This frenzy attracted in all sorts of punters who began trading tulips, sucked in by the hope of large profits. At the height of Tulipmania, bulbs which had traded for twenty florins were changing hands for 1,200 florins. Holland was overtaken by a frenzy of IOUs written by desperate buyers hoping to get on the tulip ladder. There was a massive transfer of wealth from those who wanted part of the action to those who wanted to sell. The market crashed on 3 February 1637, leaving some people very rich with plenty of cash and others very poor and up to their gills in debt. In general, the society was no better or worse off.

The same carry-on can be seen in the dot.com mania which engulfed the US, and to a lesser extent Ireland, in the late 1990s. At the time the received wisdom was that stocks of internet, technology and telecoms companies could only go up. Many thousands made a fortune and when they fell, many more lost a fortune. Ask anyone who owned Baltimore Technology shares here. The Eircom flotation was similar. People who sold in time made strong profits, those who held on, lost out badly. There were large transfers of wealth from one section of society to another.

When markets crash, it's not to say that businesses are bad, just that their price is too high. Take Eircom for example: it has been sold twice since its initial flotation and still makes buckets of money for its owners, who just happen to be an Australian venture capital fund rather than the citizens of this country who actually make the phone calls and lost the money in the shares in the first place!

So, what we see in booms are huge transfers of wealth. Housing booms are different only in the sense that what should be a home turns into an asset in the upswing and a liability in the downturn. On the upswing, thousands are enriched by the fact that the equity in their houses rises, as if by magic. In Ireland, in the latter stage of the housing mania from 2004 to 2006, hundreds of thousands of people were 'making' more money on the rising value of their houses than they were taking home in their annual salaries. This created a class of drone millionaires whose wealth was rising as they were sitting on their bums doing nothing.

To see who made most, all we have to do is look at the date when they bought their houses. In relative terms, the earlier you bought your house and therefore the smaller your mortgage, the bigger the transfer of cash. If you bought your house in the early 1960s for example and its value went from £1,000 to €1,000,000 by 2006, obviously, you are in clover. But anyone who bought before things started really getting out of control also saw an enormous increase in their wealth.

The €500-billion Wealth Gap

In the context of our history, the return to land today and the fundamental inequality to which it has led, is more dramatic now than at the height of the Land League's campaigns in the latter half of the 19th century. We have succeeded in replacing one system dominated by foreign landlords, with another dominated by local landlords. The worker bees continue to feed the drones. After nearly a century of independence, that's quite an achievement!

The system obviously ensures that some people are making a fortune. Suffice at this stage to point out that site costs accounted for 42.5% of the final price of a house in Ireland in 2004.[4] This is way out of line with international standards. In the US, the site cost is on average 20% of the cost of a new house, in Portugal it drops to 15%.[5] Landowners have a huge vested interest in keeping the zoning as it is.

Clearly, such a system would lead to revolution if it weren't for the fact that enough people have also been made sufficiently wealthy as a result and if not quite a 'let-them-eat-cake' approach, the attitude is one of general support for the status quo. So apart from a minority of mega-rich oligarch landowners, a huge passive group has also made money beyond their dreams out of all this. They are the Hitchers— the people you used to see thumbing to Rory Gallagher concerts on the sides of the highways and byways of Ireland.

They have hitched a ride on the most electrifying asset-price rollercoaster the country has ever seen. This explosion in house prices has pushed the overall value of Irish housing stock to €671 billion.[6] Irish housing debt is €161 billion.[7] So there is just over €500 billion in housing equity in the country. This is a phenomenal figure. Who owns it? Well, the Hitchers do. There are 1.49 million households and of these, 73% belong to owner-occupiers, implying that there are 1.087 million private houses in the country.[8] This means that on average there is just above €500,000 equity in each house. Over half of these homeowners have no mortgage, just pure wealth. Close to 600,000 homeowners have no mortgage and half of them are between 40 and 50,[9] the type of people you see doing Jimmy Page 'Stairway to Heaven' air guitar impressions at 50th birthday parties. They are in their prime, have never been healthier or wealthier. They are releasing equity for themselves, having a blast and sitting pretty. They are the Accidental Millionaires.

In contrast, we know that first-time buyers have no equity as they have been chasing the market and four out of five first time buyers are under 35. So we can see that there is a massive wealth divide in Ireland between the young and old. The young are getting into huge debt, while the old are basking in unparalleled housing wealth.

The lion's share of the €500 billion in wealth is held by the Hitchers and looking at bank figures, the vast majority of the €161 billion debt figure is lumbered on the under-40s.

When you look at the population breakdown, you see that the demographic divide is democratically explosive and deeply unfair. The Hitchers are those people who bought their houses before 1996. Today the youngest Hitchers are in their early 40s, the oldest in their early 60s. They constitute only 33% of the population,[10] yet own practically all the wealth. In addition, they are at that stage in their careers where they are paid most. So they are asset rich and income rich. On the other hand, the generation coming behind them, in their early 20s to 40, have been caught on the wrong side of the property boom and are paying 14 times their annual salary for a starter home.[11] They account for close to 44% of the population, yet find themselves locked out of the House Party.

This enormous wealth gap is the Generation Game.

Just over four out of ten people in their 30s have mortgages while 20% of those in the 20–29 age bracket are encumbered.[12] In contrast, after the age of 45, the amount of people with mortgages falls away dramatically as they have paid off their debts and are living on pure profit. Since 1996, they have seen their wealth explode. People younger than that are sitting on less but they have equity. However, the real danger point is those in their early 30s who are sitting at that uncomfortable spot where equity is gobbled up by debt. These people, our first-time buyers of the past three years, are looking into a financial abyss as the market corrects. The contrast with the Hitchers couldn't be greater.

Research undertaken by the IMF last year, reveals that in contrast to the norm in other countries, where people start saving when they are in their early 40s and this pattern peaks when they are in their early 60s, the Irish Hitchers are spending rather than saving. Savings don't pick up in Ireland until after 60. This suggests that not only are the Hitchers enormously wealthy, but they are blowing it. The Hitchers are on the lash. And the younger generation is picking up the tab.

The Financial Body Clock
This obsession with property means that those who have it want more of it and those who don't, want a tiny bit of it. The net result of this is

that the Irish tend to buy houses young. In fact the average age of the first-time buyer is falling all the time. Today, 63% of first-time buyers are between 26 and 35. 16% are under 25. So taken together, four out of five first-time buyers are under 35.

In recent years, the financial body clock has taken over from the traditional one of having babies. This clock chimes incessantly in the heads of our young workers such as Ms Pencil Skirt urging them to buy houses earlier and earlier. In fact, the housing body clock starts ticking much earlier than the baby body clock. In most countries couples move in and out of each others' places. The places are usually rented and the relationships fickle. But in Ireland, many couples move in together for cold financial reasons rather than just lots of sex as was the case for Irish couples in the past and is still the case for many foreigners. So the fastest-rising household is the couple without children living together. In 1996 there were 31,000 of these households. Today, there are 122,000.[13]

In the past, first-time buyers were typically married. Today, only 27% are married, while 73% are still single or living with their partner.[14] They are the people who will suffer as the market slumps.

While changing attitudes towards living together has to account for some of this, a significant amount of these people are couples who've shacked up to get on the property ladder rather than wait any longer. They are bringing forward house purchasing and postponing having children. This, in the extreme, leads to the rather startling statistic in the 2006 census that, in the third quarter of 2006, more babies were born to women over 40 than under 20.

As house prices rise, the key is to get in early and put the rest of your life on hold. This means that the experience of many thousands of Irish workers in their 20s has been profoundly different to that in other countries. Many young Irish workers are now lumbered with huge mortgages while their Australian, British or German counterparts are bungee jumping, backpacking or hanging out. In Ireland, the housing mania has truncated the youth of thousands.

So in Ireland the housing obsession is changing people's behaviour in fundamental ways. And now that prices are headed down, whether you are going to experience crushing negative equity or just the mild annoyance that you are not notionally as rich as you thought you were, depends on your date of birth. So, by a process of elimination, the factor that affects your wealth in Ireland is the year you were born. This seems as bit arbitrary, doesn't it? Particularly, as it obviously means that the younger you are, the more debts you will have. Most countries pass wealth down the generations; at the moment in Ireland, we pass it up. The young pay for the old, not the other way around.

Many will say that this is only a postponement of the transfer of wealth because the wealth of today's middle-aged Hitchers will be passed on to their children in time. But times are changing and those who expected inheritance at a productive stage in their lives have been caught out by innovations in health care. Look at poor old Prince Charles across the water. The poor lad will be ancient by the time he gets the crown. He is trapped by his mother's longevity. Prince Charles' dilemma will also happen to Ireland's young prospective heirs and heiresses because their parents are living longer than any generation ever. And as the Hitchers were the last generation of Irish people to have children in their early 20s, there is every likelihood that their dauphins will be in their 60s when they get their mits on the lolly. Inheritance will come late and won't be what it used to be.

So when seen through the prism of demography, in terms of housing wealth alone, if the Accidental Millionaires were the luckiest Irish ever, the unluckiest were those born between 1970 and 1980. Contrary to much of the media reportage, not surprisingly penned by editors and columnists born in the Hitcher era, the younger generation is not some feckless bunch of hedonists who can't do a good day's work. In fact, they are the first-time buyers, who have splashed out for the most expensive commuter houses in Europe, just as the market peaked in value. A financial trap has been sprung and they are caught.

Chapter 8 〜
| THE JUGGLERS

6.45 a.m.
'Just hit snooze love, be up in a minute.'
'Don't forget about tonight, ok?'
'Yeah, yeah, see you later.'

7.20 a.m.
'Shit, shit, shit, we're late.'
'Where's my uniform?'
'On the radiator downstairs.'
'Where's Dad?'
'He's gone.'
'He's always gone.'
'Well, someone has to pay the bills.'
'What are bills?'

OK, Wednesday. What's Wednesday? Playball, hockey, swimming, piano or football? Make the lunches, get the football gear out of the car, do the spelling, remember the rice milk. Jesus, those grey bits are showing, need to get them done today. Hoover bags, fix loo downstairs, do manicure, money for the school trip, buy goggles, tights, something for husband to give his mother for her birthday, a thank-you card, plasters.

Juggler Jane is not even out of the shower and already she's making lists. She could organise the Normandy invasion down the side margin of an ESB bill. Like many thousands of young Irish mothers, she's juggling, keeping all the balls in the air, keeping the show on the road— half desperate housewife, half military planner.

> *'Can't hear, I'm in the shower.'*
> *'Fiach's hitting me!'*
> *'Get dressed both of you, or no treats.'*
> *'That's not fair, you're so mean.'*
> *'Just finish your Weetabix, all of it and I said no telly in the morning. Christ!'*
> *'You're not allowed to say "Christ", that's a bad word.'*
> *'Just hurry up.'*

The New Provos

Juggler Jane is a Provo. She's part of the New Provisional Army. She is leading a provisional life. She believes that this part of her life is just a stepping stone to something greater. This is a long war. History is on the Provos' side.

As she sits in the traffic at the Dunkettle Roundabout, Juggler Jane knows that this is not why she went to college and did the extra degree at night. This is not the end point. This is part of the great sacrifice on the journey to achieve the New Irish Dream. The New Irish Dream is a vision of the future, a future that will be better than the present. The here and now is provisional.

This belief in the future is new to Ireland. Not so long ago we were shackled by the past—past heroes, past struggles and past voices. The Irish present could only be understood by how we got here. This explains the oddity of Civil War politics in Ireland. For hundreds of thousands of Irish people, their entire political identity was forged in their view of the past, rather than their vision of the future. But this is all changing and now, we are future dreamers.

This is a profoundly American psychology. Many writers who comment on the American psyche come back to this wide-eyed belief that tomorrow will be better than today. For example, in *On Paradise Drive*, David Brooks observes that because America in many ways is a land of the future, people's 'relationship to a place a job or a lifestyle is provisional'. What he means is that in the US, because people believe that something better is always around the corner, everything they do today is provisional. The Irish Jugglers, living in the commuter belt, feel the same way.

The rise of the Provos is the result of the Americanisation of Irish society. Sometime in the mid-1990s, we disengaged from Europe, with its melancholic memories, and attached ourselves to the US with its blue-sky future. These days it is normal to hear people say that the country has become more American. This is usually meant as a criticism. The speaker is typically referring to an America which stands for a large gap between rich and poor, a country of low-rent, instantly combustible celebrity, whitened teeth and a seething trailer-trash underclass striving to get by on the minimum wage.

But of course there is the other side of America that appeals to Irish people. It is the Great American Dream which relies on the belief in a bright, ever-improving future. It is a place where people can say, as did Henry Ford, 'history is bunk' and not be sniggered at. It is a culture where a noted academic, Francis Fukuyama, is fêted for writing a book entitled *The End of History*. It is a country where an excessively Panglossian President can hold a 'Mission Accomplished' jamboree a few months after what would evolve into a disastrous invasion of Iraq, as if the present was in some way a staging post for a brighter future.

Ronald Reagan, the Irish-American President who epitomised the American Dream more than most, declared that, 'The difference between the American and any other person is that the American lives in anticipation of the future because he knows what a great place it will be.'[1] The basis for the Dream is that America is so essentially democratic that social status is always up for grabs. Wealth, rather than birth, is the ultimate arbiter of worth. Supporters of the American system contend that all Americans start with a blank slate and how you get on in life depends on the individual's efforts. (The evidence suggests something much more complex. In fact recent studies suggest that social mobility might be falling in the US.)

However, the basic dreaminess of the American psyche allows them to believe that everyone has a chance and that the system facilitates, rather than hinders, social mobility. Even in the 1830s when 100,000 Irish emigrants arrived in the US, Alexis de Tocqueville observed: 'I never met in America any citizen so poor as not to cast a glance of hope and envy at the enjoyments of the rich or whose imagination did not possess itself by anticipation of those good things'.[2]

As in Ireland at the moment, the handmaiden of this collective futurology is an appetite for risk and speculation. You pay your money, you take your risk. Americans conclude that inequality is a reflection of ability and balls. European political culture has made the elimination of inequality the cornerstone of its political philosophy. The Irish system was once somewhere in the middle, but in the Roaring Noughties we have veered rapidly towards the American Dream. This bias is not surprising, given that the Irish are part of the fundament of the American project. The New Irish Dream is the American Dream with bad weather.

The essential ingredient for the Dream is a bull market. The strapped Juggler in Castledermot knows that his starter home, for which he paid €330,000, is not heaven. He probably can't stand his neighbours, believing them to be beneath him, but he's on the ladder. He's on his way up. This is the first step. As long as he feels that he can sell on to another younger Juggler in a few years, he's on his way. The journey from Castledermot back to Castleknock is only a matter of time. The bull market keeps the conveyor belt of social enhancement going.

Societies that are characterised by risk-taking are exciting places. If there is an opportunity to thrive, the place is more open, fearless and ultimately, more tolerant. When the majority believe that the future is bright, it doesn't really matter who shares it, so long as you are improving your situation or at least not falling backwards. Thus, immigration is tolerated or even encouraged. It is normal to hear Irish people today praise many of our immigrants for their attitude, their enthusiasm and their contribution. Yes, there are pockets of discontent, but the general view has been welcoming.

People are so wrapped up in tomorrow that they are not too concerned about today. Speculative societies are renewed by constantly reassessing risk. What's around the corner? How am I positioned? The neurosis of on-going rejuvenation and reinvention is only possible when you believe in the future. The tolerance aspect of speculative societies is sometimes overlooked. But it's not hard to see how speculative societies, where prices are rising and the economy is expanding, become more tolerant and social barriers are reduced. If we decide that legislation is an outward sign of what a society thinks is right and wrong, we see a flurry of equality legislation in Ireland when the economy is booming, not stagnating. The link between huge advances in social aspirations and huge advances in material wealth is so unambiguous as to suggest that those who argue the opposite simply are not looking at the facts.

So, as Ireland becomes more American, it becomes more liberal. As we become more American, we absorb more foreign people without racial tensions. In fact, this is where Ireland's behaviour has been exemplary. In the dark days, when the economy was on its knees, had you suggested that we would absorb 400,000 immigrants without race riots, people would have thought you were mad. But it has happened.

The problem for speculative societies is that the headiness, optimism and dreaminess are intertwined. One can't flourish without the other. You can't sustain the dream without taking the risk and return, but you won't take the risk unless you feel the market is going up. And this is where some problems emerge: if the promise of wealth in the future dies, the dream will die too. At the moment the social contract in Ireland is holding, but as the housing market falters this could unravel, with serious implications for the social peace. Today, everyone is still acting as if the dream is alive.

Because the New Irish Dream is all about an invented better future, everything you do, say and achieve has to reflect the fact that you are on the Yellow Brick Road. In the future, all your children will achieve more than you, they will be smarter, brighter and more accomplished. To achieve this state of grace, today they must have the tools to equip them for this climb.

Once tooled-up, they can achieve their potential. They can fulfil today's promise of tomorrow's genius. However, everything you do today will impact on your child's chances in the future, so you have to ensure the best for the precious little one. This is why we have crèches called Little Harvard in Naas, complete with mortarboard-and-gown graduation.

But the social contract works as a conveyor belt. As long as it keeps moving up, the Jugglers know they are going in the right direction. The locomotive for the conveyor belt is the housing market. Given their provisional outlook, the Jugglers are prepared to put up with poor infrastructure, long commutes and expensive crèche fees if their house prices and wealth are improving. Once that stops, all bets are off and politically, the status quo which saw Fianna Fáil through the 2007 election will change profoundly.

Back to Reality

The Juggler's beginning to resent the very women she used to admire. Suzi's bloody mother works all the time, running around the globe leaving the other mothers to pick up the pieces. This is the snag: no matter what Germaine Greer told us, it's almost impossible to have a brilliant career and be a fantastic mother. Something has to give.

Jane can't believe it. How come she's making the children's lunches at twenty to one in the morning, worried about a client meeting in eight hours' time, plucking bits of pasta out of the filter of the dishwasher, wondering why the unpaid phone bill has gone unattended, all the while screaming at the dirty iron for staining her only clean shirt for the morning.

Jesus, get me out of here, she thinks. Washing, ironing, cleaning, picking up, dropping off, kitting out, strapping in, making snacks, raising funds, ferrying children to play dates—it's endless. If this is women's liberation, what's slavery?

She's caught in the middle of the modern tug-of-war between the two great institutions of our time—the family and the company— while being weighed down by the mortgage, which means she can't give up work, even if she wanted to.

She's pulled from pillar to post all the time weighing things up, assessing and making choices between being the alpha-female and the caring mother.

Also, the novelty of motherhood has worn off. When the babies were tiny, she was the centre of attention. Everyone had time for her. Now, as the children have grown older and less cute, she's invisible. The mother's world, in a period of four years, goes from being big, open and accessible to small, closed and cut-off. Today in Ireland there are thousands of young working mothers like Juggler Jane, who have become invisible—worried about bankruptcy, infidelity, five take away two and how they measure up in the Good Mummy league.

For Juggler Jane, the enemy is those earnestly virtuous stay-at-home mums at the school gates, the ones who joined the slow food movement and know that Wednesday is 'show and tell' day. Well, of course they do, what else is going on in their feather brains all day?

But before she negotiates that lot, she has to get the little one to crèche before 8 a.m., if she's to have any chance of meeting that client at nine. She's only just back to work after maternity leave and already she knows the whispering campaign has begun. She can hear the boss on the golf course talking to his friends:

Two children in four years and she's still young. I mean what does she think we're trying to run here, a bloody nursery?

She feels awful dropping her daughter every morning, she's only eight months old, but what can she do? She's in a trap. She goes to work but most of her cash goes on childcare. She forks out €925 a month for Ladybug crèche. That's €11,100 per year. It's more expensive because little Savannah is under eighteen months. Next year, it will come down to €850 a month. But with four-year-old Troy's after-school care at €500 a month, it's not worth her while to work. She's caught in the two-income trap.

In the US this dilemma was recognised in the 1990s and is documented in a book by Elizabeth Warren and Amelia Warren Tyagi, called *The Two Income Trap*. According to the authors, double-income middle class families are flirting with bankruptcy at an alarming rate. They are getting into debt and financial difficulty considerably easier and earlier than single-income families did in the 1970s. They contend that the double-income family, with mothers going out to work, is the reason that costs have gone up to such an extent. It is argued that financially at least, the family would be better off if the mother stayed at home.

However, as working mothers themselves, they are the first to point out the equality dilemma, which is that society has educated thousands of women who want more out of life than to slip back quietly into the kitchen as soon as the children arrive. This is the conundrum facing thousands of middle-class Irish women as they grapple with the delusions of the equality dream. They were told they could have it all, careers and children; they would look beautiful at thirty-five, cellulite-free, angst-free, sugar-free. They would juggle the spin cycle with the business cycle effortlessly.

Juggler Jane is one of the 44% of Irish women between 25 and 34 who have university degrees.[3] We have the highest proportion of highly educated young women in Europe and as the average mother is having her first child at thirty, we have the highest proportion of young mothers facing the same dilemma. Should she stay at work and juggle children and career or should she turn her back on everything that she believes in and throw in the towel?

Juggler Jane is depressed, what will people think of her? Will she become one of those women at the school gates who seem to hang around with other women with whom they have nothing in common except children of the same age?

That's her great fear. She was educated to believe that a girl should work, should make the best of her career: a girl should achieve. This is what the culture wars of the 1980s were all about, the right of Irish women to fulfil their potential. Today at least she is a marketing manager. Will she be taken for granted if she gives up work? Who would take her seriously if all she could discuss was baking, spinning classes and the thermostat on the immersion? Her choice is now to give up work or plough on. She can't give up yet because they couldn't afford it and she can't go up, as she's hit the glass ceiling. She's stuck and most of all she's tired. She's running flat out to stand still, juggling and worried about the size of her bum. She's even back on the Pill for fear of having another child.

The Prisoner's Dilemma

Jugglers are driven between yearning for security in an insecure world and the enormous costs of a New Irish lifestyle in a highly competitive society.

The Jugglers are products of the 1970s' baby boom and are the first generation to go to university in large numbers. Today, they are the fuel that drives the economy forward. They commute, live in expensive shoe-boxes and have children out in the Irish baby-belt. The Jugglers are keeping all the balls in the air: child-care, work, family and trying desperately to maintain appearances. It's not that they are not having fun; they are just exhausted, burning the candle at both ends.

In one of the hundreds of white-collar institutions that suck them up after they leave college, many Jugglers tailored their little space to send out a clear signal to everyone that, behind the conformity of the corporate man, there's an exciting, irrepressible individual trying to get out. The desk becomes a shrine to extreme sports. There'll be a large photograph of a certified accountant snowboarding in Chamonix, bodysurfing off Tarifa or paragliding in the Peruvian Andes. That's me, the bloke with the ice-pick, half way up the North Face. They don't play snooker.

The desk will also be festooned with lots of personal paraphernalia. Photos of children, wives and mates at a stag night, dressed as Elvis. And, of course, the obligatory Homer Simpson quotation somewhere on the side of the PC screen. All this signals 'my real life is somewhere else', I'm only here for the cash and, in three years' time I'll be running a surf school in Sligo, playing the Electric Picnic or, the refuge of people who don't know what to do, becoming a freelance photographer.

As Jane acknowledges, you can tell a lot about a Juggler prisoner from her screen saver. The screen saver is where they would rather be. A typical one is the tropical island, which for some unthinking reason has been equated to paradise by millions of melanin-deficient Paddies who would fry in an afternoon there. But it doesn't matter; we are in dream-world here. The blue skies, palm-trees and turquoise waters, they all scream 'get me out of here'. Give me a one-way Trailfinders ticket, a Rough Guide and I'm in Patagonia.

They don't want to be here. They don't want to be employee of the month, year, or decade. They realise that the walls are closing in. They're living for the weekend. They are beginning to feel trapped. They text the Ray D'Arcy show.

This dilemma is a function of the demographic divide that we saw earlier in the Irish economy: the two-income family has pushed up the cost of a middle-class lifestyle to such an extent that the middle classes are trapped. They have been sold a pup.

In the natural drive for equality for women, no-one asked who would replace Mum. If Mum is in the workforce, who will do all the things Mum used to do? And as there is no going back to the old days, how are we expected to pay for all the stuff stay-at-home Jagger Mum did for free 20 years ago?

In the past, the tiny fraction of Irish middle-class mothers who worked full time were bailed out by young girls who usually left school early to work as domestics. They worked for a fraction of the average wage, got their keep and provided a limitless pool of labour. So the career ambitions of some Irish women were facilitated by the limited horizons of other Irish women. Now this has changed. Young Irish women naturally won't work for under the average wage or at least close to it. This pushes the cost of childcare up enormously. And this is going to get worse because the population of 30-year-old women will rise for the next five years.

To keep this show on the road, we face a choice. Unless we have mass targeted immigration of poor women who are prepared to work for well below their Irish equivalents, the two-income trap will lead to financial ruin for Ireland's Jugglers. This would mean opening our system to thousands of poorer Europeans, like Bulgarians and Romanians. At the moment they are allowed to come here but not to work without a permit, which is virtualy impossible to get. So, if a working mum employs one, not only will she have to worry about fairy cakes, school runs and goggles for swimming, she'll have to deal with questions from the Revenue about a black market employee.

The trap will get tighter in the years ahead, made worse by two added policy initiatives. First, the Lisbon Agenda—an EU-wide objective which Ireland signed up to in 2004—has committed us to increasing to 70% the amount of Irish women in the workforce from the current 60%. Secondly, we are likely to see tighter not looser immigration policies.

This is very relevant in Ireland where the demographic divide in wealth created by the property boom is forcing the Juggler generation into huge debt. Now, the wealth gap is reinforced through an income gap because the cost of bringing up children has risen so substantially. It is not that the Jugglers' income is considerably less than the Jaggers', it is that their costs are so much higher.

––––

The jockeying for position begins before birth. In recent years, women in the catchment area of the Coombe Women's Hospital have been avoiding the hospital, risking driving, in labour, through the clogged city traffic, to have their children in Holles Street because, as one young mother put it, 'I'm not having my baby born in Africa'. Figures show that in the Coombe over 30% of births are to African mothers.[4] Irish mothers do not want to be in the same hospital, let alone the same ward, as the immigrants. This is not PC, but it's what's happening.

Jugglers want to give their children the best start in the world and have clearly decided (without evidence, it must be said) that being born in the Coombe will carry a stigma in later life. This is part of the trend we are now seeing towards separation. There is nothing particularly new in this but when it is demarcated along colour lines it is obviously clearer. The Jugglers are opting out of the public system early.

The first enormous expense that the Juggler is facing now that the Jagger, her counterpart 20 years ago didn't face, is crèche fees. The cost of crèches is rising at twice the rate of inflation and in some places three times. It costs more to send your child to a crèche full time, which most Jugglers have no choice but to do, than to send your child to one of Dublin's elite schools. It costs less to send a boy to Blackrock College than it does to send a child to a crèche in Tallaght. The average crèche cost in Dublin for one child is €800 per month or a crippling €9,600 per year.[5] One in three parents is paying more in crèche fees than they are paying for their mortgage.

The Jugglers, like Jane, are getting squeezed. They can't give up work lest they default on the mortgage but if they stay at work they are pinned to their collars with childcare. Remember, in most cases, the take-home wage for the household with their first child will be around €5,500 a month. A recent survey[6] calculated that the average cost of a child in Ireland is €12,000 in the first year and this rises in years two and three, particularly if the parent chooses extra activities to give their children a head start such as Montessori schooling.

On top of this, most double-income families now have private health care insurance, which is no longer seen as an option but a necessity given the problems in the healthcare system. Whether the health system is as bad as the media suggests is up for discussion, however, the cumulative effect of the negative coverage is to frighten people into private cover. The impact of this is seen in the fact that ten years ago there was no waiting list for private hospitals. Now there is. So, the burgeoning demand for private medical insurance is actually clogging up private hospitals! Again, this is a significant Juggler expense, as, on average, health insurance costs well over €1,000 a year for a family with two children.

If you take these expenses, together with things we don't sometimes see as a direct consequence of two parents working, such as two cars, two insurance policies, two car tax bills and two NCTs, it doesn't take long to realise how the take-home wage gets eaten away.

———

Juggler Jane spots Suzi's perfect Mum, the one who gave up work, the one who goes on about how she's sacrificed everything for her kids. There she is hovering around the teacher like a sheep worrier, thinks Jane.

Of course she walks to school. Arm in arm with her little angels, like some Danish yogurt ad. Only the very rich walk to school. Research by *Daft.ie* found that living close to a private school in Dublin can add up to €250,000 to the price of a house.[7]

'Hi Jane, going to swimming this afternoon? Should be fun!'

'Oh, yeah!' Jesus, how will she get out of work and the client meeting to drop Fiach? Maybe she could ask little Miss Perfect. No way, that would only be game, set and match in the Mummy Wars to that sanctimonious, judgmental tart. She of the self-control, the successful IVF and the converted basement. She of the pointedly effortless four children, the ultimate status symbol. Only the very wealthy and Romanians have big families these days.

Juggler Jane, the cash-strapped new Provo, kisses her kids and promises to collect Fiach for swimming at 3 p.m. She hops back into her messy car with no idea how she's going to keep all the balls in the air. She calls Sean.

'Hi Babe, can't talk. No, I'll be late. I've gotta go to some poxy team-building course. I'll try to be back to tuck them in.'

Chapter 9 ∿

DENIAL

In January 2007, when addressing a group of bankers on the issue of the future of the economy and the housing market in general, I offered a sale-and-leaseback arrangement on my suburban Dublin home. After all, the bankers, from the country's biggest banks had been positive on the property market, saying that they thought it was only going one way. If this was the case, they should have jumped at my ten-year sale-and-leaseback deal. They could buy the house at the market price and I would undertake to lease it back to them at the market rent so that they would get a stream of income. I would guarantee their rent for ten years, while they would guarantee the family's tenure for ten years.

No-one budged. Not one taker.

Surely these bankers weren't telling porkies? They couldn't be, could they? They were all confident of the market, yet not one was prepared to put their money where their mouth was. Strange that, particularly when you see how much money they are prepared to lend other people to bet on the market. Can you smell a rat?

Then again, in the past twelve months, two of our largest banks have been selling off their own property portfolios in the same type of sale-and-leaseback arrangement. So they are prepared to sell but not to buy. How bizarre. Do they sense something that we don't? Do they know something that they're not telling us? Or is there a more simple explanation? Bankers are, in the main, corporate suits who really don't play the market, so middle-ranking bank officials—the Skoda Octavia class—are therefore the last people to be able to gauge when a market is peaking or troughing.

Forget the bankers, what about you? Can you imagine an Ireland where house prices begin to fall precipitously? Already we are seeing price falls around the country—could you imagine if this became widespread? Imagine an Ireland without property supplements, without gushing descriptions of 'outside spaces' and cocky estate agents in shiny suits and plastic shoes? You know, the modern day gel boys who man the phones at isolated estate agents in the suburbs, with their excessively wide ties, Sioux Indian-chic mullets, five-button jackets and Toyota Celicas? Imagine a country without them and their grubby calculators—the ones they use to tell you the monthly cost of a mortgage rather than the overall price of the house—just in case it scares you.

The one common theme that binds all recent property collapses together, whether they are in the US, Scandinavia or Japan, is that despite all the evidence on the table before the slump, people are still taken by surprise. After the event, people are bemused by their own blindness. How did we not see that coming? What were we thinking about?

One possible reason for this is that at some stage the housing market becomes more of an exercise in psychology and greed than economics. Investors hunt in packs and markets are not rational. John Maynard Keynes once commented on falling markets, 'These markets can remain irrational longer than you can remain solvent.' Anyone who has experienced a booming market that once looked so promising only to slump, will substantiate Keynes's observation. Housing markets do fall to earth and the evidence is that there are pretty few exceptions. Mostly, there is no obvious reason or trigger other than loss of that most ephemeral of attributes—confidence—which evaporates, sometimes overnight, sometimes over a period of years.

Economists are always looking for signals that can rationally explain why something may or may not happen. The problem with this is that the baseline assumption is that housing markets, when they get into the frenzy phase, are logical. No-one who has seen Irish people queuing up to buy second and third homes can suggest that what they have seen is rational. No-one who has travelled abroad with a tour bus of Paddies with chequebooks open can proffer that these people are in any way sensible. They are members of the cult of property.

This cult is like any bunch of religious fanatics. They have their own rituals, and more than anything, they are filled with self-righteousness about their mission. They are zealots. Nowhere is safe from their converting craze, from the back boreens of Roscommon and Cavan to the oddest destinations of Ryanair. The cultists are everywhere. The café in Kilbeggan, Co. Westmeath, which serves up eggs and beans to truckers is called Kusadasi after the Turkish resort beloved of Irish property cultists.

When people come under the spell of a property or any asset cult, all logic is thrown out of the window. Looking back at history, there is precious little evidence of logic in any financial craze. Were the stoic Dutchmen of Den Haag logical in the Tulipmania craze which overtook Calvinist Holland in the 1630s? Were the smart Jewish financiers behind the junk bond mania of the US in the late 1980s calm and logical? Were any of the great Irish-American speculators during the Wall Street crash informed by sensible projections? Is there anything vaguely logical about paying in the region of €50 million for a house on Shrewsbury Road?

In fact, all the historical evidence condemns the Irish housing market to follow a pattern of six stages. Initial sound judgement gives way to euphoria, then mania which is accompanied by large borrowing, followed by panic, and then a run for the door.

If the pattern of house-price cycles in 40 other countries since 1970 is to be repeated here, according to Morgan Kelly, an economist working in UCD, we are in for real house-price 'falls of between forty to sixty per cent in the next eight or nine years.'[1]

Many readers will look at this prediction in horror, thinking that this can't possibly happen here. Yet large falls in house prices after a boom are commonplace and, in fact, much more normal than house prices remaining at stratospheric levels. The problem with Irish commentary is that it gets involved in what could be termed 'Irish exceptionalism'. This is a significant blindspot premised on the idea that what is happening here has never happened anywhere ever before, which is at best, patent nonsense and, at worst, a conspiracy.

Indeed, the possibility of a conspiracy is not so outlandish because so many of the commentators are in the pay of vested interests. More often than not, the pay check of the person analysing the market depends on the market going up.

Commentators working for the banks, the brokers and the estate agents who last year were saying that the market could only go up, have been revising down their forecasts with every piece of negative news.

So, to get a handle on this, altitude is always necessary. Let's take the long view. If you examine the patterns in OECD countries over the past 30 years, the evidence suggests that housing booms fall back to earth. Typically, the period of a slump is five to seven years but in at least three recent cases—Switzerland, Holland and Japan—the housing market stagnated for a decade. The severity of the fall is always a function of the steepness of the rise.[2]

In the Irish situation, Morgan Kelly concludes that 'the evidence of nearly forty cycles in house prices for seventeen OECD economies since the 1970s shows that real (adjusted-for-inflation) house prices typically give up about seventy per cent of their rise in the subsequent fall, and that these falls happen slowly'.[3]

So, why won't this happen here? Most of the cheerleaders for the boom argue that house prices are a reflection of strong growth, demographics and immigration. But there is no economic evidence of this unless every immigrant is a buyer, which is a ludicrous proposition. If house price rises were simply a function of economics, why did rents stagnate from 2000 to early 2007?[4] Why are rents now yielding hardly anything in Dublin's best areas? Why have rents in the baby belt—the large new suburbs where the population is growing quickest—done nothing in the past five years? The reason is simple: people chose to buy rather than rent. Why in the past few months are rents rising? Because people are now negative on the market and prefer to rent rather than buy. Contrary to what estate agents might say, rising rents are only a good sign when there's no supply. And if the construction boom is in response to demand, why is the countryside dotted with ghost estates of empty properties? The reason is that we are in a bubble, where house prices are not a reflection of the laziest expression known to modern economics, the 'fundamentals'. Rather, it is a reflection of a buying frenzy.

If we look at what has happened to house prices since 2000, we see that prices have increased at twice the pace of rents and three times faster than wages.[5] Either this means that people believe that Ireland has achieved some sort of permanent economic advantage over the rest of the world which entitles our house prices to be higher than everywhere else, or we're being conned. The problem with the 'Ireland is unique' angle is that it goes against everything we know. The growth rate is slowing down, the public service is the bigger job creator and exports have stagnated. Have we been sold a large, bricks-and-mortar pup? History certainly suggests so.

The reason why the slump can go on for so long—a minimum of five to seven years—is that we are all reticent to drop the price of our houses, so we hang on, holding out for the mythical buyer who will walk in, smell the freshly brewed coffee and take our beautiful home off us at the price we want. Thus, it takes time for prices to fall and even when they do, it doesn't seem like it. For example, if our house price doesn't increase this year and inflation increases by four per cent, meaning that the price of everything else has increased relative to the price of the house, adjusted for inflation, the price of houses has fallen by 4%. In the course of the next ten years this story is likely to repeat itself here.

Why do we think that we can buck the patterns of the past 30 years as seen in Denmark, Netherlands, Norway, Sweden, New Zealand, not to mention the mega cycles of Japan and the UK as well as the regional boom/busts in the US over the same period? Maybe the reason is that Ireland wasn't a proper economy up until recently and as we had no credit, we hadn't the conditions necessary to experience a boom. Now, however, the world's credit markets are open to us. There is cash everywhere and yet only so many places it can go. In addition, because our banks are under pressure to lend as much as possible, there is money for practically everyone. Nowhere is too exotic. Irish buyers are everywhere. Last year Bulgaria was hot, this year's favourite is Dubai. Now there's a place for a summer hollier for a melanin-deprived Paddy, 106 degrees in the shade.

Of course the slump can happen here and because we are so

integrated with the rest of the world, the trigger could come from anywhere.

Many argue that the so-called 'soft landing' is all that you need for the market to reverse. The reason for this argument is that so much of the market is now held by investors who are in the game for capital gain. They are constantly making the back-of-the-envelope calculation: should I wait or should I sell? Many thousands are not concerned in the slightest about news that the market is falling—they bought years ago, what do they care? But the problem is that over 100,000 investors have come into the market in the past two or three years, none of whom have made any money, when you take the costs into account. That's a lot of people. To put it in perspective a population the size of Cork City is facing a financial crisis. Once this begins to unravel, thousands of others who think they are fine now with a well-managed web of debts and overdrafts, get sucked in.

Financial crises behave like a swimmer being sucked into a vortex. Initially the current is manageable, perhaps a bit strong, but the swimmer is powerful, experienced and sensible. Suddenly he feels the pull, his strokes become more powerful but he's going backwards, he panics, tries to grab on to something, anything, then he's sucked into the epicentre of the whirlpool.

But today, like the swimmer, we deny that there is any problem. This denial phase can go on for a while and looking at the desperate efforts to pretend that the market is not softening in the past few months of 2007 can leave you in no doubt that we are in the denial phase. Estate agents, practically by the day, release factoids about the success of auctions and the off-the-plan new developments that have been snapped up. In the denial stage, everything is done to prevent the idea taking hold that house prices are falling. The sellers know that the market reacts like a herd and they, understandably, try not to frighten the horses. But everyone knows that it is an effervescent confidence trick and if we are being really honest, we know that there is no relationship between value and prices. It's all a pyramid scheme but this can never be admitted.

So we get developers paying the first year's mortgage repayments or kitting out the kitchens and bathrooms, things they wouldn't have dreamt of this time two years ago when the queues were out the door. Or we see the banks offering 100% mortgages and allowing buyers to roll up the costs of all the white goods into a new super-sized mortgage—a sort of jumbo, whopper, Big Mac mortgage. The reason the banks do this is very simple. In most cases they have financed the development of the homes that they are now issuing mortgages for. They want the first-time buyers to hold the risk, rather than the developer. They believe that first-time buyers don't go bust.

History indicates that they have a point but financial trauma changes everything. Up to now the evidence has suggested that most people will do anything to try not to default on their mortgage, so the banks naturally feel better if they have the risk spread over thousands of small-fry commuters rather than one big-fish developer. The first phase of this process is to make sure that the developer sells the apartments and if this means giving a 100%, 40-year mortgage to a double-income application, so be it. In recent months, developers have been offering to pay the first six months' mortgage if the couple will just sign up for the show-house.

Soft Landing

There is a structural problem with the financing market. In the past three years, the banking system has abandoned all decorum by moving from an income-based ratio to determining how much can be prudentially borrowed to this delinquent expression, 'affordability'. This approach ramps up the price of new houses to the maximum the misfortunate can afford to pay which, in turn, ratchets up the prices further. This is because the income of the couple becomes an accelerator rather than a cap on financing. A 10% increase in a person's income in an atmosphere of falling interest rates can have a 50% or 60% impact on affordability. So for every €1 we spend, we can get €6 into debt.

It also has the effect of persuading people to borrow when interest rates are at their lowest, making it virtually guaranteed that there will be problems when rates rise. Objectively speaking, the best time to borrow is when interest rates are high and falling rather than the worst possible time when rates are low and rising.

When you think about it, 'affordability' ensures that the major determinant of the price of houses is not supply and demand, the underlying price of land or the cost of materials or labour. The only thing that now affects the price of land is how much debt the bank can foist on the poor borrower who is dementedly trying to get on the ladder.

Not surprisingly, the banks are the arch deniers in the early stages of a housing slump.

The government is also a serial denier. It realises that the feelgood factor is entirely inflated by the sense that house prices are rising. Also, the tax take from property is now close to 30% of the price of a new house. But more importantly, the entire system now depends on the housing market; if this goes, so too, does the government's painless tax strategy upon which, in the Irish case, it has expanded public spending and employment enormously. The government and the construction sector created 90% of all the new jobs last year. The financial implications of a slump are devastating for the national balance sheet because expenditure goes rocketing up as revenue shoots down. For example, Finland's budget deficit moved from a surplus of around 2% in 1988 to a deficit of 15% by 1991 as a result of a property bust.[6]

We are all deniers. No-one wants to entertain the idea that the property they have just bought, whether it is a palace or a shoe-box, was a bad investment.

In the denial phase a mantra gets repeated—as if, by repetitive incantation, we will ward off the evil spirits. This year's Responsorial Psalm is 'the soft landing'. Let's cut through the cant to see whether the soft landing stands up to scrutiny.

Doors to Manual

Every time you turn on the TV, listen to the radio or open a newspaper, you will hear some expert talking about a soft landing. Unfortunately, this is about as plausible as a rain dance. A soft landing in the property market, without aggressive cuts in interest rates, has never been seen in any country, anywhere in the world at any time. In the Irish case, the term is even more fanciful because we do not have any policy levers at our disposal.

Think about the imagery of a soft landing. It is aeronautical and describes a skilful pilot bringing a plane in to land from high altitude, in bad conditions and swirling winds, using all his skill, dexterity and understanding of how aerodynamics keeps the plane aloft. We have a picture of a superhero with a Rolex in the cockpit pulling levers, fighting with the elements, decelerating and getting the angles right.

The key to landing is to remove the uplift from the air using the tilt of the wings, so the plane almost drives smoothly into the runway. The tilt is controlled by the pilot using his cockpit instruments. Remember, he is disoriented so he has to trust the tools at his disposal to give him altitude readings and speed of approach. The margin for error is minimal: if the pilot releases the uplift too late, the plane will smash nose-first into the runway; too early and the aircraft will drop like a stone onto the ground, bounce and try to take off again.

The pilot adjusts the rudder, wings and balances the machine. He straightens the plane, eyes up the runway, drops the wheels and engineers the aircraft towards a soft-landing. Everyone claps.

Now, try to picture this with no pilot, no flight instruments, no air-traffic-control tower, no tail fin, no fuel and most importantly, no power over the wings. Yes, I'd be saying the Rosary too.

The Irish property market is an out-of-control aircraft, full of petrified screaming passengers, with neither a pilot nor working controls. We abandoned our economic levers when we joined EMU in 1999. Like a doomed plane, the market can only go up and when it stops going up, as it is doing now, it falls to earth. The severity of the fall is based on the pull of financial gravity.

Because of EMU, we now face the added problem of a housing-market slump when interest rates are going up, not down. No other country has ever faced this dilemma. Typically, at the first sign of trouble a country cuts its interest rates to as close to zero as possible, in order to avoid a credit meltdown. The US did this in 2002 after the dot.com crash, avoiding a recession. Our housing market is now falling but our interest rates are actually going up. Something else will have to give.

And as house prices fall, the Generation Game will be exposed. So while the Jagger Generation and the Bono Boomers might be inconvenienced, the real pain will be felt by the generation born in the 1970s and early 1980s who have bought into the property market at the peak. These are the commuters from Deckland, the people who have the 100% mortgage and live in the new towns and estates out in the great Irish Baby Belt.

Warren Buffett, the American investor, once famously said with regard to financial markets, 'it is only when the tide goes out that you see who is swimming in the nude'. In our case, the wave has been the tsunami of cheap cash which washed over us in the past few years, pushing up house prices, enriching the middle aged and indebting the young. To see how this tide might ebb and flow and to assess what might happen when house prices fall, it is important to understand where all this cash came from in the first place. If it isn't ours, whose cash is it?

Chapter 10 ～

OSAMA'S BOOM

9/11 Fallout

Let's rock up to Croke Park in June 2005. This was U2's homecoming gig. In the space of three nights, over 240,000 people, wrapped in that weird U2 look of tricolour and Stetson, kind of half-Óglaigh na hÉireann, half-Garth Brooks, paid homage. The gig was brilliant; underlining that for all our bragging about being world class at this and that, U2 are the only Irish act that is truly global. They're the only ones who've done it.

Half-way through, the band's Third-World-debt message was beamed on large screens, images of starving children which might have made the overweight Paddies who'd forked out €80 on their credit cards a little uncomfortable. If it did, they didn't show it. For a nation that prides itself as a bastion of charity, we spend more on tickets for music festivals than we do on all charities.

But if we want to understand the story of how starter homes in Clonmel can cost over €360,000 and why thousands of these mortgages are likely to be defaulted on, a good place to start is to listen to Bono's story of Third World debt. Bear in mind that at one time these Third World countries were seen as safer bets than the less salubrious end of the Irish property market, less overvalued, with better prospects. As noted in Chapter 4, small changes in a far away place can have an enormous financial impact, thousands of miles away. Today's highly leveraged property on the outskirts of Irish country towns is, in fact, an updated version of the same process that caused the Third World debt crisis in the first place. Let's follow the money.

Live 8

The story of Third World debt is a complex one, but it has more to do with international finance than neo-Colonial policies, as some would have us believe. It begins at a time when, like today, the prices of oil and gold were soaring. In the mid 1970s, when Walter Wriston, longtime chief executive of Citibank (now one of the biggest employers in the IFSC) was asked whether lending to the Third World was risky, he responded, 'countries never go bust'.

Around the same time, the American comedienne and gay icon Bette Midler demanded that she be paid her $600,000 fee for a European tour in South African gold krugerrands because she felt that in a time of uncertainty, gold was the only asset worth holding on to.

As things turned out, the banker was wrong, the joker was right. Midler would have seen the price of her gold rocket to $653 an ounce by January 1980, up from $43 an ounce in October 1973.[1] In contrast, countries did go bust. In 1982 Mexico defaulted on its loans. Brazil and Argentina followed and by 1984, the Third World was stuck in a debt quagmire that some of it remains in to this day.

The common factor between Midler's gold and Wriston's Third World debt was oil. Today, oil is also the indirect lubricant of the unstable Irish property boom.

On 3 October 1973, the decision of OPEC leaders to restrict oil production (in response to the West's and in particular America's, support for Israel during the Yom Kippur War) changed the world. The price of a barrel of oil rose from $2 per barrel to $10.50,[2] inflation in Europe and the US took off and the price of gold rose dramatically as people went back to hoarding the precious metal as a hedge.

The oil shock resulted in one of the largest single peacetime transfers of wealth ever seen as rich, oil-consuming countries transferred billions of dollars overnight to relatively poor oil-producing Arab countries. The biggest problem for the Arabs was deciding what to do with all the cash. They had little choice but to put billions of dollars on deposit with the world's biggest banks. The headache for the banks was what to do with all the money. The mid-1970s' recession in the US and Western Europe meant nobody in the 'rich world' wanted to spend or invest, so the international banking system's biggest and most reliable clients weren't interested. Japan was hurting and the Asian Tigers were still very much developing countries. Traditional investment banking business had dried up.

The only place the cash could possibly be put to work was in the Third World. Within a matter of months, Brazil, Argentina, Honduras and Mexico were awash with Arab dollars. By 1975, African countries such as Ivory Coast, Liberia, Mozambique and Tanzania had easy access to what appeared to be cheap credit. Another huge lender was Russia which, as an oil producer, benefited enormously from OPEC's actions and, as an ideological superpower, lent money to prop up communist countries around the globe.

The assumption that 'countries don't go bust' was based on the understanding that the World Bank and the International Monetary Fund would not let their darlings in the Third World go under. Private investment bankers believed that if the worst came to pass, the IMF, financed by Western taxpayers' money, would bail out the likes of Congo, Uganda and Angola. Bankers turned a blind eye to the sort of ludicrous projects that were often financed by this African credit bonanza. A mountain of debt built up.

Typically, poor countries based their ability to pay back their loans with revenue from the sale of commodities like sugar, rubber, diamonds and wood. Therefore, countries had to increase production of commodities in order to service their debts. The more supply, the lower the price.

So when the world went into its second, oil-inspired recession in 1980-81, there were far too many commodities out there that nobody wanted to buy. The price of rubber, cocoa and sugar collapsed while at the same time—due to huge budget deficits in the US associated with the doctrine of Reaganomics—American interest rates and the dollar skyrocketed. Third World countries couldn't pay their bills and began to default, led by Mexico in 1982. Most of Latin America had defaulted by the mid 1980s and most of Africa followed suit. A large sucking sound was heard across global financial markets as money rushed out of the Third World, back home to the safety of London and New York.

Fast forward to today and substitute the extremities of the Irish and global property market for the 1970s' Third World countries. Think also about places like Bulgaria, Cape Verde, Romania and China. All these places have benefited enormously from the investment-of-last-resort idea. For every basket-case Third World economy with its deluded projects, seven-lane highways and dams which dam nothing, there is an equally ludicrous White Elephant in the Irish property market, a development of houses, where no-one wants to live, sixty miles from Dublin, built to get a tax break and now sold off plan in the past twelve months by mortgage brokers masquerading as auctioneers.

Today, the world is similarly awash with Arab money and the trigger this time was the attack on 9/11. The financial instability in the West associated with all this Arab cash is Osama's revenge.

Where were you when you heard about the Twin Towers? Did you ever think that a lasting impact of the September 11 attacks would be the explosion of hire-purchase trampolines in the suburbs? Strange as it sounds, there is a direct link and here's how it happened.

When you fill up at the pump, do you ever think about where the cash goes? Obviously, much of it ends up in the hands of the oil producer after all the others take their cut, particularly the tax man. Since the attack on the Twin Towers and particularly since the occupation of Afghanistan and Iraq, the price of oil has increased from $23, peaking above $80 a barrel.[3] At the time of writing it is somewhere around $70. Once more, Arab oil producers benefit from a huge windfall as millions of Western drivers hand over cash to the Sheiks. This is Osama's handiwork.

The best way to gauge just how much of your cash has ended up in the Gulf as a result of Osama's oil boom is to look at the foreign reserves of the region. The IMF calculates that the balance of payments of the Gulf went from a $30-billion surplus on the eve of September 11 to $212 billion by 2006. The crucial oil-trade balance has rocketed up from $159 billion to $451 billion.[4] This is your cash and the cash of every Western punter and company that depends on oil for our daily existence.

But because the Gulf States are small places, this new cash has to go somewhere. It can't all be spent in the Gulf. Also, given that the atmosphere in the US is one of overt suspicion and barely concealed hostility towards Arabs, especially Saudis, the recycled cash is not going back to buy Manhattan penthouses for rich Arab playboys. Not surprisingly, many Arabs have taken the hint and moved themselves and their money back home, the result being huge price rises and rampant speculation in property in the Gulf, leading to the extraordinary emergence of Dubai out of the desert. This new metropolis is sucking in workers from Bangladesh and Pakistan, hookers from Russia and money from investors reading the property ads at the back of the *Sunday Independent*.

Because the Gulf States have pretty modest economies (Saudi Arabia is a smaller economy than Denmark), the bulk of the petro-cash, as happened in the 1970s, has gone back out into the world economy, looking for a profitable home. All this recycled cash has had the effect of keeping world interest rates lower than they would otherwise be. As well as having old Germans to thank for our lower interest rates, Ireland has to acknowledge Osama's role in the liquidity bonanza of the past few years. His attack on the Twin Towers, triggering the invasion of Iraq, has ensured that a tsunami of oil money from the Gulf is currently washing over us. We are the new Third World debtors.

Irish banks have been watching these developments and have gone out in the past two years, borrowing Arab money and then lending it out here to finance the last phase of the property boom which is now peaking.

Figures from the Central Bank reveal that our dependence on this foreign money is now verging on the addictive. Over four euros in every ten lent to you and me is now borrowed directly by the Irish banks from foreigners. Who says we're not living beyond our means? The Botox Nation is now hooked on oil money.

Like Third World countries in the 1970s, the extremities of the Irish housing market are receiving cash, not because they are great investments, but because the surplus cash has to find a home somewhere. Ultimately, the wisdom of the investment is based on the underlying strength of the system. To assess this we have to drill a little deeper and examine the impact of all this credit on our society, because it has changed us in a profound way.

Who gets all this lolly once it is converted from Saudi dinars into euro? Does it make the rich richer and if so, are there any social ramifications of the credit free-for-all? A cursory glance at the Irish landscape now indicates that credit has made those at the very top very wealthy. It underpins a new class who have emerged as the key players in the property game. They have used the new oil money and turned it into gold in Ireland. Let's explore the financial alchemy that has created the newest and most conspicuous tribe in Ireland to add to the Jaggers, Jugglers and Bono Boomers—the oligarchs.

The Oligarchs

If you want to see what's going on at the top of the tree in Ireland but want to save yourself the bill at Sandy Lane this Christmas or the cost of a round at the Quinta do Lago golf course on the Algarve, either go for brunch in the Four Seasons Hotel or have a gander at the latest edition of the marvellously plutocratic *Who's Who in Ireland*. This publication sums it up. Be prepared to be asphyxiated as all that social climbing can make you breathless. But there are a lot of people who take this seriously, so let's not be flippant: when you combine *Who's Who* with the *Sunday Independent/Sunday Times* Rich Lists you see where the power nexus in Ireland lies.

The first thing to note is that the ground is shifting quicker than before. For example, there was only one *Who's Who in Ireland* published between 1982 and 1999. In 17 years of economic stagnation the authors obviously took the view that nothing was happening at the very top of Irish society or maybe more pointedly, that none of us cared very much. Since 1999, however, there have been two editions and there will doubtless be many more.

The combined Rich List and *Who's Who* reads like a *Top of the Pops* of the mega rich. The most notable factor in the past six years is how the lists have become dominated by property magnates, reflecting the property boom and the phenomenal amounts earned by the big developers. The *Who's Who* charts the emergence of a property oligarchy, who took cash from Osama's oil boom, invested in large tracts of Irish property, safe in the knowledge that the zoning system would favour them and so made their fortunes. Using borrowed money, the banks have created the oligarchs and now they dominate the Irish business landscape.

The Irish oligarchs are a novel breed. Some are flashy, overdrawn, full of chutzpah with a fondness for helicopters, fast cars and public sporting events. Others are intensely private. Some have adopted all classes of affectation, others are still prepared to do a day's work on the sites (if needs be). Some publicly flaunt their money with beautiful women at 'society' events; others stick close to their family and shun publicity. They are a mixed bunch who can't be pinned down socially: what binds them together is their fabulous new wealth.

The figures are truly startling and for our democracy, many would argue, quite worrying. The Bank of Ireland[5] estimates that the 'top 1% in Ireland own 20% of the wealth, the top 2% own 30% and the top 5% hold 40% of the wealth'. This is not healthy. If you take houses out of that equation and calculate only financial wealth, then the top 1% of the population owns 34% of the financial wealth.[6] This is reminiscent of the Gilded Age of the US at the end of the 19th century, when figures such as J.D. Rockefeller, Andrew Carnegie and J.P Morgan made their fortunes.

This inequality may well be the focus of popular anger when the economy turns down. For the moment people have not realised quite what is happening.

Other figures about the oligarchs are equally arresting both in terms of how rich they are and how recent this wealth is. For example, the top 1% of the population has assets of €92 billion—that's close to half of our national GDP.[7] In the past ten years, Irish wealth has increased by 350%,[8] but at the very top the increases have been much more fantastical. In a country that was almost bankrupt twenty years ago, it is estimated that there are at least half a dozen billionaires in Ireland.

According to Bank of Ireland, there could be as many as 100,000 millionaires in the country or 2.5% of the population.[9] This dwarfs the figure of 0.7% of the population in the allegedly plutocratic US.[10] However, at the very top, it's estimated that there are at least 300 people with net assets of over €30 million, close to 3,000 with assets of between €5 million and €30 million and at least 27,000 worth between €1 and €5 million.[11] This is a Kremlin-style concentration of wealth. The one snag is that practically all these Fabergé eggs are in the one basket: leveraged property. Without property there is hardly any wealth.

The oligarchs are making the running with no deal too big, no price too outlandish and no place too foreign. If you examine the mega-deals of the past two years, the same fingerprints appear again and again. The oligarchs are keeping Ireland's best lawyers and bankers rotund with Guilbaud lunches. They are the kings of the charity ball circuit, princes of the Ice Bar and, most importantly, they are close to the banks. And as a result, money is no object.

The oligarch's great wealth is infectious and it throws down the gauntlet for the rest of an aspiring society to play the game. For every big oligarch, there's a little one trying to emulate him. In addition, the interaction of the oligarchs and banks ensures that there is enough credit around but on profoundly different terms, for people with different balance sheets. One of Dublin's top bankers once described his job to me as 'to make rich people richer'. There is little doubt that he has been highly successful.

But wait a second, you might say, 'Aren't oligarchs those mega-rich Russians like Abramovich who have become rich by getting their hands on the mineral wealth of Russia? Surely our super-wealthy couldn't be compared to those characters?' Well, curb your indignation, because there are many similarities between our resource-based boom and our oligarchs and their resource-based boom and their oligarchs.

Our boom is based on land; theirs is based on what is under the land. Ultimately, both are extractive industries. Our oligarchs live off-shore and pay no tax, their oligarchs live off-shore and pay no tax. Some of our oligarchs are accused of bribery and corruption, some of their oligarchs are accused of bribery and corruption. Our oligarchs come home for sporting events, so do Russia's, and ours prefer the PR opportunities to nominate charities and good causes rather than the grubby drudgery of paying tax. So, too, do the Russian-speaking versions. Our oligarchs see no conflict between residing offshore but having their children educated here at the taxpayers' expense. At least the Russians have the decency to pay full whack for their children to go to Eton. Our oligarchs live in walled residences with security, so do theirs; our oligarchs buy football clubs, their oligarchs buy football clubs; our oligarchs compare Ireland to a communist state, their oligarchs compare Russia to a communist state. The list goes on.

But we aren't concerned here with these issues (and I'm sure you have your own opinions). What concerns us is how the oligarchs, together with the banks, have used foreign money to make huge fortunes on Irish land and how this hyper-speculation has destabilised the market, making a slump more likely. Remember what is going on here, an infinite supply of Osama's money is buying a finite resource, zoned Irish land. This has obvious consequences for everyone, including the trophy buyer.

Nor are the oligarchs immune to the cycle. In many ways, they are more geared to it than most of us. In all downturns some of the really big guys fall, exposed more as bull-necked frauds than clean-hands businessmen. Remember, in the great Third-World debt crisis, the biggest countries with the best prospects—Mexico, Argentina and Brazil—fell hardest.

Before speculating on what might happen in the years ahead, let's try to explain how the system works and how the rich in Ireland get money for nothing, while the struggling class have to pay through the nose for much smaller amounts of the same cash.

The Champagne Pyramid

An easy way to imagine how lucre gets divided up by the banks once it cascades into an economy like ours, is by thinking about a champagne pyramid. Imagine a tacky wedding with a pyramid of champagne glasses and a blushing bride who begins to pour from the top. Eventually, the champagne finds its way into even the most remote glasses (the guests who've only been invited to the afters) as it overflows down the pyramid. As each layer of glasses fills up, the next layer begins to do likewise.

Now think of the Irish financial markets. When the banks go out and borrow all this Arab money, it is the equivalent of popping the cork of a jeroboam of champagne. Credit flows initially into the top, triple-A assets, such as the Jury's site in Ballsbridge or the Burlington.

Then this market overflows, so the excess cash finds its way into other, more risky, assets. As these fill up with cash and yields fall, the speculative cash goes further afield looking for a return. Eventually, as long as the taps remain turned on, even the riskiest projects, regions and ventures get cash. Two-bit developers slapping up townhouses in rural wastelands get some of the action as do sub-prime borrowers (who we will look at in the next chapter) who wouldn't get a look in had it not been for all this recycled liquidity.

As a result of the champagne pyramid, credit seeps everywhere. So we are left with a situation where at the top of the boom, so long as there is money sloshing around in the global financial market, every single development gets built and most mortgages get financed.

However, the price of that money, like the amount of champagne you get, depends on where your glass is in the pyramid. If you are close to the top of the pyramid, like the oligarchs, your cup is constantly overflowing. However, if you are at the bottom, you realise that there is cash everywhere but it's not quite reaching you, so you have to pay more to get your hands on it.

If you want to catch a glimpse of how this system works, to see who is getting all the cash they want and who is struggling, pick up a paper today. Look at the business section. Doubtless you will see details of some mega-deal orchestrated by some new oligarch or other. Then flick to the small ads, the ones that start by asking if you've been rejected by a bank or if you need to roll all your debts into one. You are down with the bottom-feeders now, the people who can't get credit. The contrast between the two borrowers couldn't be more stark.

One Money, Two Prices

It is often said that the richer you are, the less you pay. In contrast, the poor get nothing for free. This may be a cliché but in recent years in Ireland, this has been the case.

Recent deals involving Dublin's grand-dame hotels, Jury's, The Berkeley Court and The Burlington, have seen a Clash of the Titans that makes *The Bonfire of the Vanities* read like *Anam Cara*. These sites are selling for between €70 million and €80 million an acre, making Dublin more expensive than New York when it comes to land. But how is the whole thing financed? How did the men involved stump up all this cash, €400 million here, €600 million there?

Well, the simple answer is that they didn't. In many cases, the oligarch buying these properties did not pay a penny for the pleasure of owning one of the most prized assets in the city. Extraordinary as it may sound, this is true. We are now dealing with the alchemy of corporate finance. The oligarchs are doing nothing illegal. This is all above board and clean. The people involved are of good reputation and have shown great ambition and energy to get to where they are. Now that they are so big, the system marches to their tune.

So let's examine how a deal in the boom is financed. The key to all this is the banks. In many cases, the developers are just proxies for banks or for a stockbroking firm. Consider a typical deal in Dublin two years ago where an oligarch is seen to have bought a property for €100 million. The property, let's say it's a premium office block, has a good tenant and a strong stream of income. The rent is €5 million per year. The yield is therefore 5%. But how does he get his hands on the €100 million he needs? Remember, the market is going up, so he's confident that he can sell on in a few years.

The bank, which knows him well, will finance 85%, taking a charge over the property. So he has €85 million already in the bag. He negotiates with the bank to roll up the charges and interest into one lump sum. Now he has to come up with €15 million of 'his own' cash. He calls his mates in the stockbroking company and says he needs €15 million. By this stage, the deal is almost secure, and as the market is raging ahead, they can re-rate the asset the minute they have all the cash in.

The broker puts together a syndicate of ten investors to raise €20 million. The extra €5 million is to cover the broker's 'costs', don't forget. The broker may also negotiate what is called a 'carry' which is a bit of the equity for himself, which he can realise when the sale is completed. However, the ten investors do not put in €2 million each of their own money. They put down €250,000 each in cash and borrow 90% from a bank, usually the same bank that is financing the oligarch. The syndicate investors get shares in a new company which now owns the asset.

The shareholders' agreement says that the oligarch owns 85% of the building (all borrowed) and the syndicate owns 15% of the building. However, their share is no longer valued at €15 million—which was the original price the oligarch negotiated with the seller and the bank—but €20 million, thus revaluing the building at €133 million already. As a result of this new price all the shares of the new company have to be re-rated upwards.

The oligarch, without putting in any cash of his own, is already looking at a huge capital gain. The interest costs and arrangement and lawyers' fees are paid for by the rental income. So everyone waits. These types of deals are happening across the country, so prices are being bid up not by fundamental value but by the effect of the syndicate's modest outlay which re-values the entire property. The oligarch is getting money for nothing.

Say they sell just two years later in 2007 for €170 million. (This figure is consistent with a commercial property market showing total returns of 20% per annum for the past five years.) From the €170 million, the syndicate investors get 15%, which is €25.5 million, based on their investment of €250,000. That's divided by ten, so they get €2.55 million each. They pay back the bank, which lent each of them €1.75 million. Each one of these investors gets back €750,000 less fees which is close to three times their original outlay, so they are delighted. The bank gets its €85 million back plus, let's say, €1 million in fees. The stockbroker gets his 'carry' of free equity of 1% of the total or €2 million. So what's left for the oligarch is a tidy profit of just over €70 million, of which he did not put up a single euro of his own money.

You don't read about this angle when you open the business pages of the newspapers. When you read that so and so has bought a 'landmark' building for €200 million, the details of how the deal was financed will never be picked over by a journalist. The press release from the PR company arrives into the news desk and the details are sketchy. The editor knows that the big news is the outlandish price, not so much where the cash is coming from. He puts it on the front page in a side bar because of the huge price and the public obsession with property. There are more details in the property section. But the 'details' are rarely more than the PR company's spiel regurgitated, a flashy photo and a gushing comment from an underpaid, overstressed copy editor.

The 'fast news' culture which prevails nowadays prevents proper analysis. No-one asks where the cash has come from or who is financing it. Crucially, in a boom, when the media is part of the cheerleading frenzy, the story only focuses on the buyer, never the seller. However, the seller's story is always more interesting. But the buyer is the sexier character; he has the balls, the bank account and the bravado. He represents the spirit of the times. He is the Indiana Jones of the property market. But for every Indiana Jones, there are hundreds of wannabes, whose stories are not glittered with gold.

The Non-Conformists

In north Kilkenny, a white van pulls up outside a house bought only three years ago. Sean, who hadn't realised that his situation was so desperate until it was too late, waits like an accused man. He's started smoking again.

The plasma screen didn't look like an extravagance. After all he still has a job, a computer qualification and a wife who works part-time. He was just doing what every father would do, responding to his kids' pestering. Luckily, they were out at a Trickey Tricksters this after-noon—another €80. But, hard as it is to believe now, it was the plasma repayment that caused the entire pyramid to collapse. He had been just about able to juggle the car loans, mortgage, crèche fees and the piano lessons, but now he'd added the plasma-screen, along with the kitchen extension loan which he'd always thought was extravagant, particularly as the house was practically new. He was holed below the water.

He pleaded with the finance company not to repossess, but it's hard to strike an emotional note with Sanjay in some call centre in India.

'Please hold the line, your business is important to us.'
'Our operator knows that you are waiting.'

Sanjay in the Punjab doesn't know what it's like to dash home from the under-sevens' training on a Saturday morning, where the car park is a monument to financial excess, to be there in time for a heavy Repo man.

When they arrive, they are the real deal. Two Lithuanians with no necks, bomber jackets and a number-one blade on top, jump out of the van. The older one groans when he hits the ground. The smaller one has a Britannia sovereign ring—Sean was going to point out that it would be the equivalent of wearing a Stalin tie-pin in the Baltics but today his sense of humour has, like his ability to re-pay, deserted him. Equally, the fact that yer man looks like he's straight out of the neck-breaking battalion of the Soviet Special Forces, renders humour not only superfluous, but risky.

Sean never thought it would come to this. He has spent the past five months coming up to Christmas desperately trying to shield his two children from the dissolution of the family under the weight of debt. To make matters worse, his job in a multinational is feeling the pinch from Poland.

He met Jane his wife, who is from Donegal, in Canada where he worked in the mid-1990s. Strolling down Spadina Avenue in Toronto, they decided to come back to Ireland for a few years and when they were set up, they'd head off again. Neither envisaged this quagmire of debt, deceit, lies and flaming rows all the time. Debt gets under your skin. At night when Jane breaks down, Sean holds her up and tells her they'll get out of this, they can hold onto their big plans. They'll get over this little hitch.

When you see them on the street, they are like thousands of other commuters. They are just like you but their lives are falling apart. Neither of them noticed the bills going out of control. For at least a year, the overdrafts seemed manageable. Anyway, when things started to go badly, they ignored everything and paradoxically went shopping, trying to be the first people ever to successfully spend their way out of debt.

The clearing loan was meant to be a clean sweep. It was supposed to bring things under control for the first year, but the interest-rate holiday in year one lulled them into a false sense of security.

Three weeks ago, at the local Italian restaurant, after a few pints with their new mates from the estate, Sean's fourth MasterCard, the one he kept for emergencies, the one with the Halifax 'first customer' €10,000 limit, was refused.

He tried again.

'Enter your pin number please, sir.'

He fumbled for the AIB one. He knew this would not work as it'd been empty for months. He smiled weakly at the waitress who would have been pretty if her eyebrows hadn't been plucked so severely.

'Maybe there's something wrong with the machine,' she conciliated, sensing his panic.

She's seen this behaviour before. Sean tried the Northern Bank plastic, the one he got when he spent four months in east Belfast putting in the new computer system in Stormont. Jane calls it the 'peace dividend'. For some reason, maybe because it was in Sterling or it had a Belfast address, they always ignored its bill. At first, they ignored only the peace dividend, but now they were ignoring every bill. The drawer in the kitchen was overflowing with red reminder notes on everything from car insurance bills to gentle nudges from the school for overdue arts and crafts money.

Sean didn't realise it but having a wallet full of credit cards is a dead giveaway. You are just above the line. Ask any waitress. It sets the alarm bells ringing. In the past, when credit was only given to the rich, if a man's wallet bulged with cards, it was a sign of wealth. He had choice. In the New Ireland, the more cards you have the closer to the bailiff you are. Living all over the country, people like Sean and Jane have bought into a middle-class lifestyle the pace of which is set by overachievers on hyper-incomes. The rest, the financially unfit, try their best to keep up.

Sean looked over at Jane, aware that the waitress was watching him. *'She doesn't think I'm going to do a runner, does she?'*

He tried to catch Jane's attention but she was in mid-flow, laughing uproariously, knocking back the merlot and ordering another one. Her bra strap kept slipping and she was constantly flicking it upwards, her hair was in her eyes. She was loving it.

This is the girl he married, not the woman who screams at him when the kids have gone to bed, not the woman who won't face up to their predicament, not the bitch who threatens to leave him and their debts.

Their neighbour, Steve, who makes good money selling garden furniture, roared over his shoulder and winked at the waitress.

'Don't worry Sean, I've no cash either'.
Yeah, right, with your fucking new Beemer, thought Sean.
'Sure, we're all only a few quid away from bankruptcy, throw another Red onto that and we'll scoot'.
'Thanks, Steve, I'll get you back next time.'

Next morning Sean answered the *Daily Mirror* ad which he'd seen first on afternoon TV. It was for what are euphemistically called 'non-conforming debtors'. They call this stuff 'sub-prime' in the US. The non-conforming mortgage could wrap up his pathetic financial detritus into one clean loan. He was on his way to being a client of Start Mortgages, whose strap line was 'Finance for Living', and their partner, The Kensington Group. It's funny, mused Sean, the people behind these companies thought that by calling themselves Kensington they could pretend that you were doing business with someone credible, someone of stature, someone who knew their Harvey Nichols from their Peter Jones.

The broker was sleazy. They always are—trying to be your friend when all they want is their commission. The enormous knot in his tie made him look like a footballer on trial, as did the vast quantities of gunk in his hair. But Sean had no choice but to do business with Mr Neo-Mullet. They met in Bewley's at Newlands Cross. Tasteful. Mr Neo-Mullet was Sean's last chance. Sensing desperation, Neo-Mullet touched

Sean's shoulder each time he signed and countersigned. This compounded Sean's difficulties. But at least this Faustian pact with Mr Neo-Mullet would allow him to breathe a little and send the kids to summer camp.

Sean is now what he has always been, a non-conformist, owner of a non-conforming loan, paying 8% interest for the pleasure of staying in his overvalued townhouse in Castledermot whose value is now falling. He is trapped. But little does he know that now he's big business.

The sub-prime market is a new development in Ireland. It reveals that many thousands of Jugglers are in financial trouble. In a research note prepared in January, Davy Stockbrokers estimated that this market would grow from €600 million today to €4 billion in the next two to three years, growing by 75% this year and next.

This would mean that of a total market of €41 billion, one in ten mortgages given out in the years ahead will be given to people who the banks won't touch. These are people who couldn't get cash in the greatest credit bonanza Europe has ever witnessed.

Chapter 11

THE DEBT-COLLECTORS' BALL

On Thursday 26 April 2007, in the Hibernia Room at the Four Seasons Hotel in Dublin, guests sat down for starters of New England crab and corn cakes with saffron aioli and Spanish pepper salsa, washed down with Sancerre from la Vieille Fontaine vineyard. Everyone was in good spirits. It was a time for celebration. This had been a good year. The coming downturn in the economy would mean an upswing in their business.

And what better place to host the ball than the brashest, brightest and most expensive hotel in the city? If anything captures the spirit of the Irish Roaring Noughties, it is the Four Seasons. By the time the main course of seared fillet of beef with Swiss chard, bacon, porcini and parsley mushrooms, garnished with fine beans, fondant potato and roasted peppercorn sauce, had arrived, the chat, like the bordeaux Chateau Lestage, was flowing.

Debt collectors are in the slowdown business and the more financial distress, the better. Around the tables were senior management from all the country's main banks along with corporate giants. Almost every type of company which sends out bills was represented. People default on all sorts of things: phone bills, electricity and water charges. But the banks and utility companies don't want to go after debtors themselves.

They outsource this nasty business to the professionals. Quite apart from not wanting to get their hands dirty, when the downturn comes, the banks will need cash. This is where the modern debt collector comes in.

The new debt collector is a far cry from the money-lending heavy with knuckleduster and baseball bat of East-End fiction. Typically, the 21st-century debt collector will be a former banker, in a Cerrutti suit with a finance degree and a good sales patter. Their world is not one of punishment beatings, but credit ratings, Q ratios and probabilities.

The banks realise that some of their loans are in trouble. If a bill or a mortgage instalment goes unpaid for 180 days, it becomes toxic. The banks start to lose money. In the old days, they all had large departments euphemistically called 'recovery departments' to go and collect the debts, renegotiate loans, extend credit periods and the like. However, in the boom when the game was to lend as much as possible, these recovery departments were run down at the expense of credit departments. Now, banks don't have the staff to do this messy work and so they outsource it.

The other dilemma is the *Liveline* factor. Banks are very aware of their public image and do not want to be seen hounding young families out of their houses for missed payments. They are petrified of Joe Duffy who will obviously side with Sean, Jane and the other Jugglers. So they sell on the debt to a debt collector, who can talk to Joe if necessary. The final dilemma for the banks is whether it's better to get some cash now for a bad loan by selling it on, or to chase it themselves. Most have decided on the bird-in-the-hand approach, so in comes the debt-collecting agency, which will look, smell and feel like an investment bank with huge corporate headquarters, marble atrium and website featuring handsome men with clipboards and power women in navy suits and Armani glasses.

Let's say you are a Juggler who is in default on a €300,000 mortgage. Over time you will pay €500,000 for the mortgage and the finance. The banks now have a problem. The loan is worth €500,000 on the bank's books, but it isn't paying. The debt collector comes in and buys the loan for €300,000. The bank bundles together all of its bad loans, sells the entire package at a discount and then the Jugglers' mortgage is not owned by their friendly bank manager any more but by a debt collector. The debt collector will be called something like Magellan

Financial or Columbus Financial Solutions: 15th-century discoverers are favoured by these outfits, as it gives them that sense of adventure, the opening up of possibilities, going on a voyage from debt to redemption. Delinquent debtors are always referred to as 'valued customers'.

Magellan then gets on with the dirty business of knocking on doors, and the Irish bank is off the hook. It is easy to see why the banks are the debt collectors' best friends, and vice versa, in difficult times.

Everyone at the 'Debt-Collectors' Ball' was expecting trade to roar ahead in the years to come as default rates have been soaring in recent months, driven by three factors. First, the sheer amount of new debt in Ireland, second, the higher interest rates and, third, the recklessness of the very banks that are now handing their bad-debt portfolio over to the debt collectors.

There is an endemic weakness in the banking system which we could call 'quarterisation'. This refers to the tyranny of quarterly results in financial markets. Every quarter, the shareholders of publicly quoted companies demand more and more from the banks. This means that the banks issue more arduous targets to their managers who in turn instruct their underlings to generate more business. You never come out of a meeting where the boss says, 'Well done last year, you can sit on your hole this year; I'm cutting back on sales for a while'.

So the bank tends to hurtle at full speed towards the abyss and in the final few years of a boom, any Juggler can get loans. This is food and drink to the debt collector who comes in and cleans up the mess.

By the time the 'assiette of desserts' was served, the talk was of defaults rising from 3% of all loans to 6 or 7% next year. On current Central Bank numbers, such a default rate would amount to a figure of between €2.5 and €2.7 billion, which is a huge amount of money. More champagne, sir?

Sub-Primal Scream

Sean had been in the company for eight years. He had gradually climbed up the greasy pole, notching up titles and favoured car parking places, getting the *Irish Times* delivered and nabbing a manager's special swivel chair. Sean was secretary of the softball league. He was a valued member of staff and had been sent on training courses, which is always a good sign.

But after the merger with another corporate giant, which he'd read about on Yahoo, the new management seemed a bit edgier. Instead of talking about relationships, they started focusing on new terms like 'shareholder value', 'the return on equity' (which individually they could do nothing about) and the 'heightened threat from the competition'.

Today all the talk is of globalisation and being fittest, leanest and meanest. The coming competitive hurricane has gripped the Plaza at the business park. You might have noticed that when a company is listed on the stock market, its language changes. As well as 'going forward', 'at full tilt' and 'leveraging diverse revenue-rich franchises into new growth spaces', which can be 'bolted on' by 'drilling deeper' into the 'core competencies' of 'our pre-existing rationalised business lines', the windswept courtyard in front of the ugly 1970s building becomes a New York-sounding 'Plaza'. It is as if a quoted price/earnings ratio allows you to talk like a corporate drone who watches too much CNBC.

The Other Face of Globalisation

White-collar Ireland is about to experience something new, let's call it the Great Culling. When it happens, many thousands of respectable people will find themselves with what is euphemistically called 'more time on their hands'. The reason is outsourcing.

There are two factors at work here. The first is that basic back-office administration can be done anywhere, and because labour costs are so high in Ireland, it makes no sense for any corporation to do any of its labour-intensive stuff here. Why not relocate to Poland or India where they speak English and where, according to Mercer, the recruitment agency, an accountant will work for €5,000 a year? You'd be lucky to get a trainee Irish accountant to work for that a month.

Secondly, because educated immigrants will do the job cheaper than our own, Irish white-collar jobs are soon to go the way of Irish building site jobs and factory jobs. This has happened in manufacturing and will happen in services. Why shouldn't it? Many jobs look sophisticated but when you examine them more closely they are functional and again, for what the company is getting, expensive. If you examine the data of what happens in countries when the immigrants are well educated, like Israel, it takes seven years for the smart immigrants to reach jobs that are commensurate with their education. Israel is a country which has seen huge immigration in recent years—like Ireland. It has also received plenty of well-educated immigrants. As in Ireland, an immigrant accountant, lawyer, architect or engineer might start out as a waitress but, on average, within seven years, will have a job commensurate with his or her skill.

If many of our most basic banking and insurance functions can be carried out elsewhere, not every banker or insurance salesman is essential. Globalisation is zeroing in on Salaryman. He is an expensive cost with an expensive pension. As the bean-counters weigh up his worth, the sums do the talking—if he can be nudged out now, at 35, all the better.

In the Plaza two years ago, the initial rumours of the hatchet falling became self-fulfilling when word came down from on high that the company wanted fresh blood, less overheads. Although Salaryman was only in his mid-thirties, suddenly, he went from being a young gun to a hunted corporate quarry.

The process of getting shafted is the same all over the world. When you are shafted you are always the last to know, usually because you can't bring yourself to admit that it might be possible. You always think you have friends who will protect you, but you are always wrong. No-one ever stands up for you. But the process is rarely sudden. It usually goes in five distinct phases.

Exclusion

First, you do not get included in run-of-the-mill meetings. Initially, you shrug this off and convince yourself that you are busy anyway and the meeting takes up precious client-driven time. However, you are hurt because you know that the corporation is run on the basic idea that knowledge is power. Access to the font of knowledge is a clear signal of seniority. In the corporation, there are the types who go to everything, not only to be seen, but also to glean a bit of information that may seem trivial, like the fact that the staff car-parking numbers are changing. But that's the thing about the corporate world, things that seem nonsensically inconsequential to the outsider are vital to the insider and will be protected for dear life.

So initially, the one who is to be sacrificed gets the first inclination of trouble ahead by not being invited to the forthcoming management meeting. The management's tactic is to let this seep in, corrosively, like lead poisoning.

Ventilation

The second phase of the shafting process is the ventilation phase. This is where the idea that a man has fallen from grace is spread duplicitously around the firm. This serves three purposes.

The first, and for the management the most desired, outcome is that the poor misfortunate, seeing the writing on the wall, will quit indignantly. This saves the firm any redundancy costs and the typically cowardly hatchet man the difficult and embarrassing experience of killing off the wounded. Secondly, by harassing the prey into quitting—ostensibly to save his own face—the management prevents any legal repercussions. He quit, what can I say? No firm which, on the one hand spouts tripe about corporate social responsibility while culling their own, wants to be portrayed as a bully. The third reason for the ventilation phase is to let would-be allies of the victim know that he/she is the corporate equivalent of a death-row inmate.

Interestingly, e-mail—the most spineless form of corporate communication—has made humiliating you all the easier. All the bullies have to do is send an e-mail out to the whole firm, highlighting the fact that members of the management group on 'internal bench-marking' have been changed and that you are no longer required. These messages are always made more palatable to the rest of the firm, but more hurtful to you, by announcing in tandem that some Young Turk has been promoted. This promotion is always heralded with a gushing endorsement by the man at the very top. This cuts you to the quick, as intended.

Airbrushing

If, after phase two, you, the hunted, are still turning up, phase three is activated. By this time, you are convinced that this miscarriage of justice is simply a case of mistaken identity. You are clinging on, improbably, to the notion of a change of luck or direction. More typically, you are grasping at the idea that a senior 'white knight' will emerge who will attest to your true worth and smite down the pretenders who are pushing you off your perch. You need a corporate alibi. But none arrives.

Phase three is airbrushing. At the height of Stalin's Terror, so many former comrades were being eliminated, accused of spying and treachery, that thousands of old Bolshevik photos had to be doctored to make sure that counter-revolutionaries were not seen to be close to Lenin. After all, if Lenin was possessed with Pope-like infallibility: surely he could not make such basic judgement errors as fraternising with enemies of the people? So old communists such as Bukanin and Kamenev were simply airbrushed out of photos; in one case, only the victim's boots remained visible.

Similarly, in the world of corporate reshuffles and backstabbing, company history is rewritten. Initially, your fall from grace is signalled in a rather child-like 'you're-not-my-best-friend-any-more' type of way. Your immediate boss, who used to be quite friendly, gets all frosty. He begins to display overt favouritism. Your expense accounts are checked thoroughly and queried. Clients that you had for years are inexplicably transferred to other colleagues. Remember, everyone is selling, so a client, he who pays the bills, is the most important man in the corporate equation. If the clients respect you, you are safe from a cull. But if you are cut adrift from your clients, you are like that baby seal who gets caught in an island of ice that breaks away from the rest in an unexpected thaw. The seal will either die of hunger or be killed by a predator. Either way, he's a gonner.

Similarly, a salesman cut off from his client base is toast. No clients, no income, no income, no future.

The Character Assassination

Airbrushing may take many forms, some innocuous, some explicit. During a reshuffle of desks and offices, for example, you are put squarely in an open-plan area rather than the private office with the view that you had for years. Your stock is falling and everyone knows it, you sense it but as you are the subject of office gossip, everyone around you is at pains to be saccharine sweet. People, particularly younger colleagues who are unaccustomed to the corporate airbrushing that precedes a shafting, are embarrassed by your presence. They don't quite understand what is happening but are sufficiently clued in to realise that proximity to you is the kiss of death. You start having lunch on your own: former friends make excuses.

Whatever confidence has not ebbed away by now, begins to seep out of you. It must be making a hissing noise like a slow-puncture because it seems that people can hear you coming. You try to carry on as if nothing's wrong, going through the silly little rituals that have characterised your world for years, checking phone messages, returning e-mails and making sure to pay your €20 for this year's kriskindle. Despite your best efforts, you have become a pariah, surrounded by the guilty long faces of people who wouldn't have missed a four-ball with you last year.

But remember, it is important for the corporation that you are ground down. Firing a confident character is no good. The corporation has to be seen to be doing the right thing. Its spin, particularly if you are popular, has to be that it had no choice. Whispering campaigns are initiated about how incompetent you have become. *Do you think he's drinking a bit too much? I hear there's trouble at home.* By the time you are summoned to your denouement, it is important for the hatchet man that you have been thoroughly humiliated, half the man you used to be, meekly walking towards your P45.

This process of de-humanising can take a long time. It is more often than not driven by age-old jealousies and the horrible realisation on everyone's part that we are all trapped—even the hangmen, who, like the hangmen of old, wear corporate balaclavas, afraid to look the condemned man in the eye. The corporation owns us, and we have traded independence for buttressed serfdom.

Execution
This is the simple, 'Salaryman, can I have a word' moment. Like a teenage affair that comes to an end after the Leaving Cert, the one who breaks it off always says, 'It's not about you, it's me. I've changed.'

For Sean, this comes as a dreadful shock. His self-worth is caught up in being a model corporate citizen. He hosted the department barbeque last year, for God's sake. Yet, when his time comes, he has no friends. No-one speaks up for him. He is radioactive, contagious and a corporate contaminant. At the final secret managerial meeting, held on, holy of holies, the 5th floor—not one of his friends who played golf with him, none of the married men for whom he had covered up and lied when they had had that hooker episode, not one shouted stop. Not one stood up and said, 'This is not how we deal with our friends'. They were all complicit, their honour and decency slowly but surely sucked out of them by the firm. When they passed sentence, they had fear in their eyes. They knew that they had crossed the Rubicon. They realised that they had destroyed something, and they also knew that the shareholders—the invisible arbiters in whose name all this was being carried out—actually don't give a toss.

When his time comes it is swift and, as personal tragedies go, fairly harmless. His boss, Billy Bunker, with whom he played eighteen holes two months back, looks terrified as he stares out the window, past the corporate logo, the American and Irish flags, the managerial car park and the half-finished apartment block. He fumbles with his keys and makes some remark about whether Sean is going to see the Stones in Slane. He then turns and, still clutching his keys, asks Sean whether he had expected bad news.

Sean is told that it is a business decision, nothing personal. He'll be able to start again, he is still young. He can take a few months off; we all have plenty of contacts, practise his swing or whatever the euphemism is. He is told that the news will be managed in such a way as to suggest that he has arrived at the decision himself. For this he is pathetically, obsequiously, thankful. He will announce the move, chin up, head high. A man in control of his own destiny—a Salaryman to be reckoned with.

He thanks the hangman for listening and walks out the door. But people flee from him. They know. Only then does he realise that they knew all along, not only the day but the hour and there he is, devastated, clinging onto the last charade that he has been the engineer, the decision-maker, that he still has some control of his life. But he hasn't and everyone knows it.

He is back in the playground in national school, fighting back the tears, desperately wanting his mum. He wants to be hugged, to be taken away. He wants his mum to tell him that everything is fine, that everything is alright and that he is the centre of her world no matter what names the bullies call him or no matter how many times he is the last against the wall when it comes to picking soccer teams.

He can't go home just yet. Juggler Jane couldn't deal with this. And anyway she'd be at her spin fitness class tonight.

Later that evening, he finds himself back in the safe surroundings of the local. He tells anyone who will listen how he's re-evaluated his life. He is going to live for himself, to do the things he's postponed. (He can't think of what exactly, but surely there are some. Luckily, no-one asks him to get specific.)

Carpe Diem, he announces as he instructs the Polish barman to put the fourth round in a row on his tab.

'No, no lads, my twist. It's my day after all.'

Carpe Diem indeed. His new life begins today.

PART 2

Getting Up

Chapter 12 ~

TRANSIT NATION 2

13 June 2006

It was Brazil's first game and the fans demanded a team performance to match their own, which was by now in full swing. As the tanned girls in yellow and green bandanas started to move their hips, the whole bar swayed effortlessly on cue.

Screams of 'Braaazil, Braaazil' rang out—even before kick-off. Flags waved, arms were raised in the air; the capacity crowd expected style, imagination, flair and of course, victory. The two Brazilian Rastas on the bongos gauged the mood and pumped it up. The Croats, decked in their distinctive checkerboard red and white, weren't fazed. Why should they be? Croatia had always been the backbone of the former Yugoslavian teams, who were known as the Brazilians of Europe. Yeah, so they were out-numbered by the Brazilians, but what do you expect from a country of only four million? The feel in the venue was pure South American, yet we were in an Aussie bar in South King Street, Dublin, where Chinese barmen serve Brazilian caipirinhas and empanadas to illegal immigrants. This is globalisation.

That morning, Charlie Haughey—a politician from a totally different Ireland—passed away. What relevance did he have to this crowd or even to the majority of the Irish Juggler population? His

Ireland was another place—an older society, evidenced by the faithful who queued for hours in a balmy Donnycarney two days later to pay their respects. Although there were a few local twentysomethings with sprayed-on River Island jeans, the vast majority of the mourners were more blue-rinse than bottle-blonde. They had grown up with Charlie. They remembered him in the 1960s when he was the choice of a new generation. This was their day. It was a day to remember, to look back.

They lined up respectfully—people from all over Ireland. They exchanged stories of his good deeds. There was not a dissenter in the house—a bit like the 1986 Árd Fheis. The mood was one of comfortable nostalgia, a sense of being in it together, captured by the sign bearing the name of the Donnycarney Community Centre, under which they queued—*Le Chéile*.

However, when push came to shove, old Ireland's hierarchy reinforced itself uncompromisingly, as it always has done. By the time the tri-coloured coffin was marched up the aisle, the old class divisions had been reasserted. Up front, Fianna Fáil grandees and property magnates embraced each other with Tony Soprano bear hugs and double-handed handshakes, whilst the *hoi polloi*—those who had queued all day and voted religiously for Charlie all their lives—knowing their place, were gathered at the back. All this was overseen by the Archbishop of Dublin and the Fianna Fáil-backed President. It was almost like the old days.

But the country has moved on, this was the old Ireland. The new Ireland was in the Aussie bar, screaming for South American and Balkan football teams, before streaming into the adjacent cheap call shops on Aungier Street to swap match notes with their mates in Brazil for half nothing.

These cheap call joints have opened up on almost every corner of our major cities and towns. Advertising calls to Serbia, Mozambique and Mongolia, these call shops are a much more acute cultural barometer than any editorial. This is where you'll see the faces of the New Ireland. Our rundown bucket call shops offer us an instant snapshot of our immigrant society.

The price list on the wall, which is updated daily, tells us more about who is here and where they are from than any official economic publication. The price list is one of the most responsive leading indicators of social change we can get, instantaneously reflective of population change, because the immigrants will go to the cheapest shop to call home. As the business is volume-based, the more time the customer spends on the phone, the more money the shop makes. The shop can't raise prices or it will lose all the business, so the price is crucial.

Call-shop economics stand the traditional laws of the dismal science on their head. If the price to a certain country falls, it means the demand for calls to that country is rising! The quicker the price falls to a certain country, the more of that country's immigrants have just arrived and are living in the budget hotels and cheap flats in the centre of our cities and towns. Taking a week in spring 2007 as an example, it seems that we saw a huge increase in Ukrainians, as prices to Ukraine in the call shops around the bottom of Gardiner Street plummeted.

When you enter these places, you look foreign. Everyone looks you up and down because you are Irish. They want to know what this local is doing here. Is he a cop?

The place smells of garlic and captures the essence of immigration, where optimism is leavened with insecurity, homesickness with adventure and distinctiveness with a desperate desire to fit in.

The most interesting place in the shop is the notice board which shows what they need and who is buying what from whom. Most of the ads are in Chinese or Polish, not surprisingly. It also captures the most dynamic side of immigration, the entrepreneurial side. Immigrants have proved themselves adept at adapting, finding niches and moving up. This is the story of immigration and immigrants will do the same here.

The question most of us want to know is whether we are all winners in this Transit Nation. Who, if any, loses out to immigrants and how do the winners react? Can history guide us? And first, what does basic economics have to say about immigration?

Winners and Losers

A surge of immigrants is unambiguously positive for a country's growth rate. They work hard, increasing the output, add to the tax take and generate more revenues for everyone. But there are losers. At the moment, the idea that a country like Ireland can absorb limitless thousands of foreigners without some social problems appears to be the working assumption of our political class. If we achieve this, we will be the first state ever to do so. There's no rule against trying, but basic economic theory tells us that there are limits unless we reconstitute the objective of the State and assert explicitly that in the years ahead, Ireland's primary objective is the absorption of foreigners. This is the way great immigrant societies like America, Canada and Australia have organised themselves. Such an explicit national mission creates a consensus around immigration and as most of the people in these countries are descended from immigrants, there is a direct link between the experience of today's immigrants and collective folk-memory of the locals.

In America, immigrants are celebrated and more importantly, they are seen as a sign that the American way is predominating, giving credence to the manifest destiny idea so central to American republicanism.

Given that Ireland struggled for independence in order to create self-rule for the Irish, the State's foundation is ethnocentric. It is our place and it is highly unlikely and vaguely implausible to think that Ireland will suddenly enshrine in our constitution an objective to become a cosmopolitan honeypot.

So until that happens, mass immigration will be tolerated as long as the costs are manageable. Consensus on immigration will ebb and flow with the economy's fortunes. This poses its own dilemma because immigration exacerbates the economic cycle. A large inflow of immigration will extend the economic cycle, making the boom longer, more effervescent and harder to wean ourselves off.

In contrast, the subsequent bust will be made more dislocating because more families will depend on the State for welfare when unemployment goes up. In addition, wages for the average Juggler are likely to fall further because there will be more immigrants competing for fewer jobs.

Economics tells us that immigrants make landowners and employers richer and workers poorer. Therefore, the wisdom of a country's immigration policy depends on who is making the policy. So far, so unremarkable. But let's have a deeper look at this.

Studies of globalisation show that over time, if the immigrants are unskilled they will drive down the wages of local blue-collar workers. This usually has two effects. First, if the government does nothing, the local workers will get angry and call for a ban on immigrants. Second, the government can introduce protection for lower-paid workers by increasing the minimum wage. That's exactly what has happened here.

However, there is a boy-with-his-finger-in-the-dyke feel about this. If the immigrants are willing to do the job more cheaply, ultimately they will. Ask anyone working in construction and they will tell you of subcontractors employing immigrant labour cutting the margins of Irish builders. The 'subbies' as they're known in the trade, are gouging the local lads with foreign labour. This type of competition will intensify, particularly as labour costs are so expensive in Ireland.

Another aspect of immigration is that it pushes up both rents and house prices. There is higher demand, so the prices go up. This makes landlords richer, but it also prices Irish workers out of the housing market. We can see this happening in Ireland at the moment where the government seems happy to allow the housing market to go ballistic, while preventing employers from getting the full benefit of cheaper labour. Think about the signal our policy is once again sending. If you invest in bricks and mortar, we will give you all the advantages that accrue to you from immigration such as rising rents and rising house prices. However, if on the other hand, you want to make stuff here, we will make sure than none of the advantages of immigration in the form of lower costs accrue to you. This seems bizarre until, of course, we look at the main influencers of government policy: landowners, developers and builders.

What do the Irish workers, who are seeing downward pressure on their wages and upward pressure on houses prices, do? They borrow and borrow again to keep up, turning the entire country into a debt pyramid. So, yet again, we see that government policy plays the Generation Game by pitting young Irish Juggler against young foreign workers in the labour market, while enriching the Jaggers and Bono Boomers who own the lion's share of the property. Without immigrants, Irish wages would be significantly higher than they are at the moment and Irish rents and house prices would be considerably lower.

There are also implications for the white-Nike-tracksuit brigade and the people you see wearing their pyjamas in the middle of the day. History suggests that the people who lose out most from immigration are those who are least skilled. They get elbowed out in the scrum. An interesting test case here comes in the declining economic fortunes of America's black population.

50 Cent

In the 1950s and 1960s, black Americans moved into the middle classes at a rate not experienced before or since. When seen though the lens of 1970, it would have been logical to foresee the American black future as a middle-class one, represented by *The Cosby Show*, Toni Morrison and Condoleezza Rice. Yet it did not turn out like that.

At some time in the 1980s, the mass upward social mobility of blacks stopped. Why was this? Why did the self-confident black civil rights movement, characterised by intelligent, peaceful protest and justified moral superiority, spawn the nihilism, boorishness and misogyny of 50 Cent?

One of the many reasons advanced to explain this development has been immigration. There appears to be a direct correlation between increased immigration and the halt in black social advancement. When US immigration is low, black people do well economically; the converse is true when immigration is high.[1]

Black Americans did very well in the 1950s and early 1960s when immigrants accounted for just 8 per cent of the increase in the US labour force—a historically low figure. Contrast this with immigrants accounting for 55% of the growth in the labour force in the first decade of the 20th century and more than 27% in the 1990s.[2]

By the 1980s and 1990s, competition for blue-collar jobs had increased dramatically as new immigrants flooded into the US again. Two things happened: blacks in particular lost out to the new immigrants and blue-collar wages in general, fell. On the other hand, professional incomes rose.

While there is little argument that immigration has been beneficial for the US economy and society as a whole, it is clear that the middle class has done better than the working class. This is happening in Ireland at the moment.

While the middle class gets cheaper laundry, nannies and gardeners, the people who gain most are those at the very top, whose firms are more productive because of the increased pool of labour, and who tend to own land.

Over time, the immigrants move upwards. Our immigrants are extremely well educated in fact, considerably better educated than us. For example, the ESRI calculates that 30% of the Irish workforce left school before the Leaving Cert. The corresponding figure amongst the immigrant population is 3%.[3] There can be little doubt that they will want to move up from Starbucks to megabucks and in so doing, threaten white-collar Ireland at some stage soon.

Countries tend to react to the process of immigration in two ways. Many Irish people will say, 'bring it on', if the immigrants force us to pull up our socks, good for them and ultimately, better for us. There will be others who react to this threat by saying that immigrants are a problem. The political response depends on where the votes are. At the moment, immigration is not featuring as a divisive political issue.

For the moment, it is all new and as the Botox Economy is flattering to deceive, we are still shell-shocked by all the changes. But the changes are real and they will impact on all of us. If the people in the cheap call shops of Shandon Street in Cork, just below the famous Shandon Bells, intimidate you, they shouldn't, because the immigrants are just the 21st-century version of the emigrant Irish. But you don't need to hang around these places to see the future. Just drive around the country, keep your eyes open and you can see a new society blossoming.

Inchicore, Saturday Morning 8.30 a.m.

A small basket of ornamentally painted eggs sits underneath the proud silverware of the Sheehan Perpetual Trophy, which is slightly obscured by the picture of the smiling girls of the 1991 Irish camogie team. Behind that again is a Dubs Millennium Tribute to the left of a crucifix and a poster of the Proclamation of the Republic. The brightly coloured eggs are an Easter present for the teacher. The wickerwork basket with its gingham wrap looks out of place in the entrance hall of Inchicore VEC on Emmet Road in Dublin 8. That's because it's from Lithuania.

In typical FAI fashion, just down from Richmond Park, the entrance to the ground announces that St Pat's are still proudly sponsored by the bankrupt Smart Telecom. Around the old stadium, the shops reveal the changing Ireland. You've got to wonder what Michael Hartnett, the poet who wrote 'Inchicore Haiku' here on Davitt Road, would think of the place now: African shops do a roaring trade in hair-straightening products, with names such as 'Comb Through', all of which are advertised by women who look like Oprah.

Up the road, within a few hundred yards of Kilmainham gaol, where the patriots were murdered for Irish freedom, the future of the New Ireland is being forged by a people who also got their freedom in the years after World War I. This nation similarly suffered from occupation by a large imperial power that was intent on erasing its culture and language. While we reacted to independence with isolation, cutting ourselves off from the world, other small countries did not have this choice.

Although economists constantly lament Ireland's lack of openness for most of the 20th century, the value of openness really depends on your neighbours. Sealing herself off was a luxury not afforded to Lithuania. This tiny country was stuck in a bad neighbourhood, wedged in the middle of two recent and three historic powers, Russia, Germany and what had previously been Poland. Lithuania's history is the history of the 20th century. Invaded twice and then occupied for close to 50 years by Russia, the Lithuanians have had a rough ride. Now liberated, they find themselves re-incarcerated in the perverted economic logic of central Europe.

Eventually, Lithuania will recover, but possibly not in time for most of Ireland's Lithuanian immigrants. They realise this and are putting down roots here. Today, as a percentage of the local population, Ireland hosts the biggest Lithuanian population in the world. 1% of all Irish people are Lithuanian.[4] This figure is likely to grow in the years ahead.

If you want to see why the insidious, creeping use of the term the 'New Irish', is entirely inaccurate and nonsensical, come to the Lithuanian School in Inchicore on a Saturday. Here you will see a people intent on preserving their culture and language. The Russians couldn't wipe it out, and certainly living in Ireland won't. These people are as much New Irish as I was New English when I lived in London.

It will take a lot to deflect these people. While we complain on *Liveline* about under-funding in education, every Saturday morning over 150 Lithuanian children, who have already done five days in school, come here to learn Lithuanian language, culture and maths. They obviously don't rate our maths. Their parents pay for this. There is no State hand-out, nor are they looking for one. This is a volunteer effort by Lithuanian parents keen to make sure that their children get the best education possible, while at the same time being able to write in their own language when they go home to Granny for the summer. These parents work in Spar, Tesco and on building sites. The mums are checkout girls and the Dads are security guards, yet they find the cash to send their children here because they are displaying what all immigrants have—unbridled ambition.

They are going to make it here. They're not going back with their tails between their legs. They have come to the New World and they are only going home with cash. Actually, why go home at all when there are six flights a day connecting Dublin with the Baltics? And it's not just Dublin: one of the interesting revelations from the census is that the immigrants have not been ghettoised as many would have expected: they are spread out all over the country. For example, Carrickmacross, Co. Monaghan is home to the largest concentration of Lithuanians in the country.

To get an idea of who is sending money home, hang out in the GPO for a few hours. In the Mecca of Irish nationalism, just beside the statue of Cú Chulainn erected in 1935 to commemorate the Rising and the final attainment of an Irish Republic for Irish people, a much more diffuse Ireland is emerging. The GPO is the epicentre of a financial web which extends from the Spars and Centras of Ireland to the kitchen tables of five continents via Western Union money-transfer slips.

Beyond the one-crutch junkie dealers at the welfare counters, past their clients pretending to be on their mobiles while scoping the place and the old women with tight curls playing the Lotto, you'll see the queues for Western Union. A dealer fishes for a wrap of heroin from the hollow of his crutch while his lackey starts a row with an African to confuse security. Deal done. Meanwhile, the Filipina nurses queue obediently.

Let's follow the money. We can create a new indicator: let's call it the An Post Index of Immigration. The Western Union Money Transfer, which allows immigrants to send money home, gives us a snapshot of what's going where. In descending order, 15.6% of all cash leaving Ireland is going to Poland, 7.6% to Latvia, 6.5% to the Philippines, 6% to the UK (obviously, people with immigrant families in Britain), 5.7% to Romania (even though they are, to all intents and purposes, not allowed to work here), 4.9% to Lithuania and 3.6% to Brazil.[5]

The top five post offices, business-wise, are the GPO, Blanchards-town, Galway, Tallaght and Cork; but if we examine the figures a little more closely we see that Clonee and Naas are the top origins for parcels to Brazil, while there are a lot of illegal Moldovans living in Leixlip. The top destination of cash from Ennis is the Czech Republic and swanky Ranelagh is the favourite post office in the country for Nigerians sending money home.

Castletownbere, Autumn 2006

At the other end of the country, Rosita scans a Lithuanian newspaper for second-hand car ads. Coming over the pass from Allihies, the last thing you expect to see down at the harbour in the shadow of the huge deep-sea trawlers with their rusting cranes and pulleys, is a Lithuanian shop. But here, amidst the smell of petrol and fish-heads, the little shop is open for business. It looks like a Londis from the 1980s, you know, the sort of place that does a roaring trade in *Ireland's Own*. You half expect a member of the Legion of Mary in a housecoat to look you up and down before serving you. This is Knorr Cup-a-Soup central, everything is freeze-packed and dried, from the flans to the Angel Delight.

But just beside the monument to the Bearhaven IRA Battalion from the War of Independence, Rosita is unloading smoked sausage, salamis, smoked mackerel, cabbage stuffed with meat and dumplings—staples of Lithuania. Rosita's children go to the local national school. In the local bar they claim that there are 800 Irish people in Castletownbere and 600 Lithuanians, which might be an exaggeration, although the census of 2006 reveals that in Durrus, just up the road in the Beara Peninsula, one in three people is foreign.

Rosita's dreaming of going home this Christmas on Ryanair from Kerry to Frankfurt and then on to Vilnius. Ryanair has opened up this part of the world and, ironically for a company that is constantly at loggerheads with the EU Commission, it has done more to promote European integration in Ireland than any EU directive or referendum.

Berger's World

The most important man in the country now is someone you've never heard of. The man who will have more impact on the flows of immigrants in and out, on the general wage rate, the rental market and ultimately where the economy will go, is not the Taoiseach, the Minister for Justice or Finance: he's an unassuming bloke called Bernard Berger.

Bernard Berger is himself an immigrant, having arrived in Ireland from Manchester in 1989. What makes him special is that he is Ryanair's route planner. He has an encyclopaedic knowledge of central European demography, political history and more importantly, the location of every former Warsaw-Pact military airport. There are hundreds of these in the remotest reaches of Europe, all of which have two things in common: the airport needs money and the people want to leave. Bingo O'Leary! And for that matter, bingo for every Irish company that depends on these industrious people for labour. When Bernard Berger ticks a remote region in central Europe, you can be sure of two things: immigrants from that place will arrive in Ireland the next day, and the price of property there will rise, as Paddies head out looking for bargains.

As far as he's concerned, the company will expand lines to anywhere. And the man who will determine this will not be Bertie, but Bernard. There's no limit to the amount of immigrants they can carry. Every one Pole who comes here generates ten trips over the next two years with weddings, birthdays, holidays and visits from friends and family. And the immigrants are now emigrating by text. They get a text in Poland saying there's a job in Dundalk, they're on the Ryanair website and within days they're sleeping on a floor in a new estate in The Saltings just outside Dundalk. Cheap travel and cheap communication means cheap labour, more immigrants and more competition in the jobs market.

Getting Ahead, April 2007

Back in Inchicore it's 10 a.m. and, as their Irish classmates are glued to the *Den*, these little model citizens are learning extra maths. With their tell-tale crew cuts and big soulful eyes, the little boys belt out their tables in Lithuanian. Their parents know that there is competition out there and to stay ahead of the pack, their children need to be smarter, quicker, more nimble and flexible. They didn't come all the way here to produce underachievers. They came to produce winners. They have put their own lives on hold for their childrens'. They are thinking about the next generation, while we're thinking about lunch.

Danguala, herself a mother, runs this school. She also works five days a week, her husband works in construction and they live in Stoneybatter. Stoneybatter has always been a crossroads. Years ago, it was the main thoroughfare to Dublin from the districts lying to the west and north-west of the city. It was known as Bóthar-na-gCloch (Bohernaglogh), the road of the stones. The name was later changed to the English equivalent, Stoneybatter, or stony road. It was also on the pilgrim's path between Tara and Glendalough. Stoneybatter was home to our first foreigners, the Vikings. Oxmantown Road refers to the Norsemen who were known as Ostmen (men from the East) who settled here. This also explains the Viking-sounding street names of Olaf Road, Sitric Road and Sigurd Road. Today, as hundreds of immigrants move into the area, we are seeing it change again.

At the little cluster of shops on Aughrim Street you can see the shifting social and demographic sands of Stoneybatter. Sandwiched between Aughrim Street Credit Union, which serves the traditional working class Dubs of Stoneybatter, and the Polish grocery Samo Dobro, which looks after the interests of the immigrants, there's a chi-chi little café called Java Bay which attends to the up-market Fairtrade-and-bagel brigade who say inaccurate things like 'Stoneybatter, it's Dublin's best kept secret'. (It's only a secret because they come from Foxrock.)

The ads in Java Bay reveal the concerns of the locals, from the secretive such as Thai massages, yoga of course, to something called *www.jo-jingles.com* which 'provides fun music, singing and movement classes for babies and young children. With the help of our Jo Jingles doll, trained and experienced presenters run a popular music and movement experience.' Well, you can never start too early. Imagine what the grannies at the credit union would make of that? For the new mums desperately trying to get back into shape after their first baby, across the road we have the Head-to-Toe beauty studio with 'medi-spa'. Finally, with a reminder of what it used to be like before the service economy took over, there's a motor parts shop blaring out, appropriately, AC/DC.

Shifting Sands

Stoneybatter is the changing face of Ireland. The young professionals drinking Hoegaarden at the Dice Bar, priced out of the areas from which they came, never even knew where Stoneybatter was before moving there. Now, they are pricing the locals out of the market and the investment properties their parents have snapped up are being rented out to immigrants like Rosita and Danguala.

Over the coming years the twin forces of immigration and hyper-competition are going to set the pace of change in the economy. This will have enormous implications for our society and will determine the face of the Stoneybatters, Macrooms, Galways and Letterkennys of this world. No-one has any real clue about how things are going to play out. But the falling housing market should focus our attention on the fact that the way we have done things up to now is not good enough. There's a lot to play for.

There are also a lot of questions to be asked: what is going to happen with our immigrants in the longer term, will they stay or will they go? Will we become a melting pot or a patchwork quilt of different colours and cultures, living side by side in ghettos, rarely meeting but rarely fighting either? Who is going to be displaced by the immigrants and will the middle classes be affected?

We will also need to consider the burgeoning entrepreneurial flair we are seeing in the immigrant population, and how that might be harnessed. Perhaps we will see ethnic Chinese multi-millionaires, as we are now seeing all over south-east Asia? Or a Polish political bloc? Will the son of a foreigner, like De Valera, rise to lead us? And most importantly, how will we react if the coming downturn is prolonged?

The beauty of globalisation is that it has all happened already. What better place to look at the future impact of immigrants on Ireland than in our own history? Using history to help us navigate the future, we are first going to go back to America just after the Famine. The experience of the Irish then, their impact on the society and their imprint on American politics, will help us understand what could happen here.

Furthermore, we are not the first country to turn ourselves into an exporting powerhouse in the space of a few decades. Other countries have done this before us. In fact, the much vaunted Irish model of economic development was originally conceived in Latin America in the former miracle economy of Uruguay. The parallels between Ireland now and Uruguay in the early 20th century are uncanny. So we are going to travel down to the River Plate to see what we can learn from Uruguay and its neighbour Argentina. In doing this we are following in the footsteps of the 500,000 Argentinians and Uruguayans of Irish descent, whose ancestors left here over a hundred years ago, following the global money trail.

In the great Irish Generation Game, the lost generations can tell us something about the years ahead, just as the experience of another lost generation inspired Pádraig Pearse in the Proclamation of the Republic, almost a hundred years ago. Let's look to our history to get a possible vision of our future.

Chapter 13

BLACK IRISH

Pedro was a mixed-race Rasta from Colombia, and he was my partner washing dishes in a lower-East-Side restaurant on my first (fairly unsuccessful) illegal tour of duty in New York City in the 1980s.

You learn a lot washing dishes. When you're at the bottom of the pile, you experience the petty nastiness of managerial power at its best. Luckily, Pedro kept the kitchen stoned for most of the time, so managerial strops about dish-stacking techniques became part of the background comedy, in the 120-degree heat of a New York restaurant kitchen in August 1986.

To my right was a barrel-chested Mexican, half Hugo Chavez, half Brian O'Driscoll. He was a man with enormous upper-body strength and a low centre of gravity. He never spoke Spanish, let alone English, but played football at breaks between shifts like Maradona, so we just called him Diego. To his right were the chefs, Fitz, Fitz and Murph, who were all black.

They claimed that, along with me, we were the four 'Irish' in the kitchen. Fitzgibbon, Fitzgerald and Murphy were proud to be 'black Irish'. (The fact that I was the only white man in the kitchen—and English-speaking to boot—attests to my atrocious waiting skills.)

The story of these 'Black Irish' is a fascinating and disputed one. It sheds light on our past, but it also gives us some indication of what might happen to immigrants and the native Irish in the years ahead. As the economy slows and the competition for jobs and income between the Irish and our immigrants heats up, a few lessons from our past might well be heeded.

Today in the US, there are as many as five million blacks with Irish surnames. From the poet Toni Morrison, to the Harvard academic Randall Kennedy and of course Eddie Murphy and Shaquille O'Neal. We all know about Mohammed Ali's white Irish grandmother and the countless other black Fitzes, Sweeneys and Kellys.

However, the relationship between the Irish and the blacks has been extremely fraught. Conventional white Irish-American lore suggests that these black men with Irish surnames are descended from freed slaves who took their white masters' names. If the masters were Irish, then they ended up with Irish names. This could be largely true because many slaves had no surname and, despite the predominance of WASPs running plantations, thousands of Irish slave-owners worked in the southern states of America in the pre-Famine years.

———

However, there is another story. In recent years, other interpretations, based on urban American population records from the 1850s have emerged. These indicate (not surprisingly) something much more complex.

Take yourself back to East-Coast America in the 1850s. If there is any place that resembles the Ireland of today this is it. America, with a population of 26 million, absorbed over two million immigrants, or just about 10% of the population, in the fifteen years from 1845 to 1860. Ireland has absorbed 400,000 or just about 10% of its population in half that time. If anything, the immigrant shock to Ireland now is even greater than that to the US in the 1850s.

In 1850, people were flooding into the US at a rate never seen before. Like America then, we are taking our immigrants in willingly now, and, importantly, not because of some imperial hangover after the fall of Empire. In this way we differ profoundly from the French and British: we have no feeling of obligation. Our immigration is economic.

Like the US in the 1850s, the vast majority of our immigrants are coming to make money. They, like most people, want better lives for themselves and for their children. There are very few refugees in both cases. Just as in New York, the majority are here to work and there are no barriers to them getting jobs.

So, in terms of a historical blueprint, New York in the 1850s is an interesting place to start assessing what happens to migrants, to the people they displace, how the local middle class responds and how the political status quo is altered for good.

Sleeping with the Enemy

The census of 1850 reveals what was described at the time as an 'alarming rise' in the number of 'mulattoes' in the Northern Free States. In Philadelphia alone there were 15,000 mixed-race children born in 1850. This was about one in thirty of the children born. Given that the poor Irish and the poor blacks lived together, it's hardly surprising that Irish women slept with black men.

According to Noel Ignatiev, in his book, *How the Irish Became White*, developments in the poor areas of Philadelphia mirrored those of all other major cities. It's the same now. Immigrants head for the poorer areas of town and, while they might work for the middle classes, if they mix with anyone, it's their neighbours. Back then in the US, the Irish and the blacks lived cheek-by-jowl.

Many freed blacks in the US were well-skilled tradesmen like coopers, carpenters and blacksmiths, because prior to their freedom, enlightened masters had invested in their education and trade. They were therefore able to survive and thrive.

So by the 1840s, the freed slaves of the Northern Union states would have constituted a solid part of the artisan class. Granted, they were not in many cases admitted into guilds but they did have work and networks. Then the destitute Irish arrived. We were disgorged from Famine ships at a rate of a thousand a day, with no skills, many without the language and with nothing to sell. As the native Protestant Americans detested the Irish for their Catholicism as much as their Irishness, initially the black freed slave was a better financial bet than the indigent Irish. So, many Irish women chose to marry the man with better prospects, who could provide for the kids and keep a roof over their heads. There is also evidence that many Irish women might have 'taken up with black men.' Imagine the consternation in this case in

Philadelphia as reported disapprovingly by a missionary in 1853 and cited by Ignatiev:

> *'Many a husband too is weeping with his offspring while the mother of his little ones is drunk on the streets, or locked up a vagrant in … prison or living with some dirty negro.'*

The newspapers of the time capture the anarchy of the tenements where any strictures that may have held in the old country were thrown out of the window and where poverty, death and filth brought all sorts together. It's essential to understand just how poor our ancestors were at the time. Shockingly, the average life expectancy of an Irish immigrant following his/her arrival in the US just after the Famine was six years. They were broken by hard work, sickness and hunger. To put our poverty and helplessness into a modern context, Professor Cormac Ó Gráda of UCD estimates, looking at financial records of the time, that the average Irish peasant farmer then was poorer than the average Somali is today.

In 1853, the *Evening Bulletin,* reporting on the conditions of the Irish, described a doss house owned by an Irishman known as Jemmy Quinn:

> *'The walls were discoloured by smoke and filth … everything was as wretchedly uncomfortable as it is possible to conceive. Yet in every one of these squalid apartments … men and women—blacks and whites by dozens—were huddled together promiscuously … keeping themselves from freezing by covering their bodies with such filthy rags as chance threw their way.'*

In New York and Boston the majority of mixed-race children were born to Irish women. To the white Protestant native population, this tied in with their view that the Irish were not real whites. We were regularly referred to as, 'niggers turned inside out' and blacks were referred to as 'smoked Irish'. Neither group took these terms as compliments. Flattery was not intended.

So how did it come about that the Irish, initially thrown together with the blacks, the Irish who slept with the blacks, the Irish whose great leader at home, the Liberator Daniel O'Connell, had been implacably opposed to slavery, became the most vehement supporters of the continuation of slavery? Why did poor Irish immigrants, not poor German immigrants, move against the blacks? How come after the 1850s the reported population of Irish mullattoes decreased when economics would have forecast a significant increase?

The first reason was competition. Wherever there is competition, there is resentment. We were both scraping around at the bottom of the barrel in 1850s' America. This was, in fact, the last time the 'Blacks of Europe' line from Roddy Doyle's *The Commitments* actually held true, and the Irish were not going to let that description stick. We were intent on becoming white, even if it meant suffering in the short-term.

This dynamic of two victim races scrapping was best summed up a few years ago when I interviewed the Palestinian writer Edward Said in New York. When asked to describe the position of the Palestinians, he explained that they were in the most miserable position of all because they were, 'the victims of victims'. As the Irish gradually became white in America, the blacks became our victims. They were the victims of victims. Every time we had a pang of conscience about what we had done to them, we could always justify it by citing the horrors that had been visited on us.

As more and more unskilled Irish flooded into the already crowded cities of the north-eastern US, they elbowed out the blacks at the bottom of the pile. But how did the WASP establishment react to this race at the bottom? It appears that—in the same way as Irish people today sometimes refer to the immigrants as doing 'jobs the Irish won't do'—the native WASP Americans were, at first, happy to see this competition for jobs they believed were below them.

The Irish made these menial jobs their own to an extraordinary extent. In 1855, of the 19,783 immigrant labourers in the city, an enormous 17,426 were Irish. And of the 29,386 immigrant domestic servants, 23,386 were Irish.[1] These were the jobs that the blacks had before the Irish arrived. Today, if you examine the proportion of immigrants working in child minding and cleaning jobs in Ireland, the same thing is happening. For example, one of the women who runs the Lithuanian school in Inchicore runs a cleaning company that only employs immigrants. Those women might be cleaners now, but they plan that their children will go to university. So the first generation sacrifices and the second generation thrives. The Lithuanian cleaners are undercutting and elbowing out Irish women who used to do these jobs.

Today, the Irish middle classes, like the skilled white Americans in the 1850s, welcome competition for these jobs because it leaves them better off. The white WASPS of New York were happy to see the blacks and the Irish fight over scraps. Today, immigrants are keeping wages down and not yet competing with the middle classes for either jobs or housing. Not surprisingly, because it is a win-win situation for the Irish middle class, it has been largely supportive of the immigrants.

This attitude is most prevalent in the Irish media today—an attitude held by people whose living standards will never be threatened by a Lithuanian or Pole. This blanket 'immigration is good for you' mantra is reinforced by a massive campaign of race awareness and 'anti-racism' slogans paid for by the public service which ironically employs the fewest foreigners of any sector of the Irish economy. But underneath the dinner-party hype, there is a significant, unreported, feeling of anxiety amongst Irish workers, who feel threatened. When a local worker complains about the immigrants, as is increasingly the case, they are dismissed easily by the media as racist.

For modern Ireland, the first significant lesson from the relations between the Irish and the blacks, is how we displaced them in the US. This is a tutorial that we could well heed. The person who claims that mass immigration will not lead to significant displacement of the average worker when the economy turns down, is naive.

The reports from the US in the 1850s are striking in that they are so similar to reports we are hearing here from building sites all over the country, where foreigners make up 29% of the workforce.[2] The following is an extract from a letter in the *Philadelphia Daily Sun* newspaper in 1849 and cited by Ignatiev:

'There is direct competition between the blacks and the Irish as we all know. The wharfs and new building attest to this fact; when a few years ago we saw none but blacks, we now see nothing but Irish.'

Substitute Poles for Irish and Irish for blacks, and it is surprisingly familiar. Furthermore, when we read how the blacks saw it at the time, it is strikingly similar to conversations that you hear the length and breadth of the country from Irish people involved in the trades. In 1860, a black writer explained the changes he had seen in New York since the Irish Famine:[3]

'Fifteen or twenty years ago a Catholic priest said to the poor Irish, you are all poor and chiefly labourers; the blacks are poor labourers. If you wish to succeed you must do everything that they do, no matter how degrading and do it for less than they are able to do.'

According to the writer,

'the Irish adopted the plan, lived on less than the Americans could do, worked for less and now the result is that nearly all the menial employments are monopolised by the Irish who now get as good prices as anyone.'

This is an example of the Irish Ferries scenario writ large. Here you have immigrants who are willing to work for less than we are. You have an employer looking to cut costs and you are looking to shareholders who want higher returns on their capital. The immigrants are simply trying to get a toe-hold and they will work for whatever they feel they are worth. Their benchmark is a combination of their wages at home and how much they need to eke out an existence here, scrimping every day to send money home. We should expect the lessons of history to be repeated in industrial relations here and, as the Irish did in America in the 1850s, immigrants to undercut and displace Irish workers in every sector in a downturn.

In the 1850s the Irish were fleeing starvation, so anything in America was better than back home, even a reduced American wage was better than what they could get in Mayo. Many socially concerned American commentators at the time criticised the cheap furniture in the houses in the Five Points district of New York. Yet having furniture at all, would have been a huge step upward for many Irish immigrants.

In his book *Workers in the Metropolis*, Richard Stott tells us that Gweedore in Donegal, with a population of 9,000 in 1837, had 93 chairs, 243 stools and 10 beds. Over half of the people were barefoot and there were three watches in the whole area! So the wage expectations of the

Irish immigrant in the US had almost no downward resistance point. It's not surprising that increased immigration caused American wages to cascade downwards.

Up in Dublin Airport, Laza, who was a tree surgeon in Slovakia, manages baggage handling at night. He is earning six times what he could make in Bratislava and he's saving to get married. Even if his wage were to fall by 20%, he'd still be making four-and-a-half times more than the corresponding wage at home. That is the calculation that counts in his head, just as it did for the Irish in the 1850s.

Another issue is cost. Laza shares a house in Santry with six others. His costs are considerably lower than the equivalent Irish worker because his lifestyle expectations are lower. If you are in your 30s or early 40s, you may remember going to the US in the late 1980s and early 1990s to work. Many of us lived four to a room in Boston or New York, in bad areas where rents were cheap. I distinctly remember a group of about eight of us appeared to be the only whites in Roxbury, Boston, which, at the time, in 1986, was in the middle of a crack epidemic. But it was affordable and seemed more or less fine. The white American students we worked with in bars and restaurants lived in palatial splendour with their girlfriends or boyfriends in proper flats. They paid huge rents and lived in good areas, while we lived as all immigrants do—cheaply.

The immigrants in Ireland today, like Laza, are doing the same as we did in the US 20 years ago and as our ancestors did 150 years earlier. This is the pattern of immigration. Immigrants undercut the locals. That's the game. We can see it here. There is little doubt that were it not for the immigrants here, Irish wage inflation would be considerably higher. For example, in 2007 wage inflation in construction, where one in three workers is an immigrant, is running at 1%, while it is running at four times that in the economy in general. In the nine quarters up to March 2007, the immigrant population in the workforce has gone up from 6% of the total to 13%.[4] This is obviously having a downward impact on the price of labour.

In New York in 1855, 52% of the city's 622,925 citizens were foreign-born. Of these foreigners 28% were Irish and 16% were German. In all, from 1847 to 1860, 1.1 million Irish immigrants docked at the Port of New York, as opposed to 900,000 Germans. The Irish constituted 3.9% of the 26 million population,[5] about the same as our Polish population today. Within a few years of stuffing the blacks in the menial jobs, the Irish started to threaten the skilled 'nativist trades', sewn up by white Protestant Americans, and this is when the political problems started.

Once Irish immigrants started threatening the wages, the housing and general hegemony of the nativists, the political pendulum swung against the Irish and when it swung, it swung violently. Crucially, it also swung with the economic cycle, when a recession in the early 1850s altered the political landscape.

Model Citizens

In the early 1850s, a newspaper appeared calling itself the *Champion of American Labour*. It emerged in response to the undercutting of native tradesmen's wages in the years of the downturn. According to Robert Ernst in the excellent *Immigrant Life in New York City 1825-1863*, in the five years to 1855, the wages of cabinetmakers fell from $15 a week to $5 a week and the price of coats from $5.50 to $2.33. In the building trades, Irish carpenters, painters and masons had lowered the cost of labour. The *Young America* magazine at the time suggested that employers *'were going aboard ships before the emigrants have landed and offering skilled ones on board 30 dollars a year and their board'.* This is precisely what Irish recruitment companies are doing in Eastern Europe at the moment by going to Slovakia and filling jobs there, rather than letting the immigrants find out about working conditions for themselves.

It wasn't only the wage structure that was threatened by the immigrants. Trades in the US, as in Dublin at the time, had been organised by a closed-shop system called the guilds. In the 1850s, the Irish immigrants destroyed that guild system by doing whatever work was going. So carpenters painted houses, plasterers made tables and joiners dug foundations. The industrial demarcation system was left in tatters as poor immigrants worked in jobs way beneath their qualifications.

Today, the same process is occurring. The trade unions are worried about the immigrants undercutting the locals and they rightly fear that the last great battle of the Left will be with poor foreign workers rather than rich domestic bosses. It is notable that the trade unions are strongest in the public service where only 1.5% of the employees are foreign.[6]

Back in New York, when it became apparent that the skilled trades were under threat, the middle classes started to slur the immigrants. For example, the *Champion* stated that America was accepting in, '*swarms of needy adventurers, cut-throats and the paupers of European jails*'.

When you look at the figures for Irish delinquency in 1850s' New York it becomes apparent that the worries of the newspapers at the time weren't too far off the mark. In 1859 for example, 11,395 Irish people were convicted of a crime in New York; the next most troublesome ethnic group were the Germans with 1,403 criminals. So the Irish, with a slightly higher immigrant population, were ten times more likely than the Germans to be convicted of a crime. In 1859, more than one in twenty Irish immigrants had criminal convictions. In 1858, of the 3,890 admissions to the poor house, 2,544 were Irish.[7]

Admissions to Bellevue Hospital in Manhattan reveal a similar picture: 5,703 Irish rocked up to casualty as opposed to 537 Germans, and of the 4,177 foreigners admitted to lunatic asylums from 1849 to 1858, 2,039 were Irish.[8] The picture is one of extreme poverty, destitution and violence.

We were not model citizens and these factors, taken together with the fact that by the mid-1850s many ambitious Irish were starting to threaten the living standards of white Americans, fuelled anti-Irish feeling and spawned a most powerful anti-Irish political party. By 1853, the pendulum was swinging against the Irish.

The Recession and the Know-Nothings

A political crisis might have been avoided had it not been for the economic slump of the 1850s. As long as the economy was chugging along nicely, the impact of immigration was positive. Indeed, the main gelling agent of the American project was immigration, opportunity and the incentive of a better life which was the American dream. However, the Irish impact on wages was so deflationary that it caused people to rein in spending. The resulting recession of the early 1850s caused a dramatic change in popular sentiment towards immigrants and in particular, towards the ubiquitous Irish.

A combination of weak government which had exhausted the nation's patience, together with renewed nationalism in the face of significant immigration, fear about the native population's standard of living and a devastating recession after ten boom years, propelled a new anti-immigrant, nationalist party onto the scene in 1854.

This background noise sounds disturbingly similar to the one playing out in Ireland at the moment where we have a weak government, a huge overhang of property and hundreds of thousands of immigrants jockeying for position with the locals.

In pre-Civil-War America, the new party's targets were Catholics who were seen as foreign and un-American. The Irish, who were both Catholic and an economic threat, were the target. Other episodes from history indicate that such a political reaction is not uncommon. When the political pendulum swings in response to a dramatic change to economic circumstances, it moves violently to the extreme before settling down in the middle again.

The Know-Nothings, as Tyler Anbinder says in his book, *Nativism and Slavery*, burst onto the political scene with a swiftness unprecedented in American history. They quickly became the biggest electoral force in the US. Before they were ultimately subsumed into what is now the Republican Party, they changed the relationship between locals and immigrants, the Irish and the blacks, the Irish and slavery, the Irish and the WASP establishment and the course of American history.

Nobody knows for sure where the term the 'Know-Nothings' came from but in November 1853, the *New York Tribune* noted that in a bye-election a Whig candidate was beaten by a man on the Know-Nothing ticket. The Know-Nothings came out of a secret society called the Order of the Star Spangled Banner which had been formed some years earlier in response to the deluge of Catholics arriving on American soil. It's thought that members of the society when asked about it, answered, 'I know nothing' and so the name stuck.

The Know-Nothings spread through the establishment of Lodges. If some of their ideas and language sound like early-1970s' Belfast, it is because it is disturbingly similar to the old Ian Paisley rhetoric of anti-Popery and religious bigotry (before he became the all new 'Paisley Lite' that we know today). The Know-Nothings referred to Catholics as 'papists' and were constantly fulminating about 'Romish plots' being hatched to undermine the Republic.

In essence, however, the Know-Nothings were an economic

movement, a backlash against the threats to their livelihood posed by immigrants. Condemning the Catholics as being non-American was a convenient flag in which to wrap their economic self-interest. It dignified their narrow interests, allowing them to state with ham authority that:

> *'The cornerstone of our Republic is political, mental and social liberty and in direct antagonism with these principles, stands Romanism. It denies the liberty of free inquiry, the liberty of speech and thus saps the fountain of freedom. There can be no Republicanism where Catholicism bears sway.'*[9]

This movement was the last thing the impoverished Irish needed and it must have made them feel that they were being followed by anti-Catholic bigotry from Ireland to New York. It all sounded more south Belfast than south Boston.

As well as being feckless, lazy, disloyal and drunken (the Know-Nothings were also a temperance movement), the Irish were accused of being fraudulent, stuffing ballots and organising riots on polling days. We were alleged to be a threat to the functioning of American democracy. The Know-Nothing newspaper, the *New York Express,* opined that *'government is a science which the Irish man, who cannot read, cannot learn in a single day'.*

They called for the introduction of a 21-year naturalisation rule to prevent the Irish from voting, stating that only after this time could the immigrant be American enough for such a lofty responsibility. The voting issue has surfaced in Ireland too, in recent years, but we have avoided this thorny issue with our own very democratic solution: immigrants can pay tax, but not vote here!

The Know-Nothings were also abolitionists which went at the time with temperance movements. They wanted to see the end of slavery in the American south—the Irish opposed this. The roots of this opposition were economic as much as philosophical. In the Irish case we are back to the 'victim of victims' idea. The Irish selfishly feared a huge influx of cheap black labour from the South on the day slavery was abolished. This influx would undermine their monopolisation of the lower-class jobs and threaten them in the same way as they had destroyed the blacks' economic power base in the previous decade.

The Know-Nothings supported the abolition for precisely the same reason the Irish feared it. They took the view that if America were to have an underclass it was better to have a pliant black Baptist who knew his station, rather than these bolshie Catholic Irish whose antagonism towards all things Protestant was palpable.

In the 1854 elections for Governor of New York State, the Know-Nothings garnered close to one in three of all votes. They began to describe themselves as the American Party.

Irish immigration slowed up in the mid 1850s. Many put this down to racism, however, New York was in recession and there was probably an element of postponing the journey until the us economy took off again.

The Know-Nothings were a logical political reaction to immigration and together with the small Republican Party they posed a real threat to the Whigs and Democrats who had dominated American politics since the foundation of the Republic. The anti-Irish stance was a populist form of easy-to-digest nationalism, while the anti-slavery platform gave them an air of respectability.

The Know-Nothings posed a threat not only to the Irish but also to the traditional wasp nationalist party, the Republicans. So, the Republicans aimed at co-opting the Know Nothings to diminish their threat while, at the same time, capturing some of their populist energy.

The Republicans achieved this by picking off leading Know-Nothing figures and by 1858, as the economy was pulling out of recession, the Know-Nothings voted to join the Republican Party. Their legacy is evident today. Their dna is all over the modern Republicans—so much so that the present American President, tee-total, anti-foreign, an evangelical Protestant, could be a direct intellectual descendant of the Know-Nothings.

———

The story of the Know-Nothings, the economic war between the blacks and the Irish, the subsequent battles between the Irish and the nativist skilled working class is instructive for us. So, too, is the implication of the 1850s' falling wages, the competition at the bottom and the massive political reaction when the economy slowed down.

In many ways, Ireland now resembles the north-eastern states of the US back then: the key difference is that back then, we were the immigrants and now we are the hosts. This idea that a society's tolerance of immigration is linked to the economic cycle is not new. However, because the boom here has been so effervescent and immigration so significant, we need to avoid our immigrants becoming the 'victims of victims'.

At the moment we appear to be extending the wishful 'soft landing' thinking which has dominated our view of the property market, to immigration and the possibility of economic tensions in the years ahead. We have made this complacency more dangerous by having no immigration policy. Irish immigration policy is made in London not Dublin and unless we want to seal off the North which to say the least, might be against the spirit of the Belfast Agreement, whatever London does, Dublin will jump. In addition, our monetary policy is made in Frankfurt. So, we have left ourselves more or less defenceless. The Botox Nation is trading recklessly in the area of immigration. With no-one taking responsibility, the buck stops nowhere. In an age of globalisation with people and goods moving across borders 24/7, this approach will not work. The centre will not hold. Somebody has to take control.

Our immigration, which has been largely positive thus far, is a consequence of our soaring personal spending. The spending, driven by cheap credit, is one of the unforeseen consequences of 9/11 and Osama's oil boom. The more we spend, the more prices rise. The more prices rise, the more wages have to rise to catch up. Yet the more wages rise, the less competitive we become and yet higher wages attract in more migrants who need places to live and the cycle starts all over again. But it starts at a higher price and this is making the cost of doing business here prohibitive, unless you can pass off these costs to other Irish people caught in the same upward spiral. However, when you leave the financial Lilliput of modern Ireland and look at the economy through foreigners' eyes, you understand that the higher our costs, the less likely multinationals will choose to locate here.

And yet, even with the best leadership in the world, international events can sometimes conspire against countries, particularly countries whose people sit on their laurels rather than constantly innovate, adjust and move forward. We will only prevent a nasty political reaction to immigration if we become more competitive. But given the pace of global change, we need to move quickly. We need a new plan.

The next chapter looks at what can happen to a country that loses competitiveness and is caught on the wrong side of globalisation. Rich countries can become poor, just as poor countries can get rich.

Chapter 14 ～

RECKLESS TRADING

Latin Lessons

The last thing they remembered was sky where the cockpit should have been. A huge ripping sound was followed by a violent explosion, throwing everything forward. Then it was the cold, unbearable cold and the stars. They were at the top of the Andes, with no food, medicine or water. Most of their friends had been killed in the crash. They had no idea where they were or how far from the nearest village: at this altitude, it could be days. Many of the survivors had broken limbs; they were going to die of hypothermia, hunger or both.

At first it tasted more like pork than steak. Some vomited at the idea, but after a few morsels, driven demented by the hunger after over a week without food, they sat and chewed their dead friends in silence. One or two cried. You knew the ones who had digested the meat because of the ghastly greenish tinge to their faces. Cannibalism is not something the Christian Brothers at the Stella Maris College in Montevideo had prepared them for.

All the members of the Old Christian rugby team whose plane crashed in the Andes in October 1972 were pupils or past pupils of the Stella Maris College. The school had been founded in 1955 by Brother Patrick Kelly to educate the Irish-Uruguayan population of

Montevideo. At the peak of its economic miracle Uruguay was home to thousands of Irish immigrants. Many were professionals or middle managers who quickly took their place in the bourgeoisie of this tiny Latin-American powerhouse.

By 1955, the Irish were well-established and the students of Stella Maris were the cream of local society attracted to the college by its bi-lingual tuition, its Irish-Catholic ethos and its rugby tradition. Socially, in South America as in South Dublin, rugby trounces football every time.

What were Irish people doing in Uruguay in the first place?

They arrived during the first great era of globalisation at the same time as their cousins were heading for America. Many people mistakenly think that globalisation is new, a product of the 21st century. It is not. We are in the second great age of globalisation. The first era of globalisation occurred over a hundred years ago. From 1870 to 1914, the world opened up to trade, ideas, innovation, huge capital flows and unlike today, huge legal movements of populations from Europe to the West and South. The Irish were at the vanguard of these movements in both directions.

Cork, January 1889

Looking back at the Cobh skyline with its stately terraces under the towering presence of St Colman's Cathedral, James Hanratty was counting on two or three years in South America.[1] Unlike most of the other two thousand Irish passengers on the *City of Dresden*, bound for the River Plate, he had a job sorted out there already. His contract would last until 1895 after which he wanted to be back in Dublin to take advantage of the property boom that was occurring in the new squares and roads around Rathmines. According to the papers, the skirmishes in South Africa would be wound up soon. Gold had been found in the Transvaal and his brother Timmy was working as a foreman in South Africa, sending home cash which James had been investing in small houses around Portobello. These houses had become the favoured territory of over a thousand Lithuanians who had arrived in the previous five years. The Litvaks, or Lithuanian Jews, formed the first wave of Lithuanian migration to Ireland in the 1880s.

Hanratty had invested heavily in the area, finding the new immigrants to be good and prompt-paying tenants. He had also heard from his younger brother in New York that the Jews would eventually buy him out. That's what they'd done to the Irish landlords in the Lower East Side a few years after settling there: they liked to own their own places.

So Hanratty, using South African money, became the absentee landlord of émigré Lithuanian Jews in Portobello, tipped off by insider information from his brother in New York.

It was 1889 and Argentina was booming. Buenos Aires was in the middle of an immigration surge that would see the city go from a population of 200,000 in 1880 to 1.5 million by 1915. Dublin would grow in the same period from 300,000 to 370,000. James Hanratty wasn't hanging around this backwater and anyway, he could live off his Dublin rent, get it wired to Latin America and wire the amount he owed his brother in Transvaal from Argentina. The financial system in 1890, like today, was solvent, integrated and, with everything backed by gold, there was no exchange-rate risk between the great trading nations of the globe.

At the time, little Uruguay's recent expansion was making Argentina's look positively sluggish. Uruguay was the agricultural miracle of the late-19th century. While most of Europe was still characterised by small peasant holdings, sub-divided between warring brothers and cousins and lads who looked like Bull McCabe, Uruguay was a superannuated version of Fine-Gael Meath, where farms were enormous tracts of land, flat as far as the eye could see. From Ireland in the West to the Junkers in Prussia and the serfs in Russia, Europe's politics were, at the time, dominated by land wars between the peasants and the landlords. In contrast, in Uruguay, the native Indian population had been wiped out, and now the place was virgin soil and its politics centred on getting stuff done.

Taking a leaf out of the North-Americans' book, the Uruguayans invested heavily in mechanised farming. They were the first to introduce industrial slaughterhouses, alongside meat-packing plants. These mega-plants exported all their output to Europe and Britain in particular. Links between Britain and Uruguay were strengthened as a result of the land agitation in Ireland. The British concluded that they could no longer rely on the output of Ireland, which was looking more and more unstable.

Investment in transport helped too. Between 1870 and 1910, freight costs from Uruguay fell by 0.7% every year. And over the period, taken together with rapid railway building, export costs from Uruguay fell by 70%.[2] Railway building in the 19th century was to the Uruguayans, what the telecoms infrastructure is to us today: the country with the best rail infrastructure could get agricultural products to market cheapest. Today, the country with the best broadband and cheapest telecom costs gains a huge advantage over those without. Uruguay was to global agriculture what Ireland is to global computers and pharmaceuticals today. Uruguay provided the raw material of cheap land and healthy cattle the way we provide tax breaks and educated people. Foreigners provided the capital in Uruguay in the 19th century, as today's American multinationals do here in 2007.

The population of Uruguay and Argentina exploded as migrants flooded into the boom areas known as the Rio del Plata. The population of both countries rose by over 3% each year from 1870 to 1920. And, like Ireland today, there was an investment boom. In the 1880s, 60% of all loans from Europe and the US to Latin America went to Uruguay and Argentina. Everyone now wanted a piece of the action. US lending to Latin America, of which Argentina and tiny Uruguay got the lion's share, rose from $308 million in 1902 to $1.6 billion by 1914. The French and the Germans were lending similar amounts but Britain remained the main investor with $5.8 billion in 1913.[3]

Like Ireland in Europe today, Uruguay was always tiny compared to the giants all around it. But it was nimble. Its population peaked at only 2% of the total Latin-American population in 1910.[4] So it was getting huge capital investment with only a tiny workforce, making the average Uruguayan worker amongst the most productive in the world at the time. It was the poster-boy of globalisation. (In 2003, Ireland caused a similar storm in the financial markets when it was confirmed that US investment in Ireland was more than two and a half times greater than US investment in China—the profits of US companies in Ireland in the same year surged by 45 per cent.) In the same way as technology has given Ireland, a country which never experienced an industrial revolution, the wherewithal to get the best out of its labour force, particularly in the multinational sector, innovation helped the Uruguayans. In 1876, the first refrigerated ship, the *Frigorifique,* sailed from the River Plate carrying frozen beef to Europe. The Irish and other European farmers, affected by the use of the steamships and railways, both of which reduced the price of wheat and grain imports were now deprived by refrigeration of the natural protection of distance. The Uruguayans were now part of our own market and with their highly efficient production methods, they were undermining Irish farming.

The place was awash with cash, leading—as it has done in Ireland in the past ten years—to a land-price boom. From 1900 to 1910, the price of land increased by close to 300% in both Argentina and Uruguay.[5] The Parisian boulevards that dominate both Montevideo and Buenos Aires were built to show the world that these countries had arrived. This was the new Europe in the South Atlantic.

The boom attracted people such as James Hanratty from all over the world. Between 1881 and 1931, 8.4 million immigrants arrived in Uruguay, Argentina and southern Brazil.[6] The influx of cash and people caused house prices to rise. All Uruguay's products were exported. The world's media carried gushing stories which documented the miracle on the River Plate. Uruguay was dubbed the 'Switzerland of South America'. Sound familiar?

As late as July 1913, when we were having our lockout in Dublin, the *Economist* wrote glowingly of Uruguay, but warned of changed times ahead:

> 'The country is prosperous, the customs revenue is rapidly increasing, the existing state debt is being paid off, and the railways are earning the guaranteed interest which would otherwise have to be made good by the government…What may happen some years hence under the combined influence of an oppressive oligarchy is beyond the horizon of present-day finance.'

Contrast the freewheeling, full-of-cash innovation and optimism that characterised Uruguay, where so many people were going to make a second life, with the *Economist*'s report on Ireland around the same time, where hoarding, a true sign of economic uncertainty, was rife. People had neither the confidence to spend money nor put it in the banks, so they put it under the mattress. In June 1911, under the title 'Impressions of Ireland: Hoarding and Investment' it wrote:

> 'But, although Ireland has been very poor, and is only now emerging, and although the Irish character (at any rate, in the novel and on the

*stage) is associated with the reckless expenditure of borrowed money,
there has always been a remarkable amount of thrift. A solicitor of
wide experience in County Kerry told me that...not long ago, for
instance, a woman died near Killarney leaving a hoard of £1,000
almost entirely in threepenny bits!'*

15 February 1889

It's hardly surprising, therefore, that the *City of Dresden*, built in
Glasgow in 1888 for Norddeutscher Lloyd as an immigrant ship which
could carry 38 first-class passengers, 20 second-class and 1,759 third-
class passengers, was full when it set sail from Cobh to the River
Plate.[7]

Unlike many of the other passengers who were going as labourers,
James Hanratty would be employed as a skilled machine manager
(having learned his trade at the Sirocco factory in Belfast) for the Fray
Bentos meat-packing factory in Montevideo, the biggest in the world.
His job was already secure. He was a manager in a global economy in
the first real phase of globalisation.

In 1900, Uruguay was absorbing more immigrants per head than
any country in the world. These came mainly from the Mediterranean,
Italy, Spain and Dalmatia. But over 50,000 Irishmen also emigrated to
Argentina and Uruguay in the years up to the turn of the century.

Property prices in Montevideo were rising faster than London and
the Uruguayan capital vied with Paris as the home of *haute couture*.
The capital markets were pouring money into Uruguay and the
domestic banks experienced a huge rise in their share prices. In an
example of how integrated and exposed to foreign capital Uruguay
was, if you add up all the foreign capital invested in the country, it
amounted to 162% of GDP—this is probably close to the highest ratio
any developing country has ever had. Who could blame the Irish for
flooding into the region?[8]

In 1875, to accommodate the Hibernians of the region, the *Southern
Cross* newspaper first went to press. It was set up by Patricio Dean. James
Hanratty had responded to an ad in the *Southern Cross* which he'd
picked up at the public library in Killiney where he had been working
on the point system for the newly-built Dublin municipal tramline at
Dalkey. The library in Killiney was a 19th-century version of an internet
café. Newspapers and journals from all over the world arrived in that

library, only a few days after publication. Young James was an avid reader and loved to consume news from all over the world. After work, he'd stroll up to Killiney and settle into such exotic titles as *The Cape Times*, *The Economist*, *The Boston Globe* and Argentina's *Southern Cross*.

On board, he was carrying a letter from his mother, Elizabeth Lynch, to her cousin, Anne Isobel Lynch, who had emigrated to Argentina 20 years earlier. Apart from the annual Christmas card, they hadn't heard much from Anne but knew she had married a Spaniard who treated her well and that her son was a doctor. In the bourgeois world of late-Victorian Ireland, a family doctor, even in Argentina, would get you at least two rows closer to the front of the church at Mass. Elizabeth knew that Anne would look out for her son James and while Montevideo was across the River Plate from Buenos Aires, it would be comforting for him to have her for the first few weeks.

Hanratty arrived in Puerto Madero in Buenos Aires—Argentina's Ellis Island—where millions of other Europeans started their Latin-American odyssey. Just across the harbour are the railway lines which transported thousands of Irish migrants out into the Pampas where they eventually took to farming and the gaucho lifestyle like ducks to water, to such an extent that Jorge Luis Borges, Argentina's favourite writer, wrote fondly of Irish immigrants in his masterpiece, *Ficciones*.

Today, Puerto Madero is the centre of this great city's docklands rejuvenation programme with expensive shops and apartment blocks overlooking the rusting old cranes which stand testament to an earlier era. The quayside, where Hanratty first touched South American soil, is now thronged with young trendy 'Porterios' as Buenos Aires' cocky residents are known. The cafés and bars are rocking and are built in the refurbished redbrick warehouses into which nearly 2,000 bewildered, hungry passengers from the *City of Dresden* were herded on the morning of 15 February 1889. This was the largest group of immigrants to dock from one vessel ever in Argentina's history.

Back then, Puerto Madero was packed with Italian, Spanish and Irish immigrants. Most were housed for free for the first five days by the Argentinan government, because, having wiped out the native Indian tribes, it was keen to colonise Argentina with Europeans. After that they were left to fend for themselves.

The vast majority of the *Dresden*'s third-class passengers arrived destitute. Most of them realised quickly that the promises made by the two charlatan agents who had sold them the Argentine dream of riches beyond their dreams, were lies. In the *Southern Cross*, Father Matthew Gaughran, in Argentina on a fund-raising mission, wrote that:

> *'...anything more scandalous could not be imagined. Men, women and children, whose blanched faces told of sickness, hunger and exhaustion after the fatigues of the journey had to sleep as best they might on the flags of the courtyard. Children ran around naked. To say they were treated like cattle would not be true, for the owner of cattle would at least provide them with food and drink, but these poor people were left to live or die unaided by the officials who are paid to look after them.'*

According to another article in the *Southern Cross:*

> *'Young girls of prepossessing appearance were inveigled into disreputable houses—a swell carriage with swell occupants drives up, promises of a splendid situation are made and accepted, and away go the unsuspecting girls.'*

A hundred years later, in an article on the *City of Dresden*, Michael Geraghty wrote in the *Buenos Aires Herald*, that this episode *'began a long tradition of Irish whores in the squalid, now-gone-red-light port area of Buenos Aires, where some of the most famous "madams" were reputed to be Irish'.*

After word of this débâcle got back to Ireland, immigration to the region began to slow down. It did spike up again in the 1920s, but thereafter, fresh Irish emigration to the River Plate region was uncommon. However, despite the slowdown, today Argentina is home to the fifth-largest Irish community in the world. Half a million Argentinians claim Irish descent. This is 12% of the population of Argentina.

The Lesson for Ireland

Hanratty made his fortune in a straightforward manner. He saw a gap in the market, using Irish labour from neighbouring Argentina to extinguish communism on the shop floor. The Irish factory workers, like their brothers in the USA, had no truck with the communist ideas spreading like wildfire amongst mainly Mediterranean immigrants.

The Irish brigades were organised. They were traditional trade unionists, who negotiated good conditions for themselves by being more New Testament than *Communist Manifesto*. Eventually, as part of his life-long dislike of communism, Hanratty was delighted when the Irish Christian Brothers set up the prestigious Stella Maris College for Boys in Montevideo. Not surprisingly, they insisted that rugby be played. Football was for Latin commoners, rugby was the game of the Irish and English in Argentina and Uruguay.

However, it was not communism that brought about the decline in Uruguay, as Hanratty feared. It was something more structural and, for Ireland in late 2007, of more worrying significance.

How could the poster boy of the world's first great era of globalisation do so well for a few decades, generate such wealth, attract so many immigrants and absorb so much investment and then go into an accelerated, terminal, decline? How could such a rich country get so poor?

Uruguay has gone from being the 11th richest country in the world in Hanratty's day to the 74th. It is doing all right by Latin-American standards, but well off the global pace. What went wrong?

The first thing to appreciate is that not only superficially, but fundamentally, the miracle Irish economy now and the miracle Uruguayan economy then are disturbingly alike. According to Jane Jacobs in her brilliant little book, *Cities and the Wealth of Nations*, Uruguay's problem was that it 'supplied meat, wool and leather to distant markets in Europe and it supplied little else but wool, meat and leather'. It was unidimensional and not particularly forward looking.

This could quite aptly be used to describe Ireland today with our Botox economy. Like the Uruguayans, we produce a narrow range of products, mainly pharmaceuticals and computer components for the rest of the world. We produce little else. In fact with 92% of all our exports coming from the multinationals,[9] we are even more lopsided than the Uruguayans.

Ireland is a link in a global supply chain rather than a sovereign, well-balanced economy. So was Uruguay in its heyday. On the surface Uruguay looked to have it all. It was not populated by peasants with some oligarchy or landlord class on the top. Uruguayans were European immigrant farmers, who were given vast tracts of land to farm, which they did extremely efficiently. They were educated and visionary. In 1917, Uruguay brought in the most comprehensive welfare state seen anywhere in the world. The Uruguayans outdid the Scandinavians. The country had the lowest inequality in Latin America, the highest levels of education and the most open democracy. In short, it was a model society and more importantly, it was a knowledge economy with levels of educational achievement on a par with Western Europe. Church and State were separated at the beginning of the 20th century (well before most European countries) and the country prided itself on secularism and tolerance. It was a new country geared to a new modern age. Wage rates were well above European rates for several generations from the beginning of the century, as, too, was productivity. And in a sign of just how sophisticated its infrastructure was, it hosted the first ever World Cup in 1930, beating off competition from Spain, Hungary, the Netherlands and Italy. Uruguay won that first World Cup and again in 1950. Thereafter, Uruguay's footballing prestige fell, along with its economy.

The Uruguayans did everything right. Railways, schools, even highways and hospitals were built, social welfare was expanded. On the surface, everything looked perfect except for the fact that the description, the 'Switzerland of Latin America', couldn't actually have been further from the truth. As Jane Jacobs suggests, 'where would Switzerland be now if it had limited itself to grazing and slaughtering cattle for export to foreign markets and divvying up the proceeds, rather than developing its industry further?'

Like Ireland, with our 'Celtic Tiger' label, countries that believe their own propaganda can lull themselves into a false sense of security very easily.

The problem with supply-region economies like Ireland and Uruguay is that if they remain supply regions, they become terribly imbalanced. Countries should always take the fruits of a windfall and invest them smartly. If they don't, they will miss a great opportunity and simply store up problems for the future.

Another problem for a supply region—although it doesn't seem so when seen through the narrow prism of modern economic measurement—is that it's possible to produce too much of a good thing. This is exacerbated by another characteristic of supply-region economies: the distant markets are highly selective about what they want from you.

When the whole world wants one or two things from you and nothing else, it can be highly dangerous because the country is vulnerable. If and when the rest of the world decides that it doesn't want the product from you or the market wants the same product cheaper from someone else, you don't have much to fall back on. This is Ireland's weakness. We are rigid in the face of change and because the country has simply married its people with foreigner's money, it hasn't learned the necessary entrepreneurial dexterity to think its way out of problems when they arise. We are like an over-dependent concubine.

Although the cracks began to appear in Uruguay as early as the late 1920s and 1930s, it wasn't until the late 1940s and 1950s that the game for the 'Switzerland of Latin America' was up. In 1947, Europe started producing more food under the CAP and Britain opened itself up to competition from New Zealand and Australian food. These countries could out-ranch the Uruguayans. They were better, quicker and cheaper. Uruguay began to go backwards. It experienced what is called in economics a 'negative terms of trade effect'. This means that the price of the stuff you export falls relative to the price of the stuff you import.

This could easily happen in Ireland. The price of our computer exports is falling all the time, being dragged down by China, while the price of pharmaceuticals is being kept up by the US policy of keeping generic drugs from its market. However, Presidential candidate Hillary Clinton has said that she wants to cut the prices of medicines in the US as they are causing the health budget to go out of control. These two developments could easily prompt a 'negative terms of trade' effect in Ireland which would be similar to the slap the Uruguayans experienced.

A cataclysm like this forces a country either to cut wages, to cut spending or to start borrowing, putting everything on the long finger. In Uruguay they tried a bit of all three. Loans were called in, the country defaulted. It ran out of foreign currency and had to try, in the face of rising unemployment and falling house prices, to replace its food business with something else. That failed. The government started to print money. Inflation rose and the slide began from 11th richest country in the world to 74th richest. The previous bastion of tolerance experienced a military government in the 1970s. Today, the echoes of its heyday are cruelly heard in the fine art-deco architecture of Montevideo, built in its 1920s' pomp.

The lesson for Ireland is obvious. Things change quickly. Unlike Uruguay, where the decline was slow due to an absence of globalisation from 1930 to 1990, we live in a world of hyper-competition where economic time is speeded up. If a country doesn't use its moment in the sun to diversify away from the narrow range of products which it is supplying, it runs the risk of being caught badly when industries migrate or when other countries undercut it.

The interesting thing about Uruguay is that it was a well-run country. What it did, it did very efficiently. It tried to educate everyone but ended up employing people in the public service rather than in innovative industries. As long as a country does not foster entrepreneurism and self-reliance, it doesn't matter how well the place is run: its people will be unable to deal with a crisis. History is full of these examples and the bragging Irish who claim that we have a miracle economy should pay heed. Jane Jacobs observes that in Renaissance times, Sardinia exported cheese to the cities of Europe but nothing else. Over time, the market changed: cheese-makers from elsewhere undercut the Sardinians and the place became a backwater.

A great example closer to home is Belfast. Here you had an industrial powerhouse of a city. The Belfast Boom is best exemplified by its population rising from 98,000 in 1851 to 378,000 by 1911. Belfast was a hub of mechanical innovation, trade and, of course, shipbuilding. It was the first Irish city that took full advantage of the golden era of globalisation. In contrast to Belfast's success, Dublin was a backwater. While Southerners emigrated, Belfast experienced rapid immigration.

Yet it was too narrow in its focus and arguably too hubristic in its sense of itself and its belief in the quasi-religious origins of its growth. Ultimately, Belfast was too British, plugged into a faltering Empire rather than a brave new world. It was a supply region masquerading as an economic miracle.

The main problem with being a supply region is that a country becomes a large extractive industry, not unlike an oil-producing country. You are extremely good at one thing and this dependence becomes confused with independence.

In the case of Uruguay, as is the case in modern Ireland, huge amounts of foreign investment led to a massive credit expansion, feeding into house prices and forcing a disproportionate amount of the credit to find its way into trophy houses and developments rather than productive investments. When credit is well spent, it can make an economy fit and muscular, but if wasted, it can make the economy weak, rather like a bad diet in people. Too much credit, like too many Big Macs, can have the same effect.

Many people will argue that while the example of Uruguay is instructive for the Botox economy and our multinationals, the major difference is that Ireland is in EMU, which means that, unlike the citizens of 1950s' Montevideo, the citizens of 21st-century Ireland will not run out of foreign currency. In fact, some might go further and argue that the opposite is the case: we can cushion the blow of departing supply-region industries by simply borrowing cash from Germany and fuelling our domestic service industries with cheap credit. Although that looks plausible, the absence of an early-warning system, such as running out of foreign currency, makes the crash, when it comes, more pronounced because the supply region is then even more dependent on foreign largesse without any basis for paying the money back.

Inca Gold

History argues against complacency—just because a country appears to have access to cash doesn't mean it will succeed. To see how this can be the case, let's quickly travel back to the Flight of the Earls, 400 years ago this year. The Flight broke the back of Gaelic Ireland. From then on we were leaderless, our society in a state of flux and our institutions broken. Historians claim that the Flight of the Earls was a direct result of our defeat at the Battle of Kinsale. So, what has this to do with modern Ireland descending into hyper-consumption using other people's money?

The people who financed the Battle of Kinsale in 1601 were the Spaniards, whose financial weight allowed them to entertain risky adventures in parts of the world they did not understand. Is this the 17th-century Imperial equivalent of Paddies buying apartments in Romania with money borrowed from Osama's oil boom? Let's delve into history a bit more to see the fallacy of trying to live on other peoples' money.

The delusion of easy credit is evident in the history of Imperial Spain, from the ill-fated Kinsale fleet to the palaces of Cadiz. It all stems from its relationship with gold and silver. In the past gold determined the amount of money you could create. If you had gold, you could buy everything and you could finance anything.

In 1492, King Ferdinand sent Christopher Columbus off with the instruction: 'Get gold, humanely if possibly, but at all hazards get gold.' Thus, in the 16th century the Spaniards plundered as much Latin-American gold as they could get their hands on. In *The Power of Gold*, Peter Bernstein suggests that the total stock of gold and silver in Europe was five times greater in 1592 than in 1492. Spain was the richest kingdom in Europe. However, as Bernstein says, 'the Spanish celebrations were celebrations of the past'. A new world was emerging, a world of freer trade where what you made, rather than how you paid for it, was the key to lasting wealth.

Thus, by 1570, Spain was no longer the richest country in Europe. To quote Bernstein again, the Spanish 'gold came in one end and went out the other like a dose of salts'.

Spain behaved like a poor man who wins the Lotto. The Spaniards became much better at spending the easy money than investing it and producing goods. The *nouveaux riches* Spaniards imported everything: the finest clothes, workmen from Italy to build palaces, guns from England and the Netherlands. Like Ireland today, all the gold and silver flowing in pushed up the price of everything. Spanish farmers couldn't compete with imported beef and cereal from France and Italy. Spain, once the biggest agricultural country in Europe, began importing food and paying for it with stolen Inca gold and silver. The landed Spaniards started to look down on those who traded for a living.

The more gold and silver flowed in, the higher prices soared for everything, particularly houses and land. In a short time, as Bernstein notes, Spain was 'characterised by a separation between money and merchandise'. It had loads of money, but no merchandise. It knew the price of everything but the value of nothing. The other problem was that because gold was seen as power, the Spanish king began to funnel the gold into expansionist wars, from Turkey to Kinsale, to project Spanish power outwards.

It's interesting to think (particularly in light of the perceptions of our empathy with downtrodden people) about how the attempted liberation of Irish-speaking Gaels at the battle of Kinsale was directly financed by the massacre of Inca Indians in Peru. This is how the world works when it's opened up to trade and financial flows: no cause is pure and noble or without repercussion.

The story of Spanish gold is like the story of Irish credit. For us, the German savers who finance EMU are like the hapless Incas. They have given us access to all their credit and we, like the Spanish, are spending it on all sorts of fancy stuff. On top of this, German money is the wave of Osama's recycled petro-dollars which have flowed out of the Gulf since the invasion of Iraq.

Ireland has had a once-in-a-lifetime windfall and we are blowing it. Like the Spaniards, the new Irish money is coming in one end and going out the other. This makes us weaker not stronger, leaving us with inflation, a flashy car which depreciated the minute we bought it and little else. We are making a hames of it.

The moral of the Spanish gold is that cheap money can destroy as well as create. Spain was initially unwilling and then later, when the Inca gold ran out, unable, to produce anything. It was denuded of skills and left lamenting the missed opportunity. Spain went from being the most powerful country in Europe to a provincial backwater in the following centuries.

Today's Irish financial profligacy is made all the more damning when we look at the Uruguayan example, because, unlike Uruguay, we have limitless finances to divert into other activities, before the lesson of other supply regions plays out here. But we are ignoring economic history—and what do they say about those who ignore their history?

30 May 2007, The Shannon Pub, Montevideo

The traditional band Grianan[10] took the tiny stage in the Shannon, led by Conrad O'Neill, a fourth-generation Irish-Uruguayan. The roar went up, as 400 Irish-Uruguayans, some the descendants of the passengers of the *City of Dresden*, belted out the 'Fields of Athenry'. Jameson flowed. They exchanged stories of their visits back to a place they call home. For the O'Brien clan who were here in force, the ancestral home was Navan; for the Lawlors, it was Wexford. There were countless other McGoverns, Kellys, O'Sheas, O'Neills and Murphys. These are the descendants of the waves of Irish migrants who flooded into this boomtown over one hundred years ago.

Today, Uruguay is the land that time forgot. 1960s' Chevrolets roll down the streets and men on horse-and-carts collect rubbish. No-one bats an eyelid. Unlike Cuba, where vintage cars are touted like relics of a different age, in Montevideo they are an all-too-real reminder of what might have been. Uruguay feels like a country which has been frozen in time. Carrasco airport is empty except for the pretty girl trying to flog a new fragrance and ads warning against foot-and-mouth disease. The highway, built in better times, is also disturbingly free of traffic. It is as if, decades ago, the city tarted itself up for a big party, a celebration of its success, and no-one turned up. They are still waiting and there is a sense, particularly from the Montevidean Irish, of a people cut off from their homeland, stranded at the far side of the world.

Uruguay, a tiny Atlantic country of just over three million people, rose from nowhere, reversing hundred of years of Spanish colonialism, absorbed hundreds of thousands of migrants, was the world's fastest growing economy, prompted an economic crisis in rural Ireland in the 1880s and 1890s, became the poster-boy for globalisation in the early 20th century, received more foreign investment than almost any other country, reinvented what small countries can do, shone brightly, basked in the accolades, won the World Cup and then vanished off the global radar screen. It was a victim of its own precocious success, unable to disentangle myth from reality, too flat-footed after years of plenty to adjust to the changing rhythm of the global economic beat.

The former star pupil became frustrated and delinquent, unable to understand what had happened. It lashed out. Immigration was replaced by emigration, tolerance by tyranny, democracy by despotism and hope by despair. How strange that the world-beater of the first half of the 20th century would become recognised not for its economic golden age, but for the forced cannibalism of a bunch of desperate Irish-Uruguayan rugby players on the top of the Andes.

Let this be a lesson to those of us who think this time it's different. Everything goes in cycles and Uruguay is our warning sign. The writing's on the wall, if we choose to read it.

Chapter 15 ⌒

MADE IN CHINA

My father has a pair of nail-clippers in the shape of a fish. Or more accurately, a fish lure. It is an intricate little thing, the gills are emerald green and the eyes and mouth reasonably realistic. It is extraordinarily resilient. Someone must have spent a bit of time and effort in getting everything in this minute piece of technology right. I can remember playing with this fish as a very young boy. Despite the fact that it looks like something he got in a lucky bag in the 1950s, it still works and it is certainly close to 40 years old, if not older. My father and mother are from the hoarding generation, those Irish people who bought things to last, saved money and never threw anything out.

An interesting thing about it is that, if you flip it over, it has 'Made in Japan' written on it. This must have been the last low-tech thing ever made in Japan. Japan is now the world's centre of technological excellence. When did Japan make this type of basic stuff? Or, more interestingly, when did Japan stop making these bog-standard, pile-'em-high, flog-'em-cheap trinket things? When did Japan move up the value chain from toys to computers, from Space Invaders to Nintendo, from hardware to software, from the Mazda 323 to the Prius?

If you ask your parents, they will tell you that in the 1960s, the image of Japan was of a cheap manufacturer churning out bargain-basement pots and pans, second-rate cars, transistor radios and nail-clippers. It was a by-word for cheapness. The Made in Japan symbol was recognised and seeped into popular consciousness: with the 1972 Deep Purple 'Made in Japan' live album, the expression had found its way into the lexicon of spotty teenagers with 'taken-in' jeans. 'Made in Japan' was a must under the arm of any self-respecting head, along with a packet of Old Holborn, a donkey jacket and desert boots.

But over time, like heavy metal, which has gone through all sorts of reincarnations from glam to thrash metal, the image of 'Made in Japan' changed dramatically. To use the vernacular of the business world, Japan 'moved up the value chain'. The Japanese realised that they could only pay themselves well by investing in technology and by increasing the productivity of every worker. The country did this with extraordinary breakthroughs in innovation. Japan went from a defeated post-War country of cheap labour to a resurgent country with the best-paid workers in the world: from an importer of capital to the world's largest creditor. Yes, it got burned in its Kamikaze Capitalism phase of the late-1980s and early-1990s, when it became infected with the Irish disease—an infatuation with property. It got over that. Today, Japan is the high end of the high end, the most sophisticated economy in the world.

It has passed the low-tech baton over to China and now China is where Japan was 40 years ago. How long will it take China to grow out of the cheap-goods phase? And what does this mean for Ireland?

The answer to the first question is simple: it will not take China long and, because of its scale, China will be at least two world-beating economies at the same time. It will be a low-cost producer of tat and a hi-tech producer of state-of-the-art exports. Things are unlikely to move at a single pace. However, one thing is clear: the 21st century is likely to be China's century. The country is on course to overtake the United States by 2030 as the world's largest economy and there doesn't appear to be anything that can stop this process. It's an economic juggernaut similar in scale to that of the US in the early 20th century.

Shanghai, June 2007

In early June 2007, strolling on the Bund in Shanghai, you get a glimpse of the new China. This place was the centre of pre-communist mercantile China, when Shanghai was the centre of East-Asian trade. It was here that Mao, always aware of the nationalist symbolism of the great foreign-banking buildings that overlooked the Huangpu River, encouraged his cultural revolutionary students to beat up members of the bourgeoisie, parading them through the streets like mediaeval criminals.

Today, a little over 40 years later, looking out over the river to the monuments of glass and light on the other bank, you cannot but be moved by the singular ambition of these people. The Cultural Revolution and any vestiges of communism have been erased and replaced with the most vibrant strain of capitalism on this earth. Twenty years ago, on the far side of the Huangpu River were paddy fields. Today, it is a glittering megalopolis with a skyline that dwarfs Manhattan. Up until three years ago, Times Square was the most photographed streetscape in the world. The Bund in Shanghai now claims that prize—testament to the emerging middle class in China as millions of Chinese tourists visit the city.

The river hosts enormous cargo ships, tugs, barges and show boats, as well as thousands of small boats ferrying people to and fro, moving goods around. This is a living river, in a massive trading city, which is home to possibly the world's most enterprising people.

The Chinese have been trading for centuries and many argue that the communist hiatus was simply a 50-year aberration in an uninterrupted line of capitalism. In modern Shanghai there is no evidence of red communism; this is capitalism, red in tooth and claw. Everything is for sale. Everything has a price.

And the world is paying attention. For those who have been doing business here for many years, the entrepreneurial flair that the world is waking up to does not come as a surprise. Sitting in his office in Park Avenue, Manhattan, Don Keough, the Irish-American former President of Coca-Cola and member of the Taoiseach's special economic advisory board, tells the story of Coca-Cola opening its first Chinese plant back in the early 1980s—the first major deal done with the Chinese State. This was just a decade after the Cultural Revolution. China was a country of citizens in olive green Mao uniforms on bicycles. Keough contrasted the grasp the Chinese communists had on marketing, selling and advertising with that of their Russian counterparts in Moscow with whom Coca-Cola were also doing business at the time. The Chinese Politburo explained to the US executives how to sell in China, where to put their kiosks, how to use pretty Chinese models on their advertising billboards and how to get inside the heads of the Chinese consumer. Coca-Cola only had to scratch the surface and the wheels of commerce began to move. By contrast, the Russians had no idea of what Coca-Cola was trying to do. They looked blankly at Keough and his team. They had no history of commerce. Even in Tsarist Russia the merchant class was tiny. Russia was a feudal society with no commercial savvy; China on the other hand, was a trading empire, open for business again.

This natural affinity with commerce is palpable everywhere in Shanghai. But the showcase centre of the city, with its designer brands, expensive restaurants and Porsche Cayennes, only tells you so much. To get a feel for the underlying dynamism of the country or at least the sliver of land on the eastern seaboard which dominates the economy, we have to drive out through the city to the countryside to observe the scale of Chinese mercantile power. Here we will see the manpower that has driven China since it started opening up.

China has grown by 9% on average every year since 1978—that's 700% cumulatively.[1] And last year it overtook the US as the world's number one place for foreign investment with outsiders spending $54 billion in the People's Republic.[2] We are seeing the age-old pattern of foreign money fusing with local labour to make goods for export.

Jump in your VW Passat (the surprising car of choice of Shanghai's huge middle class) and navigate the narrow streets behind the Bund. These were once home to the French, British and German concessions as zoned by the Chinese Emperor in the last age of globalisation. Here, the architecture is turn-of-the-century French colonial. Drive up past the Blarney Stone Pub, run by a man from Ballaghadereen, under the willows planted by French *fin-de-siècle* traders, past the nail bars, henna tattoo parlours and enormous billboard ads for L'Oréal, DKNY and Nina Ricci. These are aimed at the burgeoning consumer class which is estimated to be in the region of 300–350 million—that's bigger than the population of the EU, before the central Europeans joined in 2004.[3] Last year, China surpassed the US as the biggest market for that all-American car, the Buick.[4] The demand for designer products underscores not just a consumer class but an upper middle class which, at 90 million, is the size of Germany's entire population.[5]

Traffic is heavy, reflecting the 8,000 new car licences that are issued a month at a cost of €4,000 a pop in this heaving city. General Motors alone sold 876,747 cars in China last year.[6] So, let's weave through the midtown traffic, dodging rickshaws, bikes and old tramps collecting paper and rubbish. Step over the beggars, past the hundreds of hairdressers (many in fact brothels) and foot-massage parlours, out past the sleazy bars and their peroxide blonde Filipino transvestites, blasting out Tina Turner covers. (Filipinos have the cover-band market sewn up all over Asia and, in a part of the world obsessed by karaoke, the Filipinos are top dogs.)

Drive past the Starbucks on almost every corner, towards the seedier parts of the strip, where the seemingly strait-laced western accountant away from the wife for a few days can buy Baileys for his $20-a-day teenage hooker. She's advertised as a 'talking girl'. In the few words of English she has, she claims that he is handsome and she 'loves him long time' as she laughs nervously, covering her mouth. He's such a fool, misguided by the logic of the transaction, that he's flattered.

Everywhere you are reminded of the economics of huge populations. Life is cheap and, like the Irish prostitutes of New York's Five Points in the 1850s, people sell whatever they can. Like so many of Shanghai's workers, Snowdrop—her working name for western clients—has only recently arrived from the hinterland. This year, ten million similar new workers will join the labour force. Snowdrop wears fake D&G well.

He, on the other hand, is kitted out in the international uniform of the gobshite. The baseball cap is on backwards, complimented by the baggy clamdiggers and the Nike boot-runners with white socks. He couldn't score in a month of Sundays in Renards, but today in Shanghai, where a hooker's alternative is a €40-a-month job in a toy factory, he's the man, and more importantly for Snowdrop, he's the first step on her stairway to heaven.

To see Snowdrop's alternatives we've got to keep heading out of town, past the rundown People's Army barracks and out towards the new city around Pudong Airport. We're motoring now on a 21st-century flyover built in the past three years, as we pass the Shanghai Rugby Club, where GAA is the second most popular sport. The Shanghai first fifteen are favourites to win the Asian Gaelic games to be held in Singapore in 2007. The rows and rows of mature trees mask the fact that this new suburb of Legoland tower-blocks, housing 120,000 people, is only two years old. Shanghai is going up as we speak. This is the world's largest building site; a new suburb the size of Cork is being built here every year.

On our journey, we pass the fetid dormitories just above the metro excavation site which are thrown up for the tens of thousands of construction workers who are bussed in from the countryside. These labourers work like chain-gangs and collapse every evening in filthy dormitories. They gaze out through barred windows at the traffic, like prisoners. Not a high-vis jacket nor hard hat in sight. Their work is changing the face of the city as they clamber up incredible bamboo scaffolding. A metro station here, the world's tallest building there. This is what New York must have felt like for the millions of Irish emigrants at the end of the 19th century. The city just can't keep up with itself. And all the while the people keep coming. Twenty-six million people a day swarm around Shanghai, working, trading, producing and dreaming.

The traffic is jammed outside the office of Oriental Securities Limited—a hole-in-the-wall stockbrokers where the gambling-fixated Chinese play the Chinese stock market. In the past few days, the market's been falling like a stone. The place is full, with women making up about three quarters of the investing public. These are not the Gordon Gekkos of Wall Street fame, they are ordinary Joes, in cheap acrylic gear sitting on red plastic chairs, whispering to each other conspiratorially, fixated. There are 80 million stockbroking account-holders in China. This is the people's market in the People's Republic. A skinny middle-aged man in a Liverpool shirt, whose trousers are falling off him, clears his throat and spits the phlegm violently with intent into the corner—a familiar sound on the Chinese street. We pass under the huge billboards for Lancôme's latest skin-bleaching product, Neurowhite Blanc Extra. In contrast with our orange tanorexics, Chinese women can never be too pale.

We move out through the new suburbs, past the industrial parks, towards the countryside under the grey Asian sky. A traditional Chinese scene of men on bicycles and women with straw hats in paddy fields unfolds. The houses are basic, little more than shacks, on either side of a vast empty motorway. The change from city to countryside is startling but the teeming mass of people never lets up. We are headed for the biggest port in the world: Yangshan Free Trade Port, which is 24 months old and already moves one third of China's $1.3 trillion exports.[7] China is the world's third largest exporter and last year its exports grew by 27%. Over the same period, Ireland's export growth stagnated.

We cross the world's largest bridge, a phenomenal 30 kilometres long, as it juts out into the filthy, polluted, brown East China Sea. Four years ago, the city decided to move Shanghai's port from the city to a new facility. This has been done with the minimum of fuss and on the most monumental of scales and this feat underscores why China will dominate the world economy in the future. Decisions are taken, not with next year in mind but with 2030 at the forefront of Chinese thinking. Once taken, the breathtaking resources of the People's Republic are mobilised with purpose and with a blatant disregard for human suffering and conditions. As a result, everything is new, state of the art and ready within months. Contrast this with our M50 road-widening fiasco where no work may be done either at night or on weekends.

Now, turn off the motorway, onto the dust path, past the paddy fields and the shallow, stagnant rivers. There are no cattle nor sheep in the fields. Here, in contrast to Shanghai, people stare at foreigners.

The first thing you hear in the teddy bear factory is the incessant tick-tick of hundreds of flip-flops tapping the pedals of the rows of battered Butterfly sewing machines. The ceiling is low and the fluorescent lights give the place a yellowish hue. The girls look up from their work, giggling. There are four hundred of them in rows of sixteen, crouched down over their teddy bear ears. Cloth and dye come in at one end of the production line and thousands of Paddington Bear teddies are shipped out at the back after a process which has not changed since the Industrial Revolution. Cheap labour is the ingredient. All that can be heard is the whirr of spools of thread and the occasional order directed from the stern looking woman under the blackboard with this hour's target marked on it. At the fluffy-tail part of the assembly line, four dozen teenage girls prick each tail with a spike to make the hair fluff up.

There is something vaguely incongruous about 40 Chinese women stitching badges with ''Twas the night before Christmas' written on it, in a language they don't understand, referring to a religion they've hardly heard of. But these cute teddy bears are destined for America and Europe and they'll be under our Christmas trees or taken to bed by our children on Christmas night. And here is where they originate: in a prefabricated factory, four hours outside Shanghai, made by hundreds of young girls in identical pristine light blue shirts, jeans and flip-flops. It is clear that labour-intensive manufacturing industry is over in Ireland and Europe.

Two hours down the empty highway and a different image of this industrial powerhouse emerges. This is more disturbing for those of us who believe that we can stay ahead of the game by investing in technology. The oddest thing about the high-tech General Motors factory is not the efficiency that produces 800 cars a day but the intermittent piped-music versions of 'London Bridge is Falling Down', 'Old McDonald' and 'Greensleeves' which disturb the hum of a factory at full tilt. The music is triggered by a fault on the assembly line and each part of the car has a different song, so if there is a problem with the chassis, 'Old McDonald' plays, thus signalling to the supervisors that they are needed in the chassis section of the production line. When I asked why they don't simply make an announcement calling the supervisor, they said they adopted the system of playing English childrens' songs from the Japanese, who pioneered it in the 1980s. This shows that the model for China is not some triumphalist Anglo-American formula championed by the *Economist* magazine which values free speech and liberal democracy, but the narrow-gauge, R-&-D-driven Japanese approach, where management and workers sing from the same hymn-sheet, industrial capacity is the driving force and Anglo-American niceties are tolerated, not embraced.

This year, General Motors will invest $1 billion in plants in China[8] and has indicated that it will continue to invest for the foreseeable future. There is no strong financial reason for cars to be made in the US in ten years' time. Given GM's difficulties in the US and the fact that the Chinese plant is the one keeping the company afloat, it is hard not to see why most of its production won't be in China in the near future.

The same goes for almost all manufacturing industry. Globalisation turns China, like Uruguay and the US before it, into your next-door neighbour. It brings China into your living room, kitchen and bedroom.

Carrickmines, 24 December 2006

It's Christmas Eve in Smyth's Toys and the Bono Boomers, Jugglers and the odd Jagger-Generation last-minute shopper all vie with each other in the cavernous aisles of this altar to the industrial might of China. There are sheer walls of toys. It is like facing a Grand Canyon of red, blue and yellow plastic tat, none of which will last the New Year. Everything is made in China, as are all the buggies, strollers and trampolines. The unfailingly polite Slovak assistants smile at the snappy, hungover Pussycat Mom who can't find anything on her list. Apart from she of the concave tummy, every other woman is heavily pregnant, testament to the baby boom Ireland is going through.

What will the impact of China be on these yet-to-be-born Irish children? It is clear that manufacturing in Ireland is over. The extra dollar invested by US multinationals will not come here as quickly as it did in the past. It won't happen overnight but the influence of China on Irish living standards will be profound. And it will work in two ways.

First, the ceiling on wages for Irish manufacturing jobs will be set in Tiananmen Square, not Merrion Square. This will have a knock-on effect throughout the economy and every reasonably-sized company, when faced with the extremely high wage-bill in Ireland, will have this 'China Factor', of whether or not to outsource, uppermost on its mind.

For those in the professions, it is a mistake to think that the China Syndrome will only impact on manufacturing. Why get architect's plans drawn up here for a fortune when you can get the same with perfect dimensions from Shanghai or Vietnam for a fraction of the cost? We can see this impact already in the newspaper industry where the twin forces of China and the Internet are affecting traditionally secure jobs. Newspapers were told that the Internet would spell the end of the traditional reading habits of the public. This has not happened. Yes, people do read blogs, on-line newsletters and the like, but they still read newspapers. However, broadband has opened up the possibility of using setters and printers in China or wherever the typesetting cost is lower. Entire Irish newspapers are already—or soon will be—set in cyberspace, allowing the papers to benefit from the China effect without ever setting foot in the People's Republic, thereby forcing down wages or eliminating jobs altogether.

The second impact of China will be a rise in Chinese emigration to everywhere in the world, including Ireland. To catch the flavour of this, take yourself up to Parnell Street in Dublin. Here under the eye of the 'uncrowned king of Ireland', we can see the impact of the Chinese Diaspora. Just stick your head into the bustling Chinese restaurants and bars and then think of Parnell's speech:

> 'No man has a right to fix the boundary of the march of a nation; no man has a right to say to his country—thus far shalt thou go, and no further.'

A hundred and thirty years after this famous speech in Cork, the sentiment rings true today. The bigger issue now is that with globalisation and immigration, no man has the right to fix the boundary to the march of another man. And no nation can say to its citizens, thus far and no further.

If the experience of other countries is a blueprint, Ireland is likely to experience a massive increase in a Chinese entrepreneurial class. The Chinese are buying investment property here and the community has three separate newspapers full of ads for property in Ireland. Check out the website, *www.emeraldtiger.ie*, to gauge this development. We don't appreciate that the polite Chinese workers we see in our bars and cafés are the children of the communist aristocracy. They are the little princes and princesses of Mao's one-child policy. We are hosting the best connected Chinese migrants ever and we should be aware that their ambitions go far beyond working in McDonald's.

If we examine the Chinese Diaspora in Asia, America and Europe, the common thread is entrepreneurial talent. We will see a repeat of this in Ireland as the Chinese settle in. Because the Chinese students who we are hosting are so well connected—their parents are communist apparatchiks—we would be well advised to cultivate this talent.

Taken together, the opening of China will accelerate social change in Ireland through its impact on wages and migration. Large swathes of Irish and European industry will relocate to Asia in the years ahead, in the same way as large tracts of European agriculture were decimated by America's arrival on the scene in the latter years of the 19th century.

There is also a geo-political game at play between China and the US which is not dissimilar to the one which took place between the US and Britain in the 20th century. The Americans made sure that their unquestionable economic strength translated into geo-political power and took every opportunity, in the early decades of the 20th century, to ensure that it superseded Britain as the top dog in the world. It did this by force of economic might, the juggernaut of demography and, of course, military prowess. China is likely to do the same thing to the US in the 21st century.

On the financial front, the world is experiencing a circular flow of income which involves America getting further into debt to China. The Chinese are exporting to the US and running a massive trade surplus with the US. But contrary to much of the talk in the US, both client and producer need each other.

China has a huge interest in the US remaining its main customer. A recession in the US would be a disaster for China because the Communist Party needs the economic miracle to bestow legitimacy on its one-party rule. So, the Chinese have to act both as America's supplier of goods but also as its banker. The more Chinese goods the Americans buy, the more money flows back to China and the more the Chinese have to lend to the US, to ensure that the Americans continue to buy even more.

The way the Chinese do this is by buying American government bonds. This has two effects which positively impact on the two motors of the US economy—government spending and the housing market. By financing the US government, the Chinese allow the US to run bigger and bigger budget deficits. This allows the US to keep taxes lower than they otherwise would be and, in so doing, facilitate US spending on Chinese goods because the average American has more money in his back pocket.

Secondly, by buying US government stock, the Chinese help keep American interest rates lower than they would be had the Americans to finance their deficit themselves. This underpins borrowing in America and keeps the housing market more buoyant than it otherwise would be. Such buoyancy fools the Americans into thinking that they are richer than they really are and so they spend more on yet more Chinese goods. So the Chinese are playing a long game, tolerating American financial delinquency, while all the while making sure that America gets into deeper and deeper debt. America gets to feel strong but in reality it is being gradually enfeebled.

One area where the Chinese do not tolerate American dominance is in energy supplies. China is actively cultivating regimes that are inimical to the US but have energy supplies. The Chinese realise that apart from Americans turning their backs on shopping malls and retail therapy, the only thing that can choke off the Chinese economy is a lack of energy and raw material supplies. China needs secure supplies of its own. So it has signed treaties with pariah regimes like Sudan for oil and the Congo for rubber. It is buying up commodity companies all over the globe and is on friendly terms with Iran and Venezuela. Last year, China, signalling its move to nuclear, signed the largest ever deal with Australia to ensure its access to uranium for the foreseeable future. As the world goes nuclear in the next ten years, uranium in Australia and Canada will become a precious resource.

So China is accepting IOUs from the US to tie the Americans up in a debt knot, while at the same time, ensuring that it doesn't leave itself victim to American leverage in the area of energy supplies. The lesson for Beijing of the American involvement in Iraq is that the Americans are prepared to fight resource wars and, if you don't want to meet them head on in the field, you'd better find the back-door route to energy security.

The impact of the Dragon will be felt via a variety of channels. It's not lose-lose, there are plenty of services that the Chinese will want from us. But to position ourselves for this we have to be smart, think long-term and go out to China, make contacts and see what they need. For now, the first wave of Chinese influence will be on wages and jobs here, particularly those in the lower-skilled jobs—the very people who are already in competition with the immigrants.

The main upshot of the presence of China in a globalised world is that there is nowhere to hide. If you have a weakness, China will make it weaker.

Chapter 16 ∾

| DEGENERATION

The Black Irish, the Know-Nothings, the Irish emigrants in Philadelphia and New York, the crestfallen Uruguayans, Snowdrop in Shanghai, the Lithuanian school teachers, Chinese teddy-bear makers and the Jugglers, Jaggers and Bono Boomers all have one thing in common: they live or have lived in an era of global economic change.

In the first great age of globalisation, from about 1850 to 1915, the Irish were at the vanguard of the movement of population around the world, creating the Irish Diaspora. In the second age of globalisation from 1990 to today, Ireland has also been to the fore, seizing the opportunities afforded by increased trade, immigration, cheap loans and direct foreign investment. In the first golden age we followed the money around the globe. In the second age, the money came to us.

Now, as we enter a new and possibly more complicated phase, the question is, what are we going to do next?

In order to know what we shouldn't do, it is helpful to examine why the first age of globalisation came to an end when it had broad political support from business, the media elites and politicians as well as small shopkeepers and tradesmen. Why did a great period of openness, cosmopolitanism and scientific advancement, which drove millions, like James Hanratty, to Uruguay, the United States, Canada and South

Africa, come to such an abrupt halt? There may be lessons for us from
the collapse of the first age of globalisation. The end of that first age is
particularly relevant as we enter a domestic economic downturn,
which could cause people and politicians to lurch for reactionary
solutions that may involve blaming outside forces for our internal
convulsions.

The opening-up of China and India will have a profound impact on
a trading nation like Ireland. To understand how it will affect us, we can
compare it to the impact on Europe of the opening-up of the US
agriculture market in the mid-19th century.

Back in 1855, little did the Famine-Irish navvies—who built the
American railroads, opposed the Know-Nothings and fought on both
sides in the American Civil War—realise just how detrimental laying
railway sleepers in Illinois would be to the lot of their families back
home. From the 1860s onwards, the price of cereals in Europe fell
precipitously as a direct consequence of competition from Ohio,
Minnesota and Kansas. This is what Professor Kevin O'Rourke of TCD
refers to in his excellent book, *Globalisation and History*, as a 'grain
invasion'.[1]

If you want to see a similar process in action today, go to any PC
World and examine the prices. The prices of PCs, laptops and mobile-
phone handsets are falling dramatically. You might remember in the
1990s that PCs and laptops used to cost over €2,000. Now you can pick
up a sophisticated machine for €600. This is the impact of China, and
the first indication of a global shift in production to the East. In 20
years' time, there will be practically no manufacturing industry in
Ireland. Manufacturing, as we know it, is part of history. When Chinese
labour will work for less than €5 a day, the Irish worker, on €150 a day,
can't compete. So what are we going to do? History gives us some clues.

One hundred and forty years ago, the European agricultural market
began to experience something it had never been exposed to before,
hyper-competition. European farming was still stuck in the small-
holding structure, leading to political movements like the Land League.
In America, however, massive quasi-industrial farming was made
possible by the fact that land was practically free. By brutally clearing
the land of the Native Indians and giving it to mainly German pioneer
farmers, the US fundamentally changed the global economic balance.
The economic axis tilted from Europe to America. The same process

was going on in Hanratty's Argentina and Uruguay, compounding the economic shock.

For centuries, the European economic system had been based on a fixed supply of land and rising populations. This caused land values to rise progressively. He who had land, was top dog. The underlying assumption for the global economic system was that land was a fixed supply. All other economic calculations orbited around this central truth.

Then almost overnight, an entire continent of free land was made available, pushing down the global price of land and decimating the livelihood of millions of European farmers. In addition, the new cheaper food from the us and the River Plate region drove down the yield on European land. This was the 19th-century equivalent of the price of your house falling and your wages being cut at once.

This process is similar to what is happening today as China and India open up. Irish engineers and computer professionals simply can't compete. Let's see how our great grandparents reacted in the late-19th century.

European farmers did the only thing open to them—they emigrated to where the land was free and the opportunities abundant. They moved to the Wild West. The American Dream was born. This promise of a brighter future had more to do with individual advancement than any ideology. At the time, when Ireland and large parts of the rest of Europe were still ruled by landlords, the American Dream of freedom and liberty must have been enormously attractive.

But another ideology, based on the collective rather than the individual, was emerging as the old order retreated. By 1880, America was fast becoming the breadbasket of the world. Falling agricultural prices meant falling land prices and falling rents. This drove Europe into a state of flux. Many emigrated, while hundreds of thousands of other uprooted agricultural labourers arrived into Europe's cities forming for the first time a waged proletariat. This gave European industry a cheap resource of new labour and it accelerated Europe's rapid late-19th-century industrialisation. Many new workers, huddled together in unfamiliar slums, uprooted from their land and villages, were open to be radicalised.

These new workers were the first victims of the breakdown of the old order. They were the losers. In contrast, the winners were a new mercantile class which emerged, profiting enormously from globalisation and trade. Urban Europe began to look more and more like a Dickensian scene of fat-cat bosses and a mass of wage slaves. The resulting division of wealth led to the labour movement, communism, Marxism and a whole host of other -isms which were to characterise the political landscape of the 20th century.

Globalisation ensures that an event in one part of the world, which seems unconnected, can have dramatic ramifications in another part of the world. For example, it's arguable that socialism wouldn't have flourished in Europe had it not been for the massacre of Sitting Bull and his people in America: by clearing the prairies of Indians, the Americans colonised the Mid-West with European farmers and the resulting fall in agricultural prices around the world forced angry landless unemployed people into European cities— workers ripe for radicalism.

However, there is one huge difference between now and then. Emigration to the New World acted as a political and demographic safety valve. Although the Americas provided the catalyst for change, they also provided the solution. Europeans, elbowed out by American farming, could emigrate to America to seek a new life. Can today's displaced Irish workers up sticks from Ireland if they lose their jobs and emigrate to Shanghai? I don't think so.

Thus, unlike the last great era of globalisation, today, emigration from Ireland will not ameliorate the political tensions resulting from economic competition. In fact, the opposite will occur. As we've seen from the example of the Lithuanian school in Inchicore, immigrants will heighten the competition at home, at precisely the time when Irish workers will be looking for a break. This implies that the dole and local politics will bear the brunt of the pain this time.

So what happened to politics, last time around? By the turn of the 20th century, it was obvious that the world was changing rapidly, but like today, no-one had any real idea how or where we would end up. Reeling from the economic dislocation that accompanied the US's appearance on the global stage, unnerved by mass emigration and falling land prices, Old Europe was tottering.

Worse still, countries and peoples which had not figured in the past began to make themselves felt. In 1905 mighty Russia was humiliated by the upstart Japanese in the Pacific and a few years earlier the British, although ultimately victorious, were given a slapping in the Transvaal by the Boers. Cracks were beginning to appear in the old order. Not only in Ireland but all over Europe, nationalist movements sprung up, based on romantic notions of lost history and the added moral and racial tale of bad Imperialist versus good colonised subjects.

Yet even when it was becoming apparent that the centre could not hold, no-one could have predicted how quickly and how dramatically the age of globalisation with all its promise would collapse: into chaos, war, nationalism, racism, eugenics and ultimately, Fascism.

Taken by Surprise

In 1908, had you stood at the bar in a Dublin pub and predicted that within 14 years, Ireland would be a fully independent state, most people would have described you as an eccentric. Had you continued to suggest that, after a Great War in which millions of men would die, victorious Britain would lose more of its territory than defeated Germany, you would have been laughed at. People would have thought you slightly unhinged, had you forecast that all the main continental European empires would have disappeared within a decade and that a radical idea called communism—which was, even in 1908, a marginal political force—would have taken over in Russia or that the ideas of Friedrich Nietzsche which called for the 'purification of mankind' would be entertained.

Amazingly, in June 1914, on the eve of the First World War, yields on British government bonds stood at 3.6 per cent. That is lower than they are today.[2] Government bonds are the tea leaves of the financial markets. If people are worried about the future or about government spending, then interest rates on government bonds will be extremely high to reflect the increased risk. Had the financial markets predicted the Great War, interest rates on British government bonds, a government that would be practically bankrupted by the war, would have been at stratospheric levels. But they weren't.

Equally striking is the fact that Europe's stock markets continued to rally throughout July 1914—weeks after Gavrilo Princip had assassinated Archduke Franz Ferdinand. According to fascinating research carried out recently at Harvard by Professor Niall Ferguson, only on 22 July 1914, less than two weeks before Britain declared war on Germany, did the European markets begin to get jittery.[3]

Until 1 August, when German and Russian armies were mobilising on the continent, The *New York Times* was still suggesting that war could be avoided.[4]

On 3 August, the world's stock markets simply shut down and did not open again for months and months. How's that for the financial market's legendary foresight? If there was a war coming, the financial markets certainly did not see it. Everyone ignored the signs. It's funny how history rewrites itself: by the time I was sitting the Leaving Cert, the 'right' way to answer the history question on the start of the First World War was to say that it was the inevitable consequence of competition between Germany and Britain for economic supremacy, the result of the Balkanisation of central Europe's politics and so on. Today's interpretation is that the war was inevitable. Yet, as we see from records of the financial markets, no-one expected it, even on the day before the guns blazed.

The Insulation Nation

Baggot Street Hospital was built in 1890 as the Royal City of Dublin Hospital. Today, just to the left of the receptionist's desk is a beautiful brass engraving over a hundred years old, commemorating a fundraising fête in 1907. It smells of Brasso; the Mongolian cleaning woman has seen to that.

The plaque lists the Dublin bourgeoisie who donated more than £50 in one sum from the day of the fête until private funding stopped abruptly in 1922. The list is a testament to Dublin's well-heeled in the turbulent first two decades of the 20th century. The fundraising fête gives us a snapshot of Irish society at the time. The stalls at the fête represented different counties. The book stall was manned by the Countess of Erroll. Dublin City was represented by Lady Ardilaun. Lady Langford ran the Meath stall which raised £153, while Miss Poe and Mrs Lyster of Kilkenny generated £142 for the hospital. These must have been the most aristocratic bunch of stallholders ever assembled and along with the representatives of the west British professional class, they were raising money as they did for so many public causes.

This was the old order, the Anglo-Irish ascendancy who were fundraising to build a new extension to the hospital. Obviously, they expected to be using the hospital for some time. As far as they were concerned, they were not going anywhere. Yet within a decade or so, most would have been forced from the country, many burned out of the houses they'd lived in for centuries. As for the civic-minded bourgeoisie, they would be terrorised throughout Ireland and Europe by a combination of narrow-gauge nationalism and socialism which held them up as class enemies. They had no defence against the polemical rhetoric of the time. And like most people at the top, they had farthest to fall.

Fast forward to today and examine how similar forces in the second age of globalisation are affecting the Jugglers, Jaggers and Bono Boomers. The lesson from the past is that the backdrop can change so quickly, sweeping away old certainties.

Since the fall of the Berlin Wall, the world's labour force has quadrupled in size as China, India and Russia have opened themselves up for business. These millions of workers will have the same effect on the global economic system and our livelihood as the free land had in the US more than a hundred years ago. In addition, international financial flows are now so enormous and so interrelated, that recycled money from Osama's oil boom is financing Touareg 4 x 4s in Kilkenny. Millions of people are on the move leading to five-foot-high Congolese teenagers in eight-inch heels breaking down in floods of tears at Dublin airport. If our jobs don't go to them, they will come to us, any way they can. And as the intensive schooling of the Lithuanian children in Emmet Road suggests, when they get here, they are here to stay.

Added to these forces, an oligarchy is emerging, where the winner takes all and those in second place live off the crumbs. Although on an income basis, Ireland is becoming more equal, the amount of wealth held in the hands of the super rich is quite astounding. In Ireland, as we saw in Chapter 10, the top 1% of the population owns 23% of the wealth. When everything is going well, these oligarchs might well be seen as the benchmark to aspire to. However, when things turn down, they will become the symbols of excess, the very essence of what is wrong with the system.

Furthermore, as house prices fall here, the Generation Game will be exposed at precisely the wrong time, when the emergence of China makes our industrial weaknesses more apparent. When the Jugglers wake up to the fact that the Jaggers and to a lesser extent the Bono Boomers, have stolen the fruits of the boom, how will they react?

The social contract, whereby the Jugglers were happy to accept relative hassle today for the promise of housing wealth tomorrow, is based on house prices rising and full employment. As we move into a downturn, neither of those foundations will hold and the old social contract will be torn up.

Although not completely apparent yet, already the mood of the nation is darkening. Compared to two years ago when the sky was the limit, people are now feeling unnerved. In recent months, survey data on consumer confidence in Ireland are picking up this sense of unease. The victory of Deckland, and Breakfast Roll Man's decision to back Fianna Fáil in the 2007 election was a defensive move. Jugglers concluded that now the outlook was less clear, it was hardly the time to go changing things.

But this political passivism will not survive a recession. We are now at a turning point and people are conflicted. Everything seems rosy, but something's not quite right. We are rich but feel poor; we are strong but feel weak. Our pensions and jobs feel less secure. We are overdrawn, overtired, overworked and overstretched. There are foreigners everywhere and our neighbours' jobs are moving to the East. For Sale signs are staying up longer, house prices are falling, yet the cost of living is rising. There are ten foreign children in your child's class, yet the building is falling down. No-one says hello anymore. The place is different, it's unravelling and we feel like outsiders.

Protection

In May 2007, at an election rally for an independent candidate in Greystones, Co. Wicklow, this feeling of unease was palpable. Greystones is a typical 21st-century Irish town. The population has exploded to 5,000 in recent years. It is Juggler territory. This is trampoline country: all you can see as you drive around the new estate called Charlesland, a development of 1,800 houses and apartments, are snatched glimpses of seven-year-old faces as they bounce over the fences of identical back gardens on identical trampolines.

Across the road, the shopping centre has a Domino's Pizza, a Boylesports betting shop, a hairdresser, a dry cleaners and a fake French café selling vacuum-wrapped, microwaveable croissants. Of course there's the ubiquitous 'coming soon' allure of Jackie Skelly's gym. This could be anywhere. The new developments in Gorey, Naas,

Carragaline, Arklow, Stepaside, Oranmore and Ongar, are all the same.

A place like this should have a confident swagger, but, in contrast to a few years ago, when everything was pumped up, plumped up and in your face, that night in the local GAA club at the pre-election meeting, the feeling was much less buoyant, as if air was escaping from the tyres. The denial stage is over, we are moving towards something else. There is a sense of foreboding. Something is happening which is beyond our control. These people, who not so long ago were open to anything, rushing along like the rest of us on the coat tails of the boom, now want protection. They want to be insulated because they realise that the economy is changing, that there are probably too many houses, not enough buses, too much credit, not enough money. At the meeting, people had 'the fear'.

The local politicians who addressed the crowd were trying to articulate what exactly the fear was. They concluded that we, the people, needed more power, more community; more us, less them; more national, less international; more Hibernian, less Cosmopolitan.

This is a new version of the old conflict between Hibernianism and Cosmopolitanism which has characterised our thinking since the foundation of the State. When there are threats, perceived or actual from outside, we regroup and want to go back to a mythical Ireland that existed before all this alien transience.

This feeling, which is neither concrete nor explicit, could be termed 'degeneration'. It is a sense that the pace of change is too fast for all but the fittest. People are being left behind. The community is unravelling and the bonds that held us together are loosening. A tiny minority are sprinting ahead. We are confused, so it's not uncommon to hear comments like, 'Yes, we like the Eastern Europeans, they are great workers, but there just seem to be so many of them'.

When the pace of change is so rapid and when people don't quite understand what is happening, we see these anxiety attacks recurring.

Degeneration

The problem for politics is that the anxiety that people feel cannot be addressed by traditional Left or Right politics. Indeed, the electorate's rejection of left-wing and right-wing parties in the 2007 election was overwhelming. The difficulty with pinning down this feeling and distilling it into a political concept is that it is intangible.

This same feeling gripped Europe one hundred years ago and was encapsulated in a best-selling book at the time called *Degeneration* by Max Nordau. He argued that social change in Europe, triggered by competition from America, was causing a breakdown of the bonds that held society together. He believed that the Cosmopolitan élite were out of tune with the man on the street and that a minority who held power, and created opinions in the media, had become degenerate, living in a pampered dream-world.

Think about the similarities between now and one hundred years ago. According to Charles Leadbeater, in his book *Up the Down Escalator*, Nordau 'painted a picture of mental and moral fatigue' where innovation and free-wheeling capitalism was creating a narcissistic élite who were disconnected from the people, from tradition and from the soil. Urbanisation and immigration, according to Nordau, left people isolated, confused and exhausted. A hundred years ago, Europeans were told that scientific progress would solve the world's problems and make the world a better place. Yet, the first era of globalisation ended not with one-world harmony but in the greatest military catastrophe the world had ever seen.

The Degeneration arguments are the same now as they were then. They go to the core of the globalisation-versus-community struggle. Many Irish people believe that we are being swept along on an external tide of change, from immigration, to economic downsizing, to multinationals, to foreign money washing down over us. Others claim that our culture has become too self-absorbed, celebrity-driven, narcissistic, cynical and self-serving. For some, we are even witnessing the end of our civilisation.

There is a risk that a form of politics will emerge which will accuse degenerate outsiders of actively trying to destabilise Ireland. The targets will be varied—foreign banks, the EU, immigrants, oligarchs. In the same way as the unease is hard to pin down, the enemies will be hard to pin down too—but the point is, the enemies are out there.

The idea of national degeneration appeals to all sides of the political spectrum, leading to what Leadbeater calls an alliance of pessimism or a 'death-wish nation'. This brings Right and Left together, urban and rural, traditional and modern, in one disenchanted soup.

If we look closely, we can see the beginnings of this movement coming together here as conservative Catholics unite with atheist

Trotskyites over the Rossport 5 campaign. Or spiritual Taoists who pin up yoga ads on whole food shop-windows agreeing with old-school nationalists on the wisdom of Queen Maeve of Connaught and the benefits of the root-vegetable diet of the Red Branch Knights. Touchy-feely psychologists and hard-nosed authoritarians agree that the mental health of the nation is at risk. Both argue that we should slow down and reprioritise. Aosdána leftist artists agree with Muslim fundamentalists that Israel is the enemy, while former Marxist IRA killers join hands with died-in-the-wool Unionist businessmen, calling for lower corporation tax in the North.

Former socialist student radicals believe we should go back to the churches, while concerned churchmen argue for a return to socialism. They all agree that something's not right. Right-wing traditionalists and left-wing utopians worry about the spread of American culture yet both are quite happy to Google and take taxes from Yankie multinationals. The Left worry about the saturation of the country with American values but fall over themselves to buy the *Sopranos* box set for Christmas.

On the other hand, pro-abortion, anti-globalisation lefties in courier chic want the end of big business; so, too do the anti-abortion, traditional conservatives in the Council for the Religious in Ireland. Both sides unite around the idea of home. Ireland is a home, a homeland, a place where we can insulate ourselves from all that's nasty. It's not nationalism, but something more cuddly. We could called it 'homeism'.

As the economy slumps following a housing crash, the lessons from history are unambiguous. Whether the specific story of the Irish in America, the Uruguayan miracle which failed or the more general and more apocalyptic story of early-20th-century Europe, the moral of the story is that as the economic pendulum swings, so, too, does politics, and long periods of openness and tolerance can be followed by similarly long periods of narrowness and suspicion. Protectionism can be missold to an anxious population as a strength, rather than a weakness. The 'guaranteed Irish' campaigns of the 1970s and 1980s which exhorted us to buy only 'GI'-labelled produce are great examples of this confused thinking. Although it sounded wise, patriotic and the right thing to do, it was only keeping uncompetitive factories open marginally longer—before they closed down. But, most importantly, it put the onus on the Irish consumer rather than the Irish producer, as if our failure to buy sometimes second-rate stuff made at home was the reason unemployment stood at above 20%.

Ireland must avoid degeneration because the fact remains that, warts and all, globalisation has made us richer; it has also made the dollar-a-day Chinese worker richer and it has allowed millions of Eastern Europeans to dream of a better future in Irish towns from Cobh to Letterkenny. We have to be sure that the combination of anti-globalisation and our own property slump doesn't cause us to lurch in a radically different direction. We must avoid fatalism, overt pessimism and protectionism. What we need in Ireland is not less globalisation, but more of it. We must remain open, trading, nimble and, most importantly, we must embrace the world on our terms. We must realise that, simple and attractive as it sounds, the promise of degeneration and purification is empty. But if degeneration is not an option, what is?

Chapter 17 ⌒

THE REDHEAD
RENAISSANCE

From Brown Thomas to Lidl and Back

Like the American Roaring Twenties, the Irish Roaring Noughties will leave a bad taste in our mouths. The Generation Game will be laid bare as the Jugglers pick up the tab for the excesses of the Bono Boomers and the Jaggers.

Initially, all our efforts will be focused on short-term recovery from the five stages of a property crash, where we go from denial through anger, bargaining, depression and finally, acceptance. This is likely to prove challenging, however, it is not the overarching concern: as economies move in cycles, the recession of the next few years will naturally lead to recovery and the cycle will start all over again. The main challenge for the country is get us onto a more sustainable path. This will involve redefining Irishness in a globalised world and learning from our recent financial mistakes. This may involve us in a more-tortuous-than-usual process of soul searching.

It is clear that the economic downturn here is going to be a protracted recession for a number of reasons. The most obvious is that we can't devalue our currency. The slump will be the result of a boom in which the price of everything went up more than we could afford. We borrowed to fill the gap. House prices went up more than rents and wages went up more than productivity. Inflation rose rapidly and the cost of doing business went through the roof. The economy became one large bonfire of spending and the more we spent, the more we borrowed to keep the entire system afloat. When all this comes to a halt, we will be left with lots of houses people don't need, lots of Mercs people can't afford and lots of anger.

Looking into the future, this slump will lead to unemployment rising and house prices falling. So both our wealth and our income will be going in the wrong direction. Traditionally, when a government is faced with this dilemma, it cuts interest rates, allows the currency to drop like a stone and borrows money to finance public-works projects with the result that the economy recovers. The State thus shoulders the responsibility. But this time it is different. We are in a bind because our membership of EMU precludes us from any of these solutions.

So we have an economic problem without economic remedies. We will just have to sit here and suffer in silence. This could best be described as the 'time heals everything' school of economics where we are caught in a monetary trap.

The best recent example of such a monetary trap is Germany. Germany experienced a post-Unification boom when West Germany swallowed East Germany whole. This boom pushed all German prices upwards, prompting Germans to take lots of holidays in the early 1990s because they believed that they could get money for free, and suffer lots of unemployment in the late 1990s when it became apparent that they couldn't pay for it. It went from being a 'designer' to a 'Lidl' economy in a matter of half a decade. In 1996, precisely the time we started booming, the Germans embarked on a long period of high unemployment, falling prices and belt-tightening. We are about to face the same process.

With this in mind, let's extend the story a wee bit. There is a compelling argument first put forward by Professor Olivier Blanchard of MIT that monetary union in Europe leads inevitably to what he calls 'rotating slumps' which shunt on through the union from country to country.[1] He argues that countries which join the euro are condemned to follow this pattern because the monetary union makes the boom more effervescent and the bust more depressing.

The reason for this is that in good times inflation rises too rapidly and the country prices itself out of the market. In addition, because interest rates in countries like Ireland don't go up to warn people that they are spending too much, we spend more than we should. Banks over-extend themselves and lend too much money. We all pay ourselves too much. Prices rise and industry finds it hard to compete. In time, this becomes problematic and industry gives up investing in making things because costs are too expensive. Investors prefer instead to invest in property than other businesses. We build too many houses which are sustained by the mirage of ever-rising prices. Blanchard claims that Spain is experiencing this now. Ireland isn't far behind.

The one indicator which captures all this is the balance-of-payments deficit which measures the difference between what we buy and what we can afford. We are now running a deficit of close to €10 billion or 5.6% of GDP.[2] Five years ago, we had a balance-of-payments surplus.[3]

The conundrum for Ireland now is how do we find a way of being competitive again? Unfortunately, this will mean shopping in Lidl rather than BTs for a while. Can you imagine all the Pussycat Moms queueing up beside the Latvians in Lidl for bottles of Muscadet at €2.99 rather than their usual Meursault at €38 from Mitchell's?

The recession will cause wages to fall and over time, the country will ultimately regain the competitiveness which drove the boom in the first place. If Germany is anything to go by, the recession could go on for four or five years as the property market unravels, bankruptcies rise and spending falls. This will give us plenty of time to think about how we want to manage the future. It will give us time to sort out where Ireland fits in and, most importantly, it will give us the chance to figure out what the big picture is and where Ireland goes next. We need a big national project. We need a national renaissance and the recession will focus our minds.

————

If the Phoenix is to rise from the flames, what will it look like?

For the last hundred years of our history, Ireland was defined in geographic terms. The national project was a 26-county vision of a country, free from London but with some unfinished business in the North. Initially, Ireland's choices were seen as revolutionary. In an age of Empire, nationalism was indeed modern and rebellious. But events have overtaken us.

In a globalised world, borders matter less, change is constant and the very essence of modernity is measured by the ability to adjust, discard and re-invent. The people who win are those who embrace the world rather than shy away from it. Globalisation means that the limits of geography and boundaries matter less. In fact, you could go further and argue that globalisation should render old-fashioned nationalism obsolete. When influences are instantaneously downloadable, people always contactable and networks always on, geographical lines in the sand are just that and no more. Hackneyed as it sounds, globalisation actually does make us citizens of the world.

This new world suits smaller countries. Smallness, which used to be seen as a weakness, is now a strength. The small are more nimble and can move quicker. In addition, races that have been pushed around in the past have learned to deal with adversity. We are no strangers to an open-access world; we were there when it all started. The Irish are one of the few truly global tribes and we therefore have a head start over other less wandering peoples. But to get the best out of the new world, Ireland will have to make it up all over again. We will have to re-imagine ourselves.

There are plenty of reasons to be optimistic. Ireland is a modern nation. When other countries hold on too long, we let go; we think on our feet when other countries are left flat-footed. We have always sought to transcend the limitations of geography and size. Irish people leave when the going gets tough and come home in better times. We ebb and we flow. For example, in the 1980s, unemployment in both Ireland and Spain was at 18%. In Ireland, this prompted mass emigration; in contrast, the Spaniards hardly budged.

We are entering the age of the chameleon when an ability to fit in, shed one's coat and blend are rewarded. Self-interested pragmatism, although not heroic, will come to dominate national thinking. The Irish have shown a unique ability to drop core values when expediency demands. This is not necessarily an attractive national trait, but it is one nonetheless.

If we think about the three attributes that make a culture unique, they are language, religion and national territory. In the past one hundred years we abandoned all three. First, as Professor Declan Kiberd points out, in *Inventing Ireland*, in the 19th century we stopped speaking our own language. This, even for colonised peoples, is unusual, but we dropped our language for materialistic reasons. As Kiberd points out, in Europe 'at the beginning of the 19th century there were more speakers of Irish than Dutch, Danish, Norwegian, Swedish or Welsh'. Yet we abandoned it in the belief that it was an obstacle to progress. Most extraordinarily, and in direct contrast to the nationalist movements of central Europe and the Balkans, the language of the coloniser became the language of the separatists. English became the official language of Irish nationalism.

In the 1911 Census, the return made by my great-grandfather, John Leary, in Macroom Co. Cork, underscores the disappearance of Irish. He had been born in the 1850s when the Irish were streaming into New York. Under the column for language, he wrote that he and my great-grandmother spoke both Irish and English. Yet, tellingly for his children, he wrote that they could only speak English. My great-grandparents had not passed their own language on to their children.

Since Independence, when other countries such as Wales managed to revive their language without political sovereignty, the Irish didn't bother with any popular enthusiasm.

Our second core value has been similarly discarded. When I was a kid, people on our road tried to 'out ash' each other on Ash Wednesday. People marched around the street with the contents of entire hearths mashed into their foreheads, looking like extras from *Dr Who*. The Ashometer was part of my life in those drab February days. Now, it's gone. Next Ash Wednesday, try to spot the mark of Twenty Major on someone's forehead. You'll be hard pressed because we just dropped another core value. Up until recently, Catholicism was a key part of the Irish DNA. It defined us for centuries. It was central to the Hibernian creed. This, too, has been jettisoned to all intents and purposes.

Finally, out of the blue, we dropped 32-county nationalism. Remember all the furore about Articles 2 and 3 of the Constitution? And then when we got the chance, we dropped those too, by voting overwhelmingly for the Belfast Agreement, which was essentially the original 1922 Treaty with nice bits about canal cooperation in Fermanagh attached.

So a cynic might say that we are a Kleenex nation, more ready to wipe clean and throw away rather than the long-suffering, irrational, dreamy romantics we like to think we are. When something is a hassle, we drop it. With such a pedigree, it's hard to argue that any arrangement we enter into is permanent and, in a changing world, maybe such expedience is the best option.

What Next for the Chameleon?
This serial pattern of discarding has significant ramifications for our commitment to the EU which will take a battering in the coming recession. In recessions, people look for someone or something to blame and the EU is a likely target. If you were a betting man what would you put your money on, a diminished or enhanced cooperation with Brussels in the years ahead?

Despite the best efforts of our political élite, it's fair to say that we've always been 'headage-payment Europeans'. They patronised us and we took their coin. We were more loyal to the deutschmark than the common market. For most Irish people, Europe has always been about money and market access. There is precious little evidence of European solidarity in Ireland. However, this fact doesn't seem to matter to our political aristocracy, who display Marie Antoinettesque disregard for popular sentiment, circumventing the results of democracy when it suits them. When, for example, a few years back, we voted against the Nice Treaty, the Europhiles told us to vote again, suggesting that we weren't quite within our senses when we voted the first time. In the second referendum we did what we were told and, surprise, surprise, it was accepted!

Behind all the Erasmus programmes, diplomatic summits and Eurovision wins, we are about as European as Iceland. The EU project was originally a flag of political convenience wrapped up in a palatable economic imperative. We knew what it wasn't—it wasn't British. It gave us an economic and political lifeline—the elusive connection to the Continent. This allowed us to by-pass Britain, the culmination of what Red Hugh O'Neill tried to do four hundred years ago. It was the logical route. Secretly, we loved that the Europeans pissed off the Brits and if we could be a thorn in the Saxon sides by being loyal Europeans then that was a bonus. The fact that we got paid for doing something we'd have done for free, was like a child getting money for eating ice-cream.

Now all this has changed; we aren't so scared of London any more. In fact, if anything we are closer to the British now than at any time in hundreds of years. We have immersed ourselves in English popular culture since our accession to Brussels' inner sanctum.

The farmers who really milked the EU are almost gone and anyway we are now contributors to the budget, so our free lunch is over and, more worryingly, Germany and France are keen to harmonise corporation taxes which would nullify our industrial trump card. The remaining plus of EU membership is market access. Would our multinationals stay here if we were to loosen our ties with Europe? My hunch is yes, they would, because what the multinationals want is market access at a competitive price. Norway and Switzerland have full market access to the EU without being members. So membership of the EU at any cost is not the given it once was. And there is now the tricky question of the currency.

As we face a downturn we are presented with the following choice, stay with the euro and face a long recession or bail out of the euro and experience a short recession. But it's not that simple because we have to answer a related question: would this apparent flippancy towards our political commitments undermine the long-term credibility of Ireland as an economic location? Would potential investors conclude that if we can't stick to our Treaty obligations, what other promises might we break?

The evidence shows that the international financial community tends to be forgiving as long as the markets are profitable. Devaluing our currency, if we were to leave the monetary union but remain in the EU, would cause our exporters to become hyper-profitable. The cost of doing business in Ireland would be slashed, yet the business conditions would remain unchanged. There are good precedents for this type of arrangement. For example, Sweden and the UK are fully paid up members of the EU without being in the euro.

Also, after the initial shock of pulling out of the euro, the financial markets will display their traditional short memory. The fickleness of financial markets is one of the central truths of international finance. A few years ago, I worked for an investment bank in Russia. When the Russians devalued, defaulted and put a moratorium on debt payments in 1998, the reaction of the financial press was to banish Russia into the outer darkness. Bankers said that they would never do business with Russia again. Within a year, they were back again looking to lend, as if history had been airbrushed away. Many might say that we are not comparing like with like. Russia is not Ireland and it is too big for the financial markets to ignore. But in the past decade the same story played out in the Asian Tigers in 1997, and the financial markets were more enthusiastic for both the UK in 1992 and Ireland in 1993 after both countries devalued. So the lesson is: don't worry about the bankers, they'll be back.

Domestically, pulling out of the euro in a crisis would allow us to cut our interest rates rapidly, recapitalising the cash-strapped financial system with cheaper money and in so doing, ensuring that the recession would be shorter and less damaging than otherwise. But this would also mean that the debts which are in euro would have to be renegotiated in the new currency, maybe a reconstituted Irish punt. Initially, the currency would be very volatile, but it would find its level in time. A quick bout of inflation would wipe out a lot of the Jugglers' debts and the economy would bounce back quickly, at a more competitive exchange rate.

Now here is where we get into the politics of the Generation Game again. Why wouldn't we do this and make our lives easier? The simple reason is because it would bail out the Jugglers at the expense of the Jaggers. Anyone with debts would do well, while anyone with savings would suffer. In one fell swoop the Generation Game would be reversed and the young would start beating the middle-aged. The economy would shift from spend, spend, spend to make, make, make because the cost of producing stuff in Ireland would fall. The banks would be furious as they would lose money; holidays in Spain would become expensive. But as we have seen, time and again, devaluations work. Our own boom was triggered by the 1993 devaluation in the punt.

However, my experience as an economist in the Central Bank during that currency crisis of 1992/93 revealed just how conservative our public service is. The lack of debate, discussion and options considered during that shambles was truly shocking. Even behind closed doors, debate was not encouraged although it was evident to the dogs on the street that the existing policy was in tatters. Up until the eve of the devaluation, the mantra was repeated again and again, 'no devalution', without one good reason other than this was not the sort of thing mature democracies do. We were embarrassed.

In the event, the devaluation kick-started the economy. Interest rates fell progressively and the financial markets were happy to back the new policy. So, policy failure led to personal success. The conclusion must be that the original stance was wrong.

The Choice

Now we have this choice, do we want a long recession in EMU or a short recession by leaving EMU? Are we going to allow the future of hundreds of thousands of Jugglers to be hijacked by the intransigence of a few Jagger-Generation public servants, who live and breathe devotion to the EU and can't conceive of making rational choices about our country's best interest?

History suggests that the policymakers of this country will display inertia and hold on to the euro as long as possible, irrespective of how high unemployment goes. The burden again will fall on the Jugglers who will suffer a debt-induced recession because of some esoteric commitment to European solidarity which no-one really cares about.

Ironically, the multinationals would welcome a devaluation as it would drive their profits upwards straight away. Yes, the prestige of the State might be damaged, but its standing, and ultimately our long-term relationship with Europe, would be more damaged by forcing us into a long recession.

At the moment this might appear radical, but as the recession continues, the population will demand solutions and entertain ideas that were previously taboo. In drinking terms, the choice is between a hangover with Solpadeine or one without.

It is not difficult to see how public sentiment could change with the economic fortunes of the country. Already, we have seen a gradual cooling of our love affair with Europe, particularly since the money has run out. Like all relationships that run their course, a combination of boredom and a roving eye will also play its part between Ireland and the EU. The first sign that things aren't what they used to be will become apparent during the slump. For example, our interest rates will be rising, not falling and we will be contributing to the EU budget to help Romanian farmers, yet our own budgetary room to manoeuvre will be capped by the EU growth-and-stability pact. In addition, immigrants from EU countries will be undermining already cash-strapped Jugglers in every area of the economy. We will complain to Brussels that we need some slack. It is highly likely that the response will be one of mild irritation. We will respond in a sulk and go into the 'you never listen to me phase'. As houses are repossessed and interest rates continue to rise, we will move into the resentful stage. We will feel ignored, humiliated and vengeful. A trial separation would be just the thing, a bit of counselling as well might help, but our *nomenklatura* won't stand for it. They will remain in denial.

The interesting thing is because we are so small, the rest of the EU won't care about our plight. Remember that in 1973, the City of New York was allowed go bankrupt. If Washington allowed the Big Apple to go under, do you think Brussels will worry about the Septic Tiger? We will be caught in a loveless marriage, with no divorce.

Such a chronology is not only plausible but quite likely and will trigger anti-European sentiment. We have none of the gelling agents that bind many continental Europeans together. Remember, we have no collective memory of World War 2 and we have no common European history. Also, since EMU we have become less European and more American—closer political ties with the EU have coincided with closer cultural ties with the US. Pussycat Moms will ask, between episodes of *Desperate Housewives*, that when the costs of the EU outweigh the benefits, what's the point?

Quite apart from the short-term financial questions, there is a second more long-term factor which is likely to make Ireland's relationship with the EU profoundly different in the future. This is demographic. As we've seen, demography explains practically everything when it comes to long-range economic analysis and developments on the Continent will have profound long-term effects here. Europe is a dying continent and the expansion to the East will make this demographic dilemma more severe. As you read this, the populations of central Europe are getting smaller. Germany's population is aging as are the Italians and some Scandinavians. Today more Poles, Lithuanians, Latvians, Bulgarians, Croatians, Russians and Ukrainians will die than be born. It's a case of 'Honey, I shrunk the Slavs.' All across the Slavic world, undertakers are doing a roaring trade. This poses fundamental questions about the appropriateness of Ireland getting any closer to the EU.

Older societies tend to hold on to what they have rather than take chances. This might not be the best economic policy in a period of global hyper-competition. If an economy feels under competitive pressure, there is every reason to fear that protectionism is possible as societies throw up barriers. Many commentators suggest that the solution to Europe's demographic problem is more immigration from Africa and the Muslim world. This is a contentious issue and, for millions of Europeans, it is a cultural bridge too far. Listen to the recent debates on Turkish membership of the EU or look at the survey data on immigration. Most Europeans want immigration to stop rather than to accelerate further.

To get a sense of this sentiment all we need do is listen to the Pope. Pope Benedict has a good handle on Catholic Europe's fears about immigration and in particular, Islamic immigration. When the Pope challenged Islam last September by making comments that were allegedly insulting to the prophet Mohammed, it was pre-meditated; he wanted to get the debate started in Christian Europe about what type of Europe Europeans want.[4]

Our problem in Ireland is that, for some, listening to the Pope is like listening to Johnny Adair: polite people simply don't do it. But he's been on the ball for some time, old Ratzinger.

The populations of eastern and central Europe have a profoundly different attitude to the cultural ramifications of immigration by non-Europeans than those in the liberal west. As a rule, Slavs don't do cultural diversity. Just examine how the Serbs and Russians deal with Muslims. The Serbs, who celebrate the fact that they stopped the first Muslim invasion of Christendom during the Crusades, have drawn a line in Kosovo. In Chechnya, Russia has carried out atrocity after atrocity in a war that it believes is less about territory and more about Russia's soul. European Russia is dying and Muslims could comprise a majority of citizens of the Russian Federation by as early as 2040. But the successors of Imperial Russia, the Third Rome after the fall of Constantinople to Islam in 1453, refuse to slide without a struggle into what Spengler calls the 'digestive tract of the House of Islam'.[5] This cultural fault-line is likely to become more obvious and more divisive in the years ahead.

When you think about it, Fortress Europe is hardly that surprising. Europe is made up of a patchwork of sovereign peoples. It was not designed as a melting pot. It is not America and the cultural strains of immigration are evident every time there is an election anywhere in the Union. In each case, you have the cosmopolitan élite of people who buy the *Economist* and believe in more immigration and more federalism pitted against a local groundswell who buys the *Irish Independent* and who want less immigration, less federalism and more local and national control.

For example, on Wednesday 1 June 2005, days after the French people rejected the European constitution, the French conservative paper *Le Figaro* broke down the vote geographically. The vote in Paris was extraordinary. Even though 55 % of French voters voted against the EU, not one district of Paris did. Every single *arrondissement* voted yes.

Tellingly, the richest ones voted yes in the greatest numbers. So whereas the slightly shabbier districts voted yes by 52% and 53%, the ritzy 16th—the epicentre of expensive, cosmopolitan France—voted yes by a staggering Ceausescu-esque 80%. The treaty was beaten overwhelmingly in the poorer, more rural areas of the South and the North. The French country voted no, the French city voted yes. A similar, but not so stark, pattern was seen in Holland when it rejected the Treaty. The message in 2005 was clear—the rich are pro-European and pro-globalisation. The average bloke feels alienated from the élite.

This division goes to the heart of the globalisation debate between nationalism and cosmopolitanism. European politics of the future will be as much cultural as economic and this is a debate that Ireland can't opt out of indefinitely. Even though we have an ace up our sleeve that practically no-one else has, for the moment, because we are not about to do anything dramatic *vis à vis* EU membership in the short-term, let's focus on the possible European landscape of the next ten years.

The Eurovision Indicator
Like the high-camp Eurovison Song Contest, the EU in the next ten years will become more Slavic. In 2007, we came last in the Eurovision. For a country that used to win it just by turning up, our fall from grace has been quite dramatic. However, this is just the end of a process which has seen the Eastern countries wrest the glittering prize from the West. It is clear that new members have changed the European club and in the politics of the EU, the new countries will have an impact on the overall stance of the Union.

Many years ago, in the late-1980s, I studied at the College of Europe, a partisan pro-European University in Bruges. Back then Europe was a French project and the antipathy towards, and from, Britain, was palpable. As I sat listening to Margaret Thatcher's famous Bruges speech, it became obvious that yes, British anti-European sentiment was over the top, but equally, there was precious little effort from the continental side to understand the Little Englanders. But this has changed both for internal British reasons and for composite EU reasons. In 1992, the EU expanded to include Sweden and Finland. Very soon they made their mark. Rapprochement with Britain came first and a much more pro-globalisation and pragmatic approach to trade, taxes and finance followed. Today, Ireland's biggest allies in the EU on economic matters are the Scandinavians and the British, while our old friends the Germans and French are constantly questioning the *bona fides* of our corporate tax regime. We are much more likely to have a meeting of minds with blonde countries than many others. We might genuflect at Easter Mass with the Catholic Portuguese but we vote with the Lutheran Swedes.

As the EU continues to expand into the East and the Balkans over the coming years, it is not unreasonable to suggest that like the Scandinavians, the Slavic countries will exercise an influence on the Union and their illiberal views on religion, people, trade and possibly finance will become more prevalent in a much older Europe. The EU for so long guaranteed our prosperity but this is no longer the case. It's not that we've to think in opposition to Brussels, it's just that we have to think beyond it.

The Consummate Hosts

All these issues pose a dilemma for us. While we can't forecast accurately how things will pan out, it would seem logical to have a plan B up our sleeves because we know that Ireland thrives on precisely the opposite conditions to those in the Europe which we now see emerging. Countries have economic personalities and these will be more crucial in the future. Whereas central Europe is closed, we are open; where they are nationalistic, we are cosmopolitan; where they are old-fashioned, we are modern; where they are bureaucratic, we are free-wheeling; where they are continental, we are Atlanticists; where they are risk-averse, we are gamblers; and where the EU sees American power as something to be tamed, reined in and possibly matched, we need a dominant America to flourish.

For the past few years we have profited enormously from being a transit nation for American capital and European labour. When we had no capital, we attracted in American investment by giving it a tax break and when we ran out of our own workers we attracted in European migrants by building Tyrellstown. Both have been hosted here with impressive results. We are an Ameropean nation, half-American, half-European. We are perfect entertainers.

This constant juggling has had an impact on us, our political system, our expectations and national philosophy. This Ameropean geo-political stance is evident in elections. Irish politicians, commentators and the electorate in general seem to think that we can have the tax system of Texas and yet deliver the social welfare system of Sweden. This can only happen if the growth rate is permanently better than your neighbours' growth rate and for this to be the case, we need a strong America.

Ireland benefits more when Europe is weak and America is strong, not the other way around. The fusion of monetary economics, demography and investment flows explains this. When Europe is in recession, Irish interest rates are extremely low to reflect this. But because we are much younger than the rest of Europe and young countries spend more, we get a free lunch. We get German interest rates that fuel the Irish boom. On top of this, when Germany is weak, the dollar is strong against the euro. This makes Ireland look cheap and hyper-productive to American investors, creating more jobs here, reinforcing the injection of German cash because as our incomes rise, we can borrow more without necessarily feeling the strain.

Unfortunately, at the moment, with Germany growing faster than anyone expected, both interest rates and the dollar are going the wrong way for Ireland.

Because we are small, we are liberated when America is the world's only hyper-power. Since the end of the Cold War, the us's grand strategy has been to maintain its overwhelming military, political and economic pre-eminence. For that, we should be thankful—not because the strategy has been remotely designed with Ireland's interests in mind, but because, as a by-product of us dominance, we have flourished economically, politically and socially. Until now, the Americans have acquiesced in that grand strategy because the costs appeared to be tolerably low.

By providing security for Britain, France, Germany and Japan, by defending their interests in far-flung places like the Gulf, and by intricately involving them in a system of mutually enhancing alliances, Washington prevented any of the old powers from ploughing their own furrow. This global policy, which is known as 'reassurance', has cost the

Americans billions of dollars. It has also facilitated unprecedented levels of economic, political and social cooperation among the states of Western Europe with the EU and South-East Asia through the ASEAN (Association of South-East Asian Nations). Without the US security blanket, it is hard to see how the EU would ever have evolved into the peaceful structure it is now, of which Ireland is a member and from which it benefits greatly.

Underneath this American military umbrella, small countries have been able to express themselves like we do in Europe, feeling like an equal at the top table for the first time ever. Do you think this would have been possible in an EU dominated by the military aspirations of France, Britain, Germany, Italy or Spain? I somehow doubt it. American hegemony has put manners on them.

Our increase in living standards has been the result of cherry-picking from both the European and American way. By attracting foreign investment on the one hand, and taking advantage of the European pool of savings on the other, we have profited in ways unimaginable only a few years ago.

We arguably benefit much more from the Pax Americana than the Yanks do themselves. For small countries it is the ultimate free lunch: we get peace without humiliation, for the first time in history. In contrast, the medium-sized old powers have been made to dine on humble pie.

Ireland has to do everything we can to maintain that position which is more akin to a mediaeval city state than a fully fledged European country. The diplomatic model we should have in our heads is Venice, the open, tolerant, affluent city state that brokered one power off each other. Venice used its brains more than its brawn and remained a trading outpost, cultivating friends and weighing up its options constantly. Loyalty was to Venice first and others second.

We also need something more than just deft diplomacy and openness, because the axis of the world is tilting to the East and we must tilt with it. It's not good enough anymore to be the link between Europe and America; we need another string to our bow. The dilemma as we are now seeing is that globalisation has changed the pace of everything: every time you are ahead of the posse, someone copies you, every time you think you've found a new idea, it is downloaded and customised.

There is nothing going on in Ireland that can't be copied better by Singapore. We have 10% corporation tax, Estonia responded with 0%. We invest in education, but Slovenia does likewise as does Malaysia, Scotland and Portugal. We speak English—well, the rest of the world is becoming bi-lingual very quickly and our inability to speak another language may soon become a hindrance. We are investing in infrastructure, well, so is everyone else. We are privatising, so are the rest of them. We have moved rapidly into services; this will give us time to breathe, but it, too, will be copied. Suddenly, it is becoming apparent that we do not have anything special that can be protected. Our shelf-life has been truncated and so we have to be constantly on the move, getting better, faster, smarter, keeping on our toes.

When once we thought we had a comparative advantage, we are now only seeing a temporary monopoly. Where once we were the only country at the multinational game, now India, China and Indonesia can photocopy the Irish game plan, implement it and execute it at a fraction of the cost. So what are we going to do? We have to find something unique.

To see how this new, interrelated world works, let's cast our minds back to slow sets. The cringy DJ with the made-up American-sounding name has just said, 'this time we're gonna slow it right down'. Close your eyes and imagine being a sweaty teenager to the soundtrack of Spandau Ballet's 'True', 'Nights in White Satin' or 'Careless Whisper'. The horror.

Wezzonomics

If, like me, you have red hair, you will be able to relate to the following neurotic way of understanding the new world in which we are now competing. The Wesley Disco Theory of Globalisation or Wezzonomics, is based on the fact that the world now works like a slow set at a teenage school disco. We can learn a lot about the challenges a country faces from looking at the challenges that our own long-suffering minority—redheads—faced at school discos.

We redheads have a secret code. We acknowledge each other privately, stand up for each other in job interviews, share each other's insecurities, remember the same playground taunts and generally know what it is like to be the silent, oppressed minority in a country of mousey-headed sameness. My carrot-topped brothers and sisters have endured the widest range of low-level psychological abuse imaginable. This begins with the innocuous but hurtful name-calling ranging from 'foxy' and 'redser' to the recently imported English derivative 'ginger' (pronounced with a hard g). There was always 'Bosco', 'carrot-head' and 'Duracell'. (My own personal favourite happens to be 'jam-rag head', levelled at me at an under-15s soccer match in Ringsend playing against an outfit called Cambridge Boys.)

As a young kid, I asked the barber in Dalkey when my hair would turn black. By that stage, Dom McClure, the barber, had cut three generations of McWilliams' redheads so he knew the score. Dom assured me that by the time I was ten, I would have a jet-black mane. You see, there were no redheaded cowboys or Action Men. Lee Majors didn't have a carrot top and even amongst footballers, there were no Keeganesque red perms.

The Redser neurosis gets more pronounced as we move into our teenage years. We tend, like Jewish comedians who build up great resilience due to childhood derision, to develop other attributes. We can talk, tell jokes, entertain and laugh, particularly at ourselves. Apparently we have fiery tempers, well, who could blame us? Redheads are always good at talking and we have loads of girl friends but no girlfriends, loads of teenagers who would tell you about their problems at home but none that would let you take their tops off.

Our problems were particularly acute, however, at the school disco because no-one would snog redhead lads when they were sober. So just when you were regaling a beauty with jokes, spoofs and general charm, disaster struck. Today, I still break out in a sweat at the opening lines of 'Stairway to Heaven'—because that was the signal for redheads to morph from witty, engaging personalities into swamp donkeys. The slow set was the pretty girl's cue to run a mile from the redhead she'd been happy to use as bait up to then. As soon as you turn around, the beauty in Sasparillas who was just seconds ago in your palm, throwing her head back, playing with her hair, giving you the glad eye, is up snogging a black-haired rugby jock from Stillorgan. You are the redhead wallflower and he is the flirt.

The global economy works in precisely the same way as a teenage disco. With no comparative advantage, the world is divided into countries that are redhead wallflowers and others that are flirts. The flirts get noticed, making the most of the assets and showing off. The wallflowers get left behind. The country with something unique, or at least the semblance of uniqueness to offer, gets the prize. Under conditions of Wezzonomics, in our world of copycat economies, where capital is mobile and no country can be pre-eminent at anything indefinitely, all people, companies and countries are at the same game. We are all trying to get noticed in the great global slow set. No country can afford to be a wallflower in an age where every country is on the make. Ireland, like all other competitive economies, has to get out there on the floor and do our thing.

If a country is lucky it might find something special, something unique that will give it an enduring advantage. What can Ireland do that might make us special? What makes us different? Education? That can be copied. EU membership? Not unique. Tax policy? Not unique. Geography? Nope. Capital? No, that's available to any country with a good idea and trade is open to almost anyone. People? Well, yes and no.

Is there anything in our history, our culture or brains that makes us different? What do we have, if anything, that no-one else has? What, to use the business vernacular, is our USP (unique selling point) or to use the technological term, what's our killer application? Remember we are small, so all we need is a tiny bit of the global action.

The most recent IDA advert for the nation suggests that it, too, is self-conscious about our ability to score at the slow-set. Our new national campaign is not a litany of stats about competitiveness, costs or the like. It is a Louis le Brocquy drawing of Bono under the title, 'The Irish Mind'. The idea behind the ad is that we think differently, the Irish have mental agility that others don't have and even if we are getting expensive, we're worth it, because we'll do your thinking for you. If that's the case, that is interesting but there aren't that many of us and capacity is crucial. Wouldn't it be brilliant if we could clone ourselves? Is there a stash of Irish minds somewhere or are we limited to what's on offer here? There's only four million of us.

——

Wait a second, are you sure that's all?

Chapter 18 ~

THE JACK CHARLTON
THEORY OF ECONOMICS

Soft Power

*'You were a crap player and you are a crap manager. The only reason
I have any dealings with you is that somehow you are the manager of
my country and you're not even Irish, you English cunt.'*

Allegedly, with that parting shot, Roy Keane walked out of the Irish
team at Saipan in 2002. But Roy had used the word that can never be
spoken in polite society. He used the E-word. He called Mick McCarthy
English and in so doing, opened up the debate about what constitutes
an Irishman. Is it enough to have Irish blood or do you have to be born
here? What about those who live in an Irish area of Queens or London,
have Irish parents and relations, feel themselves to be Irish, sing 'The
Fields of Athenry' yet sound Scouse, Bostonian, Cape-Townian,
Cockney or Canadian? Is the Diaspora truly Irish? Have we, the Irish
born here, forgotten that these people are the Irish footprint around
the world?

Ever since I was a kid, English and Scots of Irish descent have played
for the Irish national team. My first memories were of Steve Heighway
ghosting down the wing, playing balls inside to Tony Grealish, a man

who first played GAA at Wembley. Ray Houghton, who scored against England in the Necker Stadium and Italy in the Giants Stadium was born in Scotland. Kevin Sheedy, who equalised against England in the 1990 World Cup was born in England, as was, from squads at the time, McCarthy himself, Mark Lawrenson, Tony Galvin, Chris Hughton, Chris Morris, John Sheridan, Tony Cascarino, Terry Phelan, Andy Townsend and John Aldridge. Both Paul McGrath and David O'Leary, although brought up in Dublin, were born in London, sons of the exiles both. The list of Irishmen, sons of the Diaspora who have played and fought for Ireland, is endless.

The best Irish football teams, the most successful ones, were those in the Charlton era who represented a widest-possible definition of Irishness. At the time many soccer commentators lamented the fact that there were so many of what was termed derogatorily 'Plastic Paddies' on the team. But these men were the demographic echo of the 500,000 Irish emigrants who left for England from 1949-1961.[1] These were the teams of men and women who were driven out by De Valera's economic nationalism. Their sons pulled on the jersey and, as far as we were concerned, they were as Irish as anyone else. When Kevin Sheedy scored against the country in which he had been brought up, we didn't question his *bona fides*. When Alan McLoughlin's drive saved us at Windsor Park, Belfast in November 1993 in a night of sectarian madness, we didn't ask whether his Manchester accent made him any less one of us than Gary Kelly, Packie Bonner or Roy himself.

The sons of exiles added enormously to the potential of the team, giving it options and talents that we would not otherwise have had. This was a post-nationalist, national soccer team, the very essence of globalisation.

Now think about the Irish Diaspora. This is the one thing we have that so few other countries have. This is our biggest and most unique resource and yet we don't use it properly. Like Roy Keane, many of us are, if not hostile, not particularly welcoming to the Diaspora. But all our great-grandparents are from the same root. Now, four generations after the Famine, it could well be that the history and culture of the Irish people, one of the world's great clans, is about to fuse with the demands of the Irish State to ensure that we remain one of the world's most successful economic jurisdictions. This is the next part of the Irish story. The 21st-century economic narrative conceived in the demographics of 19th-century emigration. This is the future Generation Game.

Answering the Call

Olé, olé, olé. The chant went up from the back of the chartered plane. The 'kooshh' of cans opening, the off-key screeching, red faces and watery eyes all poured into Eircom jerseys. Itchy acrylic on skin and sweat stains—these tops had seen many battles. Lads hugging each other like brothers in arms: the Green Army was on tour again. Draped in the tricolour, Dutch in one hand, joking with the pretty airhostesses, the biggest non-Jewish tourist invasion Israel had ever seen was only four drunken hours from Ben Gurion Airport. 'Here we go, here we go, here we go.'

The notorious Israeli security treatment was seen as part of the fun, so when the guards kept apologising, the Green Army just sang on, unfazed. The echo in the airport made it seem like all of Ireland had rocked up. In truth, there were only a few thousand. Once we were kosher, it was out into the buses and off to Tel Aviv. A few thousand pink fellas hit the beach. The beautiful people parted like the Biblical Red Sea and the Paddies plunged into the void. A pageant of undaunted, blubbery ugliness played itself out. The buffed Israeli beach-volley-ballers had never seen the likes, nor had we seen Adonises like them, so both clans were equally fascinated.

The tribe was starting to gather. Two days before kick-off they were answering Ireland's call. Throughout the global jungle the drums had been heard. We were converging on Israel from all corners of the globe. We were recharging, replenishing and returning to something that gelled us together, something much greater than football. Unlike any other international soccer team, the Irish team's support is a miasma of accents and attitudes. When the tribe comes together it's a reunion. They were from everywhere, because the Irish are everywhere. Plastic Paddies with Gary-Barlow Manc' twangs mixed with Goodfellas from the Bronx, west-Belfast lads laughed with those just in from South Africa and Glaswegian Billy Connollys mixed with thousands of natives. Everyone was celebrating his roots, his place and his country. Shame the team was so poor. But you can't have everything.

Tel Aviv was buzzing, the bars were jammed and Molly Malone's was heaving. Pints were downed and stories of past campaigns swapped.

Amongst the footballing cognoscenti there's a distinct hierarchy of commitment. The highest rung on the pecking order goes to he who can credibly claim to have been at the most esoteric games the longest time ago. This is the footballing equivalent of the music snob who says that he preferred their 'earlier stuff'.

Anything from the pre-Jack era suggests a true trouper. An away trip from the 1970s is top-of-the-tree material. Anyone who remembers Gerry Daley's 1976 penalty against England at Wembley gets extra points automatically. Into the 1980s and any trip to Sofia counts. This was a time when Bulgaria stood for dodgy off-sides, brutal referees, redheaded Irish players getting sent off and points dropped, rather than what it stands for now—apartments, snake-oil salesmen, buy-to-let and equity release.

So the conversation ebbed and flowed as the fans tried to sort out who was an official, who was a provisional volunteer, who was a continuity member and who was the real deal.

When it was time to go, two of us hopped in a taxi. The driver, Yonni, chatted away about the traffic, the game and the fact that the Israelis expected to be beaten. Such humility is unusual for Israelis. He learned his English in the States. As we sneaked through the traffic, we spotted two Paddies looking like a demented Asterix-and-Obelix pairing, head to toe in the tricolour with giant green inflatable plastic shillelaghs, hammers and orange wigs. Surrounded by orthodox Jews, with ringlets in full 16th-century Polish shtetl garb, it's hard to say who looked weirder. We pulled in. The lads were desperate and with a few thousand Micks trying to get to the game on top of the 40,000 locals, they might have got stranded in the no-man's land between new Tel Aviv and the stadium.

Asterix and Obelix were from Cavan but had been in New Jersey since 1984 and had that odd American twang fused with pure borderlands drawl, not an 'r' to be heard. We started chatting, four Irishmen and an Israeli. It transpired that Yonni had worked in the Garden State as well.

'*Where did you work in Jersey*'? asked Obelix.
'*A moving company,*' said Yonni.
'*Which one?*'
'*Moishe's Movers.*'

'No way, so did I!' piped up my mate from the back of the cab.
'So did we!' said Asterix and everyone started roaring.

Sitting in a cab in Tel Aviv, four Paddies and a Jew, and four out of the five had worked illegally for the same removal company in the United States. That's globalisation for you.

The similarities between the wandering Irish and the wandering Jews have long been apparent, to the extent that a former American Jewish boss of mine described the Irish as the 'Jews who booze'. The main similarity is the fact that both are globalised tribes. Both only acquired a self-governing homeland in the past hundred years, having been persecuted for centuries, in our case by one bully, in their case by many. No two races have a Diaspora quite like us pair and in a globalised world, these exiles are an enormous resource for the homeland. We can learn from the Jews.

The Unbearable Lightness of Power

In the years ahead, the country with the best brains is going to thrive. The world will be divided by those countries that inherit 'hard power' and those that generate 'soft power'. Brain power is the ultimate soft power. In the past, hard economic power, such as steel and coal reserves, large populations and political or military clout mattered enormously. The country with the best and most natural resources won. Britain, Germany and France had these resources and for years, they were the most successful nations in Europe. Today hard power matters less. Take Russia for example. It still has more natural resources than any other country on earth, yet its population is falling. Russians see through the vanities of hard power and have decided either to emigrate or to stop having children. Hard power guarantees nothing.

We in Ireland are now in danger of becoming beguiled by hard economics because there is nothing harder than land and our land obsession has meant that most of the country's resources have been sucked into this most useless of assets, property. It is also the least modern, least tradable asset in a modern world and is the polar opposite to brain power. Land is fixed, dirty and unimaginative. Brain power is flexible, clean and, most importantly, renewable.

The problem for Ireland is that land is wrapped up with politics. And because of this, economics is replaced by what could be termed

Strokeonomics at times. Strokeonomics is where the State, through a licence, makes some asset artificially expensive. The State needs to abandon Strokeonomics and focus on the power of the future, soft power because soft power means brain power and creativity.

In general terms, the problem is that hard power is concentrated, soft power is diffuse; hard power is rigid, soft power is malleable; hard power is absolute, soft power is conditional; hard power is masculine, soft power feminine and ultimately, soft power is democratic, hard power autocratic.

Globalisation rewards countries that invest in their soft power. Look at the countries that have thrived in the past few years, such as Ireland (because of the multinationals), Singapore and Hong Kong. None of these countries is remotely capable of defending itself in the traditional sense of the word. Soft power is light power, power you can't measure. It is the power of imagination, the muscular strength of creativity. It is inspiration over perspiration. The lighter the economy, the more grey matter applied the better. The world will pay for ideas and the ideas are created by frontal lobes, wireless networks, imagery and branding.

Ireland has an extra advantage over the off-shore Asian city states: we are, or at least have become, tolerant. The link between political tolerance and intellectual curiosity and economic growth has been well established. Intolerant countries, as this place was up to 1980, stifle debate, exile their critics, hound their dissenters and strangle their economies. Intolerance makes light economies heavy. Business acumen flourishes when people are free to think up ideas, question authority, reinvent new ways and look at the world from a different angle. A free society and creative society can thus foster great artistic spirit and great entrepreneurial flair. The questioning mind can turn its hand to anything.

Joycean Economics

Trieste is an unusual place. It is an Italian city with Austrian habits. Rather than the typically Italian names, such as Totti, Fusco or Scappaticci, Triestine cafés have names such as Elsmansberger, Hinterseer and Bergdorff. It's a halfway house.

Coffee is served with strudel as well as biscotti. The architecture is pure *Mitteleuropa*—pastel shades and stark columns. Wiener schnitzel competes with pasta on local menus. One of the most interesting buildings is the old stock exchange, echoing the city's mercantile past. In its heyday, Trieste was the Austro-Hungarian Empire's main port. It was a bustling centre of trade, commerce and speculation.

And it was here, in September 1909, that Eva Joyce, James's younger sister, suggested that there was money in cinemas. For a city of 400,000, Trieste had loads of cinemas. In contrast, there wasn't even one in Ireland. Joyce was sold. He knew four local businessmen (with typically ambiguous and non-Italian Triestine surnames: Messrs Rebez, Caris, Machnich and Novak) who were making good money in cinemas and theatres. His sales pitch began.

'I know a city of 500,000 inhabitants where there is not a single cinema.'[2]

Joyce didn't give his secret away at first. He then produced a map of Ireland and pointed to Dublin, then Cork and finally Belfast—not one cinema among them—and close to a million people. Spreading his arms wildly over the whole territory like a demented general, Joyce persuaded the businessmen that if they moved quickly, the entire country was theirs for the taking.

They agreed instantly. Joyce had his venture capitalists. But what was in it for the original entrepreneur, James Joyce? As he had no capital, he negotiated 10 per cent for himself. Today, this capital would have been known in the jargon as 'sweat equity'.

Joyce set off for Ireland in October 1909. By December, the Volta cinema was open on Mary Street in Dublin, with Joyce as proprietor, Novak as manager and an unknown Italian on the projector. The *Evening Telegraph* covered the Volta's opening night on 20 December: 'James Joyce, who is in charge, has worked apparently indefatigably and deserves to be congratulated on the success of the inaugural exhibition.'

Two other ventures captivated Joyce at this time. The first was a plan to import skyrockets into Trieste, and the second (which would become enormously successful for subsequent Irish entrepreneurs) was to import Irish tweeds into Italy. Both projects were dropped and the Volta folded, but all three ventures reveal a portrait of the artist as a young entrepreneur.

Joyce, arguably our finest and definitely our most celebrated writer, saw no contradiction between artist and the entrepreneur. Rather, they

are complementary and at their root the artist and the entrepreneur are
similar. A fine business brain is as interested, irreverent, creative and as
alert as a fine artistic mind. The artist sees himself as outside the
mainstream. So, too, does the entrepreneur. Both celebrate the
individual over the collective. Both regard security with a certain
distance.

There is a striking similarity about their worldview. Both regard the
rest of society's obsession with certainty and security as bizarre.
Neither can bear the idea of working for someone else for a wage. The
very thought of taking orders from a bureaucrat strikes fear in both.
Working is about creating, beating the competition and expressing
themselves, not about pointless committees, political games and
promotion. They don't do corporate away-days. Tony O'Reilly, Dermot
Desmond and Sean Quinn have much more in common with Neil
Jordan, Colm Tóibín and Pat McCabe than either group imagines.

In the end, artists and entrepreneurs are the only people in society
who do not retire. They rarely become jaded or washed up and they are
precisely the type of people that give a country a competitive edge in a
period of globalisation, where hard power, borders and armies won't
contribute an ounce to national wealth. In addition, they are the only
people who can pay their way. They live on their wits. Ultimately, they
are both disobedient and the future will go to the disobedient, the
questioners—the lads at the back of class who asked why. The future
belongs to the messers. They are the ultimate soft-power exponents.
Globalisation demands that a country promotes these non-
conformists. If you don't have your own, then host them.

Another lesson that Joyce and Trieste teaches us is that geography
counts. Being in the right place at the right time helps enormously;
being in the wrong place means you just have to work harder. Distance
matters less than it used to, but it still matters.

One hundred years ago, Trieste was at the centre of Europe, nestled
under the Alps between the great Slavic nations to the east, the
Austrians to the North and the Italians to the west. In the first era of
globalisation it couldn't have been better placed. Like Dublin today it
boomed and was sufficiently interesting to attract the likes of Joyce in
the first place. It was loose, cosmopolitan and inquiring. Then disaster
struck; two world wars and Trieste went from being the centre of a
trading web to an isolated outpost stuck up against the Iron Curtain,

with no-one to trade with, no-one to engage and no-one to learn from. Trieste went into a tailspin. It became a remote eastern outpost of an Italy that had re-oriented herself completely to the West. By 1992, when I first visited, after 40 years of isolation, it had a death rattle about it.

Today, the city is flourishing. Life has been breathed into it by the opening up of Eastern Europe once more. The city hums with traders from the East. Chinese entrepreneurs have set up in the cheap rent areas down by the train station and the city has renovated the docks. It is a sophisticated Italian city with cafés, bars and, once more, is attracting creative people.

Attracting and keeping creative people is crucial to the making of a city or country. The lesson is that when the geo-political axis of hard power is shifting to the East, you do this by exercising soft power. In the years ahead, Ireland's geographical position, which in the past twenty years has been an overwhelming positive, will not be any more. We will need to become softer, not harder, more knowing rather than certain. Everything's up for grabs. But first, we have to turn economic logic on its head and look at things differently.

The Reverse Angle

From a certain angle, one of the many coincidences of the Irish economic boom is the correlation between the legalisation of homosexuality and the economic lift-off in the mid 1990s. Obviously, this sounds facetious but in the US, according to recent research, there is a direct correlation between the size of a gay community in a city and the city's economic prowess.[3] The Gaydar reading of a city is quite instructive. (A gaydar is a gay radar system for gay men who claim to be able to spot another gay man at fifty paces.) The stronger the Gaydar reading for a city, the more likely it will be rich.

Richard Florida observed in his excellent book, *The Creative Class,* that tolerance of a gay population implies openness and inventiveness. Societies that allow a gay scene to flourish are also likely to be more open-minded and attract in people who are, like Joyce, prepared to take a risk. We have seen this idea down through the ages, where tolerance and the values of the Enlightenment have gone hand in hand with economic growth. Back then, like Leopold Bloom, the only real foreigners in our midst were Jews. Societies that were tolerant of Jews were normally ones with the other attributes that aided wealth creation such as curiosity, education and vision. In many ways, today gays are the new Jews.

In the past, a tolerance of a Jewish population went hand-in-hand with political liberalism, economic adventure and, ultimately, wealth. The very word 'ghetto' comes from the Mediaeval Venetian word for Jewish area. Venice was also, at the time, the richest, most enquiring and most sophisticated society in Europe.

When that son of the Diaspora, Ray Houghton, scored against Italy in the 1994 World Cup, the majority of the Italian-Americans at the game on that balmy night were Sicilians. Why were a disproportionate number of Italian-Americans from Sicily? What happened to this prize of the Mediterranean that it got so poor and its people had to emigrate?

Up until the 15th century, Sicily had a lot going for it. It was rich, sophisticated, tolerant, mixed, multilingual and important. Empires from Rome to Carthage fought over this most significant of nautical prizes. He who controlled Sicily, controlled the Mediterranean, and he who controlled the Mediterranean, controlled the world.

Then, in 1492, a great tragedy befell Sicily.

The island was under the control of the crown of Castile and when Ferdinand and Isabella ordered the expulsion of all Jews and Moors from Spain, Sicily had to follow suit. Although there had been pogroms on the island, Jews had lived in Sicily since the time of Christ, in reasonable harmony with the locals.

They had played a disproportionate role in trade as well as in the professions, particularly those of medicine and pharmacy. Jewish astronomers had used their knowledge of the stars to guide Sicilian adventurers for years.

Realising this, the viceroy of Sicily dithered, sending emissaries to Madrid to explain the vital role the Jews were playing, but to no avail.

Gradually, a series of orders was passed which compelled Jews to sell their assets, pay all their outstanding debts immediately and, most ominously, barred them from bearing arms.

Eventually, in 1515, they were all expelled but were granted 'benevolent' permission to take 'the clothes on their back, a mattress, a woollen blanket, a pair of sheets, some small change and some food for the way'.[4]

Within a few years, what had been left of Sicilian trade after the devastating first decrees, collapsed to almost nothing. The Sicilian tradition of medicine and enquiry disappeared and entire neighbourhoods fell into rack and ruin. Economically, Sicily went into a tailspin.

Without the Jewish traders (who had formed only a tiny percentage of the population), no-one traded. Without trade, there was no cash and without cash, there were no jobs.

About two hundred years later, Charles II realised that he had to do something about the plight of Sicily and in particular something directly to promote trade. So what did he do? He tried to import Jews!

A New Hibernia

There seem to be two economic lessons we can draw from Sicily. The first lesson is that tolerance works. The Jews were creative, freewheeling and enterprising. They used their heads and tolerating them reflected a certain attitude in Sicilian society towards enquiry, irreverence and adventure.

Kicking out the Jews was emblematic of a more profound malaise. It represented an intolerance of creativity, an inclination towards censorship and a strangling of freedoms among the more inquiring minds of the greater Christian population as well. Economic history tells us that this is the road to ruin.

The second lesson is that intolerance, ignorance and superstition are much easier to acquire than to uproot because such attitudes pertain today in Sicily, contributing to its persistent backwardness.

Today, our flourishing gay scene is testament to a new openness in Ireland and a tolerance of the difference. Tolerance is a sign of strength and confidence. Once you tolerate the different ones, the questioning ones and the irreverent ones, you begin to build creative capital. Creative people who think on their wits are attracted to each other and congregate in clusters. Creative people build centres of soft power and, just as the Jews in the old days transcended restrictions placed on them by using their brains, creative people will also celebrate and contribute to places that encourage their disobedient minds.

But the Jews have their place now. They don't need to congregate together living in fear of persecution. The general view in Israel is that international Jewry doesn't need Israel as a last resort anymore. All the Jews that were likely to be persecuted have made it to Israel. Now the

Diaspora provides another function, one of money, influence and brainpower. Jews around the world, most of whom have no traceable ancestors there, come back to Israel to recharge their Jewishness. They support Israel materially and Israel gives them a feeling of authenticity and a sense of belonging. They are part of the tribe. From an economic perspective, the Jewish Diaspora expands Israel's human capital. By giving all Jews the right to return, the right to settle there, the country has created a tangible modern link with an intangible spiritual yearning. Both sides benefit.

Now look at Ireland, the country with a huge pool of well-educated exiles in America, Australia, Canada and Argentina. Not to mention the six million English people who have at least one Irish grandparent. How do we use them? Do we make them feel at home here? Do we see them as part of our human capital? Do we see ourselves as the dynamo for Irish culture or Irish belonging? Will we be the mothership for the tribe or will we, like sleveens, snigger behind our backs at our genetic cousins, while ripping them off?

It is time to see the island of Ireland in the 21st century as the cradle of a global nation. This nation extends all over the world, gelled together by the shared experience of previous generations. The exiles could be our labour force and in the new, soft world, their brains are invaluable. This is a feather-light economic army of grey matter who are at our disposal. All we have to do is imagine a New Hibernia.

Chapter 19

THE GLOBAL TRIBE

Homecoming

Sheila and Eileen Geoghegan turned up at the Irish Embassy in Buenos Aires in 2002, just months after the collapse of the Argentinian economy. The sisters, aged 18 and 20, wanted to claim Irish citizenship through their great-grandparents who had arrived on the *City of Dresden* in 1889. They wanted to come home. Sheila and Eileen have Irish blood on both sides going back to their eight great-grandparents. As far as they are concerned, Ireland is their homeland. They are from a town called Duggan north of Buenos Aires where 60% of the people can trace their ancestors back to County Westmeath. English is their first language. They were taught by Irish nuns and priests. They know the words to 'Danny Boy'. Their parents still speak with midlands accents. They are part of a 500,000-strong Irish Argentinian population.

Yet both were refused entry visas. They did not merit consideration. They were one generation too late. Had their grandparents been born here, they would have qualified, but as their grandmother, Mabel Ryan, who speaks with a flat Mullingar accent, was born in Argentina, the family were not Irish enough.

We refused entry to two young women, educated, sophisticated, willing to work, with invaluable ties to Latin America, fluent in the second-most-widespread language in the world and most crucially, committed emotionally to Ireland. If brain power is soft power, networks are invaluable and people are the only asset that counts in our new competitive world, then surely this refusal makes no sense.

These people are potentially pioneer immigrants. People who want to come home, with a deep, vested interest in our culture and we snub them. These are the people who keep the Irish flag flying in the remotest parts of the world, the people who suffered most under our colonial past, who sent money home to Ireland when we hadn't a bean and who took other destitute Irish into their communities when wave after wave arrived on the docks in Argentina. They are emotionally drawn to us, they are our history and yet modern Ireland gives them the finger.

But the Diaspora is our best economic asset. We have little else. There are 3.5 million Irish citizens living outside the country. But the greater Diaspora is considerably bigger. In economic terms, the 70 million-strong Irish tribe is the 21st-century equivalent of a huge oil deposit. In the same way as oil guarantees Saudi Arabia's future, the Irish tribe is the key to Ireland's prosperity in the next century.

Unlike oil, because the tribe exists inside the minds of millions of Irish people around the world, if we cultivate it properly, it is a resource that won't run out.

People are the natural resource of the future and we have the smartest and most numerous global Diaspora. For example, of the 34 million Irish-Americans registered in the 2005 census, 31% have bachelor's degrees or higher. That's over 11 million people. More than 30 million Irish-Americans have a high-school diploma. At 91% of the total Irish-American population with secondary education,[1] our American cousins are considerably better educated than us, both proportionally and actually.

40% of Irish-Americans are either professionals or work in management and 72% are home owners. The average income of an Irish-American household is $53,000.[2] This puts them at the top of the ethnic league after the Jews, in terms of education, income and social class. Close to 900,000 Irish-Americans speak another language other than English. Their average age is 37, but there are over 10 million Irish-Americans under 18.[3]

This is an extraordinary reservoir of talent in our feather-light, weightless world. The Irish-Americans define themselves as Irish: as far as they are concerned this is where they come from, this is their homeland and while they are American, they have a deep affection for and affiliation to this country. The 3.8 million Irish-Canadians, the 1.9 million Irish Australians and the half-million Irish-Argentinians have similar profiles in terms of education and income.[4]

As the world is involved in a global talent war, a talent aristocracy will emerge in the years ahead. The country that thrives will be the country that either has or can attract the best and brightest. Think about the economic areas where soft power is most in evidence: it is in the service area. Last year service exports from Ireland increased by 16%.[5] This is the impact of the soft-power industries such as banking and insurance which we are good at. In contrast, the Chinese can compete with us in the export of hard stuff such as manufacturing goods. In Ireland, these exports have been flat for six years. As we saw from our visit to Shanghai, there is no point playing this game. The future is services and the key to services is brainpower and the key to brainpower is capacity and the key to capacity is the Diaspora. It gives Ireland the largest, best-educated, English-speaking network in the world. This is not a virtual community. It is the real thing and it is waiting to be tapped. It is our lever into the 21st century.

In the same way as the sons of exiles such as Ray Houghton, John Aldridge, John Sheridan, Andy Townsend and the rest, fused with homegrown Irish talent to create the most successful Irish football team ever, the Diaspora would have a similar effect on the economy. It would expand our reservoir of talent and open up opportunities that we could not otherwise avail of.

The exiles come in all shapes and sizes. Some are highly educated, some are not. But what they all have is an attachment to this country and while integrating into the host country, these people have preserved an Ireland in their heads which is enduring. A few days spent just across the Irish Sea in Liverpool sheds some light on the various different shades of green to be found all around the globe.

7 November 2006

The 7.55 am Ryanair FR442—one of the hundreds of jets Mick O'Leary bought in the post-9/11 Boeing fire-sale—takes off on time, bound for Liverpool. Out past the suburbs, over the giant steel-and-chrome motorway slug of commuting morning traffic and straight across the Irish Sea. It is only thirty-five minutes to John Lennon International.

As you come through security, the first sign welcoming you to England tells you that 'Blackpool is Brilliant'.

Surely John Lennon's granddad—the Dublin seaman, Jack Lennon, or his grandmother Mary Maguire—never thought anything would be named after one of their own when they both, like millions of other Irish, made the same trip, never to return home?

The Croxteth orchestra of sirens, shouting kids and screaming mothers is momentarily drowned out by the traffic on the East Lancs. This place is home to the longest continuous Catholic congregation in the North of England. The Blood of the Martyrs Catholic Church—named according to the local priest, Father Inch, because Catholicism in this part of England was maintained by the blood of the martyrs—is where Wayne Rooney was baptised and confirmed a Catholic.

Father Inch is a Toffee true and true. Everton Football Club is the Irish team in Liverpool and it's no surprise therefore, that Rooney is a Blue.

Bob Pendleton, the Evertonian who scouted Rooney, remembers seeing young Wayne for the first time aged nine. Jeanette, his mother, would take him and his two brothers on the bus down to Fazakerly to play for Copplehouse in the Walton and Kirkdale Junior League. Wayne was simply in a different class to all the other kids. Other second-generation Irish kids, Jamie Carragher, Danny Murphy and Steve McManaman also came from the same schoolboy league in the years before Rooney, but talented as they were, none of them had the scouts whispering the way Rooney did. Bob remembers that Rooney was so keen to play and get on with the game that when the ball was kicked over the walls into Everton Cemetery next door it was always Wayne who hurtled over the wall to get the ball.

The cemetery itself tells the story of Liverpool's immigrants. You can see that Liverpool was a pretty multicultural place way before most other English cities. There is a huge Jewish part, host to Ringo Starr's people, who arrived in the great Jewish migrations from Eastern Europe of the late 19th century, while today, enormous Chinese mausoleums testify to the changing immigrant aristocracy in modern Liverpool. Quite apart from the other immigrant tribes, the names on the headstones evidence the presence and passing of the biggest minority—O'Briens, Forans, O'Haras, McCabes and Kellys.

It saddens Bob—given the joy Wayne brought even as a child playing here—that the roof of the dressing rooms at Fazakerly was daubed for weeks on end with 'Rooney You Scab', when he signed for United.

Down the road, past East Derby, is The Western Approaches, the Rooney family local. There's something about the smashed car windscreen glass, which has fragmented into thousands of particles, that tells you you'd better walk in here with a local. It's early afternoon, school's just finished and skinny young lads on bikes are doing wheelies, trying to avoid the teenage mothers whose top-of-the-range strollers suggest that, despite the recent Revenue assessment, the Giro alone isn't the only income in the house.

There's a small lad with no neck poured into an Everton strip, swearing at a William Hill betting slip, while a few women in pink pyjamas are hanging around Cost Cutters, having a smoke and a natter. No-neck steals up behind one of the grans and takes her from behind. Everyone pisses themselves and no-neck makes off bright red from the laughing.

A Citroen Saxo, weighed down by an enormous subwoofer blasts rap out at the traffic lights. 'Slapper', shouts one of the young lads, as he grabs his crotch and thrusts in her direction, spitting at the same time. The girl in the passenger seat, in pristine white Juicy Couture, hoop-de-hoop earrings and full Croydon facelift, gives him the licked finger as she pulls off. Older ladies with tartan trolleys wait patiently at the bus stop, oblivious to the pubescent girls from Saint Swithin's Primary scratching their fellas' names on the shelter.

Bob, the local Everton scout, who met his missus in the Western, points me up to the bar. Gerard Houllier was amazed, he said, when looking for talent that there were no black kids in Croxteth.

This is an Irish neck of the woods. Most people here are straight from Scotland Road—the traditional home of the Liverpool Irish. In fact, Scotland Road was so Irish that, in the late 19th century, it returned an Irish Home Rule MP for years. The Western is simply Costigans on Scotty Road 40 years on—the same people, same names and the same culture.

The door opens grudgingly. We are in familiar surrounding of red carpet, screwed-down barstools, flock wallpaper, posters advertising bingo and tired men and women. Skinny old men with hollow cheeks scan their betting stubs, while local brazzers' reveal a bit too much on top, as they shout across the bar for their fourth Smirnoff Ice. We get hunkered down, chatting with a few punters on the Irish theme.

> 'Alright Bob.'
>
> 'Couple of lagers please.'
>
> 'Wayne Rooney's never,' says a visiting Geordie whose two loves are Newcastle and Everton.
>
> 'He is, you know, just look at the name. No Longshanks were ever called Rooney. Pure Paddy.'
>
> 'Not one English ounce.'
>
> 'Not a drop?'
>
> 'He's pure Scotty Road Irish.'
>
> 'On both sides?'
>
> 'Yep, Holy Cross parish.'
>
> 'On the Morry side too?'
>
> 'Sure Jeanette's ma's name's Patricia Fitzsimons.'
>
> 'Good job Jack Charlton didn't see him when he was a nipper.'
>
> 'Too right.'
>
> 'How far back?'
>
> 'Four generations.'
>
> 'No fucking way.'
>
> 'He's hardly English at all.'
>
> 'Just look at him—he looks like a GAA player!'
>
> 'Two more pints of lager please, a whiskey chaser, a pack of Lamberts and one for yourself.'

An old lad with a cap pulled down over the side of his face, swaggers up to the bar and starts singing. He's introduced as Billy. We buy him a pint and talk about football.

Billy Morry married Patricia Fitzsimons in St Dominic's Church, just off Scotty Road. When the priest, Fr McNamee heard Billy's name, he double-checked with Patricia that he wasn't 'Orange'. Once it was established he was a good Irish Catholic, the marriage went ahead.

Their daughter Jeanette married Wayne Rooney and had three sons Wayne, Graham and John.

At a small table, close to the loo, sits Patricia Fitzsimons, Wayne Rooney's nan. Even before Wayne exploded onto the scene, Patricia

Fitzsimons, whose lot are from Derry, was famous locally for being born on the 17 March, St Patrick's Day—hence the name Patricia. The first thing you notice is the crucifix and her clear, strong blue eyes. Straight off, she starts referring to herself as Irish and to me as 'one of our own'. Within seconds she's back in 1960s' Liverpool, sharing memories of running away from the King Billys (as she calls them) on the 12th of July, reiterating just how sectarian the city was until recently.

The Western is rocking now. A few winners, a few pints and the place is alive. It's Monday afternoon, late October and Patricia is talking about some German professor who claims to be Wayne's half brother. Billy's still reminiscing about sectarian scraps in the 1960s and 'orangies' throwing bricks at his Patricia when she was looking beautiful in her finest Hibernian Irish dancing costume at the top of the St Patrick's Day Parade.

The Western is the type of pub that works. Located at the end of the street where young Rooney first went to school at Our Lady of St Swithin's Catholic Primary, it might not be pretty, but it, and the adjacent Our Lady of the Martyrs Church, where Father Inch baptised Wayne, are at the heart of this community.

Across the road is St John Bosco Catholic School for girls where one Miss Colleen McLoughlin graduated three years ago and within a hundred yards, is De La Salle Brothers Catholic Secondary School for Boys, where the man-child Rooney honed his footballing skills.

All the older people, like Patricia Fitzsimons, were moved here in the slum clearances of the late 1940s and 1950s. They, like thousands of Irish before them, lived in the Catholic area of Scotland Road or 'Scotty Road', as they call it. Scotty is down by the docks, the first port of call for desperate Irish emigrants who flooded Liverpool for over 100 years after the Famine.

Like its black community, Liverpool hosts the oldest Irish community in Britain and Irish immigrants and their descendents have been central to the development of the city. As Liverpool's economic strength declined, so, too, did new arrivals from Ireland. Yet, even today, when only 10% of the population of England is Catholic, 60% of Croxteth's children are baptised Catholic. They are Irish, Catholic, Evertonians and proud of it.

'*Could Wayne have played for Ireland?*' I whispered, thinking of all those Plastic Paddies who'd worn the Green. And what about the

Diaspora lads who'd played the other way—four recent English captains, Kevin Keegan, Steve McMahon, Martin Keown and Tony Adams?

'*Nah,*' replied Patricia, '*He's English on the outside.*' She looked up, '*but, pure Irish on the inside.*'

Patricia Fitzsimons paused. She checked her betting slip, looked up again: '*He's a half-breed.*'

———

That is what the exiles are—they are half-breeds. In England, they are genetically Irish, environmentally English. They are the echo of the millions who left and many millions like Wayne Rooney's granny are emotionally connected. Whether in sport or business, these people are our unique resource.

Like Rooney's great-grandparents, in the past we Irish have revealed that we want to play on the bigger stage and to do this we will travel, trade and settle, if necessary. We have never been afraid of the big bad world, in fact we have always wanted to get out there and breathe it in. Consider Dublin airport: in 2006, 21 million people used the airport, coming, going, buying and selling. There are only four million of us. Think about what this means in proportional terms. If the English—a great mercantile nation—travelled as much as we did, Heathrow would be carrying 252 million people rather than the 67 million it carries at the moment. Use of the airport reveals just how globalised we are.

History suggests that the Irish have always wanted to transcend the physical boundaries of geography and demography. In a globalised world, the Diaspora gives us this opportunity.

We are in a world where the notion of borders is gone and Ireland has adapted well to this new arrangement. Just think about the fact that the proportion of foreign workers has increased from 6% of our workforce to 12% in barely two-and-half years.[6] Few other countries have experienced this level of penetration of its culture with little or precious little racism. We can adjust, we can jettison, we can reinvent.

That's not to say that there are no limits to immigration; there are, and indeed, in the new world, foreign workers can only bring us so far.

But just think about the opportunity we are missing by treating these people simply as economic migrants rather than economic ambassadors. Think about the enormous waste of talent that is the Chinese doctoral student working in Centra. In a weightless world their connections to their home countries are priceless.

It is very clear that the world now is one where manufacturing will be done in the East and the services bit, the branding, the banking, the accounting, the taxation and the marketing will be done in the West, where the goods will be sold. Ireland needs to be a hub for all the better-paid service jobs in that chain. But how do we do it?

First, we've got to recognise that we have things that the East doesn't have. We have one of the most sophisticated banking systems in the world and our legal system, our insurance industry and our professional backup, like lawyers and accountants are as good as any. These are all things that China, Russia and even India don't have and will not have for some years. We can offer them these services but the key is not to do this via the traditional IDA route of trade delegations and the like. The key is the Chinese students working in Spar, the Polish lab technicians working on the site or the Lithuanian scientists cleaning our houses. These people are our new trade delegations. We should position ourselves as a hot-house facility for immigrant talent so that future Chinese businesses are domiciled in Ireland, make things in China and export to Poland. This is the web that we have to weave around the world, so that our immigrants achieve their potential and we become the mercantile capital of the new world. In the same way as our Diaspora emigrated to transcend the limitations that geography imposed on them, hot-housing immigrant talent could allow Irish firms to transcend the same limitations again. Remember, it is people who count in the weightless global economy and we now have them in abundance. One answer to the global talent conundrum is staring us in the face every time we order a skinny latte in Insomnia. Let's galvanise it.

New, Old Voices
As well as the global reach these new citizens of Ireland give us and the professional service infrastructure we could give them, we have a unique resource. We have to look back to look forward. And here we find that the ace is our exiles who are our passport onto the larger stage. The global Irish tribe is a club of which we are the founder members.

It is difficult to conceive of Ireland or Irishness without the Diaspora and yet we are snooty about their bona fides. Many of us seem to be caught in a narrow view of Irishness. For some reason, we don't consider the Diaspora authentic. Maybe we are still stuck in the peasant mindset that has caused generations of small-minded people to somehow look down on those who left. However, given the peculiarities of the tribe, it would seem illogical to consider the Irish and the Irish story as beginning and ending at the borders of the 26-county Republic. If anything, the Republic is a phase in Irish development. A phase which was totally appropriate in a period of closed borders, of unfettered national sovereignty and of post-Occupation neurosis. But that's all over. Think about the behaviour of the fans at Croke Park during the singing of 'God Save the Queen' in February 2007. Most of us understand why the English national anthem might be problematic at Croke Park. We are not unaware of our history, but we can put it in context and move on. The only people making an issue of the English national anthem were atavistic nationalists and the Jagger Generation media commentators who seem obsessed with these tokenist gestures.

Ireland is a post-nationalist country, where one in ten is foreign-born, where we travel more than anyone else, are open to every influence imaginable and where the vast majority are flexible about the issue of what it means to be Irish. So in 2007, many of us celebrated the Irish cricket team's victory over Pakistan in the World Cup, a team made up of a mixture of Australian and South African sons of exiles, local lads, Ulster Protestants and immigrants who have arrived here in the past few years, to play a game which was hounded out of this country when nationalism was a narrow furrow. The world has changed and so have the Irish.

The exiles have paved this way for us. Without them Ireland wouldn't be a global brand, we wouldn't have the disproportionate footprint we have, nor would we get the welcome we do in every small town in the US, Australia, Canada or South Africa.

Where we, the 'marooned Irish' were traditional, they, the 'wandering Irish' were modern; we were atavistic, they were progressive; we were closed, they were open; we were a failure, they were a success; we were definitive, they were mercurial; we were rooted, they were free; we were rural, they were urban; we were narrow, they were broad; we were fixed, they were nomadic; we were protectionist, they were free-marketers; and above all we were exclusive, they were promiscuous. We were Hibernian, they were Cosmopolitan. They are our alter-ego. We need them now as much as they ever needed us. It was, and will be, a perfect fusion.

In narrow terms, the emotional attachment of the Diaspora has been instrumental in the boom of the past 20 years. Taxes and education apart, the sentimentality of many third- and fourth-generation Irish-American corporate executives has contributed greatly to the build-up of the multinationals here.

'Of course it mattered,' responded Jack Welch, former CEO and Chairman of GE, when asked whether being of Irish descent was a factor in investment decisions to Ireland from America. He is in no doubt about this. GE Capital has invested heavily in Ireland and Dublin has been its European headquarters for years. Welch, probably the most fêted executive in American corporate history and grandson of a Cork small farmer, was brought up in what he described as a 'working-class Irish area of Salem, Massachusetts'. When it came to attracting multinationals, Ireland was pushing on a half-open door that was hung by Irish Americans.

Politically, this resource is best illustrated by the fact that we are the only country in the world guaranteed a day in every US President's diary to focus purely on our issues. This level of political access, coupled with the enthusiasm of millions of exiles who, if given half a chance, would build this country, is a combination that other countries can only dream of. Our prominence in the United Nations is also helped enormously by the Diaspora because the collective image of Ireland as an honest broker with a post colonial empathy is as much a function of the exiled millions as any initiative of Iveagh House. The Diaspora is our story, our most unique resource and our future.

Yet we ignore it. This is a bit like the Arabs ignoring oil.

'Oh, yes, Mustafa, Tariq tells me that there is oil under the desert. But not to worry, I'm just going to carry on being a nomadic camel-herd!'

'Too right, Ahmed, couldn't have put it better myself.'

Culture Matters

We refuse two Irish-Argentinians entry visas. A third-generation Irish American, who has been told from boyhood that he is Irish, whose entire identity is wrapped up in the history of our people, who attended the Irish University Notre Dame, is not allowed to work or live here without a visa. Yet we allow in others with no affinity to the country.

In the early months of 2007 several thousand Bulgarians and Romanians who have no connection with Ireland came through Dublin airport. The logistical tasks associated with their assimilation should not be underestimated. But what greater right do they have to live in Ireland than our Irish-American, Irish-Australian or Irish-Argentinian cousins?

Although it is not politically correct to say so, it is easier to integrate a third- or fourth-generation Irish-American family who have a vested interest in this country than it is a Moroccan Muslim family with French passports who don't speak the language, some of whom wear the veil or believe in arranged marriages. In a world of migration, the idea that everyone is the same is nonsensical. If your objective with immigration is to enhance the economic growth without undermining the fabric of society, then not all immigrants are the same. By contrast, if the Irish project over the coming century is to erase Irishness as we know it and create a multicultural jigsaw where 'Irishness' in Ireland is seen as being on a par with other cultures and nations in Ireland, then maybe the idea of embracing the Diaspora can't fly. However, reason suggests that there are ethnic bonds, commonality and traditions that, as a nation, we value and that we would like to keep. At the moment, the free movement of people around the EU is creating an immigration policy in Ireland which is at odds with our history. If we wanted to embrace our Diaspora, it would put us on a collision course with the EU. The cultural implications for Ireland of an EU open-borders policy are not in Ireland's interest.

Culture matters and immigration is about broad culture, not just narrow financial calculations. Sometimes economics doesn't understand that. The limitation of messianic economic solutions which we can read in the *Economist*, *Time* Magazine, *Business Week* or the *Wall Street Journal* is that they ignore culture. If you read an MBA textbook or listen to spokespeople from IBEC, the answer to the talent conundrum seems to rest with importing a hundred thousand Indian or Pakistani computer programmers or whatever the decided talent deficiency is. Problem solved.

But as we have seen, you import 'workers' and you get 'people' with their own different customs, religions and values. These may well be consistent with our values, as is the case with Poles and Lithuanians who are white and Christian, but these are a tiny fraction of the potential immigrants that want to move. Our population may have increased by 46% since 1966, however, we are still just 0.06% of the world's total. We are tiny and the global migratory flows are enormous.

This year, migration has reached its highest level ever, according to the International Organisation for Migration (IOM). The Geneva-based organisation says there are now about 150 million people on the move worldwide—just under 3% of the world population. That is 30 million more than 10 years ago and 37 times the population of Ireland.

If immigrants' values are stronger, less cosmopolitan and more alien to ours, they will not integrate and whatever economic value these people bring, it will be undermined by the social tensions they inflame.

The trick is balancing economic and cultural goals, so that the economy doesn't suffer by us being too closed, nor does Irishness get washed away by us being too open. We have to achieve the fine balance between Hibernianism and Cosmopolitanism. This dilemma is at the heart of many people's fears about globalisation. How can we become more global without losing everything that makes us Irish in the first place?

This question is being asked in every country in Europe constantly. Denmark, for so long a country associated with tolerance and liberalism, has enacted some of the most restrictive immigration legislation in Europe because the Danes have decided that their culture is not strong enough to withstand mass immigration and their culture matters. The Netherlands, for centuries the country which offered sanctuary for dissenters and outcasts, from Spain's Sephardic Jews to Protestant sects of every sort in the 17th and 18th century, has now said enough. Pym Forteyn in 2002 tapped into the popular mood when he claimed that Holland was full and that further immigration threatened the very tolerant society that welcomed immigrants in the first place. France has always insisted on allegiance to France over multiculturalism. In recent years this has been challenged but President Sarkozy has made it clear that France will not tolerate any further erosion of French values. Even Britain, for so long the model for multiculturalism, has begun to question its policies.

The political lesson of immigration, as we have seen from our Diasporic history, is that the mass movement of people always causes dislocation. That dislocation is easier to deal with if the immigrants are from the same tribe. We can see this in Israel which is the quintessential immigrant society. When waves and waves of Jewish migrants, most evident in the one million Russian Jews who touched down between 1989 and 1992, arrive in Israel, the society goes through internal turmoil but it settles again in time. Immigration is easier to deal with if there is a sense of a national project, where the home culture is being strengthened, rather than diluted, by the new citizens.

If we get this right, Ireland will ascend into the aristocracy of talent that defines the modern global economy without risking a culture war and the type of problems we are seeing in European countries. If we get it wrong, we will possibly see racial tensions, allied to an economic underperformance if some immigrants decide, as certain immigrants to the UK have done, to opt out of the mainstream. Many Muslim immigrants in the UK regard themselves as an exception, as different and ultimately, in opposition to the host country's values and traditions. No country should willingly entertain this type of death-wish. We can avoid this, if we think on our feet now. The choice is either the aristocracy of talent or the risk of social unrest.

Opening up to the Diaspora is the only option which allows us to become more globalised and more Irish at the same time. Equally, by recharging the latent Irishness in the Diaspora, we extend our country's reach all around the globe. This can only be good for business and culture—a delicious Joycean fusion of the artist and the entrepreneur playing itself out in the mind of the Diaspora. And this in a world where there are no comparative competitive advantages, only temporary monopolies, where every country is trying to attract the right type of immigrants, where brain power, networks and know-how are key, the Diaspora gives us a permanent advantage. The Irish labour market goes from two million to a possible 70 million. This is 70 million new ways of doing things, new ideas and an almost missionary zeal to build the country, to make the place that their ancestors fled from, better for good.

This is a muscular, almost Zionist project. The difference between Zionism Irish-style and Zionism Israeli-style is that we have no-one to kick out. There are no Palestinians here. There were eight million of us here in 1841: there are only a little over five million on the island today. This threatens nobody. In fact, our exiles include the Ulster Scots exiles in Canada and the southern states of the US as much as the Catholic Irish Diaspora all over the world. The St Andrews Agreement and the welcome change in the rhetoric of Ian Paisley, implies that what is good for the goose is good for the gander. Seeing the economy in terms of the island is doubtless the only way forward. And most crucially for all of us, the labour market would expand exponentially without the cultural or racial downside of new ethnic tensions.

In terms of concrete steps, the first move would be to extend Irish citizenship to the Diaspora, with ancestors going back at least to the Famine. At the moment there is a two-generation cut-off point. The central aim is to encourage a certain proportion of the Diaspora to come home and emigrate from wherever they are, to settle in Ireland. Many people might argue that we can't do this as we are not prepared infrastructurally for them. Are we any more prepared for the Bulgarians, Romanians and others who can come here and settle every day without having any connection to the country?

Bringing home some of the Diaspora hits the sweet spot where the economic logic of the market state fuses with the traditional concerns of the nation state. It would leave Ireland in a win-win situation. We could be more Hibernian yet more cosmopolitan at the same time.

Do the Right Thing

But would they come? Why would someone from Savannah, Georgia or Cape Town or even Camden Town pack up and emigrate to Ireland?

This used to be the type of question that knocked ideas like this down in the past, yet in the last five years, thousands of immigrants have come to see Ireland as a viable place to live. We are now receiving in more migrants per head than any other country in the Western World; the idea that this is not an attractive place to live is nonsensical. For example, while there are 39,000 Italians in London,[7] there are 15,000 in Dublin. Of the new immigrants to Ireland, 200,000 have come from Britain,[8] suggesting that although money is driving many Poles, Lithuanians and others here, because the gap between Irish and

English wages is small, there is every reason to believe that second-generation Irish people come here because they want to.

But traditionally migration has always been more driven by push factors rather than pull factors and, as the Irish have been successful migrants, the tribe now lives in sought-after parts of the world such as America, Canada, Britain, Australia and Argentina, followed then by smaller groups in New Zealand, South Africa and continental Europe. The tribe isn't going to be pushed out of anywhere. So how would we pull them here, how would we make Ireland accessible to the sons of our ancestors? How do we make Ireland the mother ship of a global tribe, so that people can come home, recharge their Irishness and go back out into the world again, satisfied that they know where they come from and who they are?

In melting-pot societies like America and Britain, the last few years have seen a surge in interest in ethnicity and authenticity. The exiles want to find out about themselves. Everyone is afraid of sameness; everyone wants a story, something that makes them unique. In the past few years there has been a boom in genealogy in the UK as people want to know who they are and where they come from. A study in 2001 suggested that one in four English people claim to have some Irish background.[9] If this is true, that is some fourteen million people. This means that today there are close to three times as many Irish in Britain as 'real Irish' in Ireland. They have answered the Roy Keane taunts: sorry, Roy we feel Irish, somewhere, deep down.

This affinity with Irish roots is particularly marked amongst younger people, 42% of whom claim to be part Irish.[10] This implausible figure may reflect the recent phenomenon whereby all things Irish are considered hip in England. Young Londoners, never slow to spot the trend, are committed. Close to 80% claim to have Irish ancestry![11]

The Irish-Americans have always had this ethnic solidarity largely as a result of their own political experience but those in Britain are now much more attached. The tribe wants to look to Ireland. This idea that people need a unique story will get stronger in a multinational, cosmopolitan world. Globalised culture leaves millions of orphans in its wake who want to belong.

This factor might explain why, in 1986, only 899,000, or 5.5% of Australians considered themselves Irish. By 2001, this figure had jumped to 1.9 million or 8.9% of the total Aussie population.[12] Ireland and Irishness has become more attractive and this is an extraordinary development that has enormous economic and cultural ramifications.

When we native Irish hear Americans longingly talking about where their grandparents came from, we do not connect with what they are saying. These rootless Irish-Americans, Canadians and Australians are homesick. Now, we have the opportunity to give them back that spiritual sense of identity for which they long, while at the same time using them to widen Irish commercial interests all over the world and to come back and help us make this economy the strongest in Europe, if not in the world. We can save their soul and they can build our economy.

A potential problem lies in the implications of this approach for our EU commitment. In fact, the EU cannot prevent countries from altering their citizenship laws and we would only be following the example of the EU's largest country. Germany's citizenship laws operate on the basis of German descent which allowed thousands of Volga Germans, native Germans living in southern Russia, to return to Germany after the dissolution of the Soviet Union. Other EU countries operate similar systems but none has a Diaspora like the Irish. Equally, the point of this move is to transcend today's political arrangements, which are based on the nation state, and proceed into a borderless world defined more by trade than territory, space more than soil.

In addition to the economic arguments, this is also the right thing to do. For years, when we were poor, emigrant remittances from the tribe kept us afloat; now that we are rich, it is time to give something back.

So, how do we go about strengthening our economy, upgrading our labour force, expanding Irish culture and making the Irish global footprint even bigger and more powerful? How do we reinvent a national project for the 21st century? How do we see our history as part of an economic continuum? And how can we refashion the historical catastrophe of the 19th century into the demographic and economic windfall of the 21st century, which consolidates and strengthens the achievements of the late-20th century?

This is the big Generation Game. How do we play it? Globalisation gives us this chance; let's grab it.

Chapter 20 ∽

THE GENERATION GAME

Re-imagining Ireland

One hundred years ago, Irish writers, academics and dreamers imagined a New Ireland. This New Ireland would be free from English domination, free to do as she pleased, free to express herself and to frame her own destiny. But the achievement of geographical and political sovereignty should be looked at as only the first chapter of independence for the Irish nation.

In the first phase of Irish independence, Ireland was a narrow-gauge 26-county concept. For the first 70 years of its existence, from 1922 to 1992, the limits of this ambition were not so evident because the world was a place of fixed borders, territorial wars, managed trade, ideological power blocks and very little international migration. Given the global background noise, such a limited geographic definition of Irishness was understandable.

In contrast, the modern world is a nomadic one, of free movement of practically everything. People are on the move constantly. Borders have collapsed and traditional governments are confused as to how to control this process. It's a MySpace world of instant communities bound together by interests, ideas, knowledge and opinions downloaded and digested in milliseconds.

Now is the age of rule-breakers, border-crossers and itinerants, where power is in the mind and not vested in some all-knowing State. Globalisation is the economic incarnation of Cosmopolitanism. It is the era of the individual and groups of individuals bonded together by choice, not force. It is a bottom-up, rather than top-down age. In this world, the winners will be urban, literate, mobile and intellectually flexible. Those who have been exiled, suffered the exodus and rebuilt the tribe in hostile environments by living on their wits, will be tooled up for the challenges ahead. In contrast, those who have depended on force, State power and hard and heavy muscle will be caught flat-footed.

Soft power has taken over from hard power. The small, like Ireland, have become rich and the big, like Russia, have become poor. What is inside the heads of all of us is far more important than what lies buried beneath the soil. In fact, in a world where speed of adjustment is crucial, smallness, for the first time in history, is an invaluable asset. The small can be quick. The future will belong not to those countries that are cheap, but those that are fast. In the years ahead, the more cosmopolitan the country, the more open to ideas, the greater willingness to learn while at the same time discard what isn't needed, the brighter its prospects.

Quite apart from the new global reality, which should of itself get us thinking, the coming slowdown in Ireland should focus our minds and be seen as a chance to go back to the drawing board. A house-price collapse is not a long-term disaster; it is an opportunity to re-prioritise. For example, in 1990, Finland suffered a dramatic house-price slump. The Finns reacted to this positively with a root-and-branch reform of their society. They realised that land and land speculation were fool's gold, so they invested heavily in technology and education. They even went as far as improving the health of the nation by successfully changing the national diet. They re-invented themselves. Today, Finland tops almost every index of political, social and economic achievement. Ireland should do something similar—not by copying the Finns, but by playing to our own strengths.

We need, once more, to re-imagine Ireland and to use all the resources at our disposal to take advantage of the new globalised world. In a sense, we need a post-nationalist, national project.

In years to come, the big political battleground will not be the 20th-century set-piece battles between Left and Right, capitalism and socialism, coloniser and occupier or rich and poor. Free-market capitalism and its handmaiden, liberal democracy, have produced unassailable results in terms of political freedom, economic self-fulfilment and societal sophistication. This is likely to remain the template for successful countries such as Ireland.

The next battle will be framed by the enormous movement of people around the globe and particularly, migration from the poor South to the rich North. Therefore, the new fault line is likely to be between the demands of the market state and the foundations of the nation state. Mass immigration and multiculturalism, which might be necessary to create an efficient economy, will not be tolerated by people who value the uniqueness of the nation. There is a trade-off between culture and economics and in the years ahead, culture will matter at least as much as economics. Whether we like it or not, mass global migration threatens cultures in the same way as mass global communications do. If people begin to feel alienated in their own country, they will wonder what the point is of having a successful economy when the long-term cost is that Ireland turns into Connecticut with bad weather. The dilemma for modern nations will be how to remain flexible and open without threatening the traditional culture that makes them different.

Too much Cosmopolitanism dilutes the very Hibernianism that makes us Irish. Finding that particular sweet spot, where we get the best economic performance point without undermining our culture, is almost impossible, because societies are fluid. The lesson from the rest of Europe is that it is easy to get the balance wrong: as we've noted, you import workers for an economy but get people.

Now that Ireland has become an immigrant nation and we have seen that the country can absorb considerably more people than any of us imagined possible a few years ago, we should consider what type of immigrants we want because in our successful economy and tolerant society, we have created something of value, something that has a price on it, something which should be cherished, not given away cheaply.

A successful economy and society is like a well-tended garden. The gardener spends time and effort thinking about which plants to plant, which will flourish, which will allow others enough light to blossom and how the entire ecosystem works. This doesn't happen overnight, but via a process of trial and error that, in most cases, takes years to perfect. The gardener will be cautious about introducing new plants which might overshadow some of the existing varieties. He is always weighing up, assessing and imagining what fits where. Societies and immigration policy are likely in the future to be similarly selective and planned.

There is nothing new in this contention. Most mature countries have arrived at this conclusion. So Canada and Australia have an exclusive immigration policy based on qualifications. If you have a skill that these countries are lacking, then you can acquire the requisite points for entry. This is a highly restrictive and discriminatory policy, but it works. At the moment, free travel within the EU, a community of 456 million people, means that Ireland—given that we are a magnet for immigrants and that we make up only 1% of the total EU population—could find its culture diluted quite easily. When you are small, it doesn't take a lot of people to alter the social balance.

So Ireland's dilemma, of getting the best economic performance, using the best people while at the same time not jeopardising the culture significantly, will not be solved by current EU policies. But if we look at the difference between us and other EU countries, we see that they do not have an ace up their sleeves—they do not have a literate, urban, global tribe of exiles. The exiles are precisely the soft power that countries yearn for and most importantly, if we cultivate them, our exiles will give us that competitive advantage while reinforcing Irishness. This appears to be a win-win situation where both the economy and the traditional culture are strengthened at once.

Like any big project, this reinventing Ireland—from a small country on the periphery of Europe into Greater Ireland—has to start small. Creating a network of global citizens, who may have two identities, two addresses, two allegiances, but one homeland, has to begin at the source. It starts young in the most precious, weightless resource known to man, our imaginations. Remember, our battle is to recolonise the minds of the exiles. This type of project aims to turn history inside out, to turn identity upside down and to turn Ireland into a flyweight and heavyweight champion of the 21st century.

Not only does this make sense from a future economic perspective, it is also the right thing to do. For years Ireland survived on emigrants' remittances. If you examine the Irish balance-of-payments figures in the 1930s, 1940s, 1950s and into the late-1960s, you'll find that the cash inflow from emigrants sending money home kept this country afloat. It is only right that we repay the children of these people who gave so much to us while in exile. In addition, embracing the prodigal sons would be a true sign of Irish economic success and maturity. In 1990, Germany extended its financial generosity to 100,000 ethnic Germans living in Russia—the Volga Germans. By doing so, the large paternalist German State was throwing its arms around people of German culture, even though their ancestors had left Germany four centuries previously. The German State repatriated tens of thousands of these people. It was a generous gesture that arguably, only a rich State at ease with itself could have carried through. Likewise, the Finnish government extended passports to Finnish communities in Kerelia, Northern Russia. This is another example of the home State taking responsibility for the tribe. If we follow these examples, the opportunities are limitless.

The Prodigal Sons

How could we construct the building blocks of an Irish Renaissance project? It is one thing to offer the 'right of return' to the exiles, but how would we nurture their Irishness and make more concrete their sense of who they are and their connection to us? To visualise this, let's go back to rainy summers in rural Ireland before Tesco, holiday villages, treatment rooms and destination hotels, to a grainy world of Cadet cola, Pete's Peanuts, Ford Cortinas and the *bean an tí*.

Odd as it may sound to many people who have been biased by hearing miserable stories about Limerick, I refuse to believe that anything bad can come out of that city. Limerick in my mind is a beautiful place full of promise. It is the centre of all things that are good about this country.

The reason for my affection for 'Stab City' is because my first teenage girlfriend came from Limerick. Holding hands as two innocent fourteen-year-olds behind the *céilí* hall is my abiding memory of the Gaeltacht. Ballingeary, a tiny Gaeltacht village in West Cork, is etched on my memory as a magical place, where every schoolboy's dreams come true. I spent three fantastic summers there, where suburban Dubs like me learned Irish, hurling, '*baint an aer*', and how to react when someone stuck their tongue down your throat. Ballingeary was part of growing up, meeting people from all over the country, learning how to inhale, rolling Golden Virginia and realising that Limerick girls were special. They wrote letters.

The Gaeltacht also served to remind many thousands of Irish children of our Gaelic heritage. We had a language that could be spoken, we had a culture that was vibrant but most of all, we had a common history. Now, plenty would argue that it was jaundiced, nationalist and limited, but so, too, is the story of any nation. We want our history and our narrative to be served in easily digestible portions.

'Give me the boy at seven and I'll show you the man.' Although there is some debate about the origin of the expression, it's been credited to the Jesuits. The Jesuits' point is the importance of education and schooling when children are young and educators believe that when a child's brain and personality are being formed, experiences can stay with them for the rest of their lives, making them who they are. Most child psychologists would agree. The Gaeltacht was formative.

As a building block of the Irish Renaissance, we could repeat this type of formative experience on a global level. It has been done before. How did Israel manage to make fervent Israeli supporters out of deracinated, secular, non-practising, fifth-generation Russian émigré Jews from New York who'd been in America since the 1890s? When asked this question, a senior Israeli advisor responded, 'Simple, we slept with them'. She was referring to the fact that so many thousands of American, British, French and Argentinian Jewish teenagers go to Israel every summer to learn a bit of Hebrew, learn a bit about biblical history, about Israeli culture and generally to recharge their Jewishness. They are doing what we did in the Gaeltacht. They stay with Israeli families, imbibe the atmosphere, go out to clubs, go to summer camp and often have their first experience with a local girl or boy. This makes them Israeli for life. The connection is fused. They return to wherever they came from, get on with their lives, but will always support Israel. They will feel a proximity they didn't have before their visit. For many, that'll be the end of it. They may marry non-Jews, as 50% of American Jews are doing at the moment. But they go back to their own country with ties to their ancestors, allegiance to their heritage, connections to their homeland. Most importantly, a network has opened up tying people of different backgrounds, languages, life experiences and different ways of doing things, together. The network is an economic goldmine, something other countries can only dream of.

We could do the same. We could involve ourselves in a large Gaeltachtisation project, where the children of Irish exiles would be encouraged to come to Ireland for a few weeks in the summer. The State would set up immersion courses for our American, British, Australian, Canadian and Argentinian cousins. This initiative would be heavily subsidised by the government and, as is the case in Israel, could also be financed by philanthropic gifts from the Diaspora and Irish business people. This would make Ireland open to as many Irish people as possible and in turn would form the basis of a commercial network that would ultimately span the globe. These teenagers could learn about the country, its history, about the GAA and literature. They could see the sights, hang out with Irish children of the same age and be hosted in Irish families. There would also be language courses to give them some idea of what many of their ancestors who left this country might have sounded like. Ireland would then serve as a recharging board for the Diaspora, making real the stories their grandmothers told them. This would be open to everyone who can trace his or her roots. We would set up an online genealogy service. This would allow them to stay in the same areas from which their ancestors emigrated and give them a real sense of place.

The second Irish Renaissance would shape their formative teenage experiences, create a bond with the country and would ultimately be fun. This would make them much more likely to come back. Some might ultimately emigrate and settle in Ireland, but this project would give Ireland access to the soft power of the Diaspora. We would have an option on their talent, a right of first refusal on the brain and so expand our labour pool. The crux is to make us economically stronger by making us lighter and deepening their sense of who they are and where they are from.

This connection, once made, can now be reinforced by the Internet, every day from anywhere in the world. The Net offers the exiles an extraordinary opportunity to promote such collaboration. The spread of BeBo, MySpace, YouTube and any number of similar sites shows the possibility of diverse communities forming around interests, identities, obsessions.

The promotion of Ireland as the homeland for the tribe would be designed to recharge their sometimes vague, sometimes acute sense of Irishness. Nostalgia is a powerful emotion and connections such as these are treasured by many of our exiles. We sometimes laugh when an American speaks with dewy eyes about his great-grandfather leaving Wexford or Cork. We doubt their *bona fides*, but these people feel Irish. This is where they are from. This is their home. Equally, if your Irish-born parents bring you up in London as Irish, how disparaging is it to be called a Plastic Paddy? The onus is now on us. It's time we respected our own tribe and appreciated the enormous economic potential of the exiles. If we give them something, they are more likely to give us something back in return.

The vision is to infuse these British, American, Argentinian, Canadian and Australian teenagers with a firm sense of who they are, their heritage and how their families came to live in Ottawa, Rosario or Perth. It would also serve to tell them that we value them. They are not in a cultural vacuum when they talk about being Irish. (There is more to Irishness than occasional visits to the Irish pub, although their success and ubiquity reveals just how strong the brand actually is.)

The enthusiasm of the wandering Irish for a connection with their past is sometimes underestimated by us, the marooned Irish, who could be accused of cultural negligence. Witness our curled-lip reaction to our own language and culture and contrast it with the way in which the Diaspora has taken to traditional music—it is hard not to conclude that Ireland has, at times, been wasted on the Irish.

And when you look at the fact that five of the giants of the first Gaelic Renaissance—James Connolly, Eamon de Valera, Jim Larkin, Erskine Childers and Desmond Fitzgerald—were foreign-born sons of exiles, you realise that sometimes, when things are in front of your face, you don't appreciate them.

As the returning Jews have done in Israel, the Diaspora will inject vibrancy and enthusiasm into both our contemporary and traditional culture while at the same time opening up economic opportunities all over the world. Anything that makes the tribe stronger makes the homeland stronger. In time the relationship becomes symbiotic. The brand gets deeper and ultimately, we could turn the Irish tribe into the largest sales force in the world, selling Ireland first to themselves and then to others. No other small country on earth has this potential.

Think about the opportunities for trade alone. Trade is made much easier if you know someone or are recommended by someone. By building a worldwide community, we open up opportunities in the remotest parts of the world with people who are equally at home here and there. This is like having a global network of ambassadors for Ireland, Irish products, Irish culture and Irish know-how. This is payback time for the exiled generations and the resulting economic opportunities are immeasurable.

Historically, the true sign of a nation's strength was the ability to project its power. This was traditionally achieved by military ends, conquering countries and territories and setting up colonies. The Irish tribal network would allow us to project our feather-light economic power way beyond the boundaries of the State, deepening the Irish brand. Ireland's prodigal sons are an ideal national weapon in an era of soft power.

At this stage, it is hard to know how many exiles would resettle here. In the case of Israel in recent years, only a small number of Jews from outside chose to immigrate for good. Indeed, permanent settlement is not necessary. Many people have and will have what is called 'modular' careers where they do one job for a while and then turn to another. In this context and given the increased mobility of global labour, a four- or five-year stretch here would be very attractive for them and highly beneficial for us. By giving passports to every Irish person, we would open the door to a new type of immigrant, a pioneering one.

Exiles who might come home will be doing so for lifestyle reasons. Like well off Jews from Terenure who emigrate to Israel, they would make such a decision for deep cultural, rather than economic, reasons. This self-selection process is more likely to attract the more educated of the exiles.

Internationally, we would be pushing on an open door because, unlike the Israelis, we have no enemies. Who could object to the Irish State seeking to look after the global Irish tribe who supported us for so long? This idea threatens no-one. We are neutral, we didn't take anyone's land and we didn't invade anyone's country. We have no need for brute strength. We live in a good neighbourhood. Ireland would be advertised as the largest English-speaking workforce in Europe, in a country the size of a postage stamp. We would be back to Enterprise Ireland's 'Irish Mind' campaign, but now there would be millions of Bonos.

Imagine, just for a minute, an economy which is high-tech, but the culture is grounded, resilient and a source of inspiration, rather than some bland counterfeit concoction. This is, as they say in the business world, the USP.

Remember that the driving force behind this type of Irish Renaissance is primarily an economic policy, with positive cultural spin-offs. This makes it the opposite of the old-fashioned nationalist initiatives which put culture first and economics second. The new idea is open-armed Hibernianism for a Cosmopolitan age, rather than closed-shop nationalism for an Imperial age. It is the HiCo manifesto, half-Hibernian, half-Cosmopolitan. Dreams of nationalism are leavened by the realities of globalisation, where no-one is threatened and everyone is enhanced by having a national rejuvenation project as a common goal.

Apart from issuing passports and giving the teenage children of the exiles an opportunity—like our Gaeltacht years—to familiarise themselves with the country, how would the plan be put in place and marketed? If we look back to the spread of Irish Catholicism in the poorer parts of the world, we see Irish priests were at the vanguard of the missionary movements. Everywhere you go in Africa or Latin America, there are Irish missionaries. We could learn from them. The State could create a new Department of the Diaspora which would target Irish communities all over the world, via bodies like the Catholic Church, the schools system and the Internet, as well as the well-established Irish networks, such as the Ancient Order of Hibernians, The Ireland Funds, Tourism Ireland, Enterprise Ireland and of course, the diplomatic service. In fact, now that the St Andrews Agreement has been signed and Stormont is up and running, there must be hundreds of idle civil servants who could be diverted from the highly 20th-century border conflict to the profoundly 21st-century Irish Renaissance project. These diplomats could be sent out to spread the word as Hiberno-missionaries, half-national proselytisers, half-trade delegates. In a project to redefine Irishness and re-position Ireland for the 21st century, it is imperative that all the power of the State is utilised.

The Hub

The Diaspora holds the key to our future because Ireland has to turn itself into a talent hub if we are to stay ahead of the game. If we can achieve this, we will not only give our economy a shot in the arm, but we will generate a renaissance in Irish culture, literature and language. We will be the only country to use globalisation to enhance, not dilute, what makes us different.

From an economic perspective, this is the only avenue open to us. In the world of Wezzonomics, capital is mobile and every economic innovation will be copied. The only difference between countries will be the grey matter of their workforces. As rich countries like Ireland can't compete on costs with Asia, we have to do something different. We need capacity and where better to get it but from the Diaspora?

This is a self-sufficient manifesto where Ireland relies on the Tribe. We are Europeans, which gives us access to the EU, but this is not enough because it is not unique. However, fusing EU access with the talent of the exile would give us an edge. They would bring their Anglo-American attitudes to work and bring capital and brainpower, networks and experience to us, making this island the most exciting business location in Europe, if not the world. Under the cloak of Irish culture and the Diaspora, we would be piggybacking on the Australian, American or Argentinian education systems, taking their graduates after their education has been paid for. (Just what the UK did with the Irish brain-drain of the 1980s, where one in every four graduates from this country emigrated.)[2]

But these homecomings are not likely to be permanent. It is probable that the returned migrant will keep the passport of his or her home country. The Irish homecoming gives people a chance to see other parts of the world, experience other cultures and use Ireland as a base from which to explore Europe.

But how does soft power translate into hard economics? In the future, with capital mobile, the country that has the best brains wins. Yet we can't indefinitely beat the competition. So, rather than think of Ireland as a home for the Diaspora, think of us a good host for creative people. We will host industry that we are good at. The exiles are the extra unique resource. We are applying the same logic we applied when we gave American multinationals a tax break in the 1990s, except today we don't need their capital as much as their brains. We also need their capacity.

Capacity is crucial. Ireland needs to reposition itself as the European hub for any company that wants to produce high-end goods and services in Europe, whether they be professional services like banking and finance or high tech services like software development. To do this we need capacity and, most of all, people.

When Microsoft's CEO, Steve Ballmer, visited Ireland in 2006, he didn't quiz Enterprise Ireland about costs or taxes; it is assumed that Ireland is a rich country now. There is no point trying to get cheap labour here: that's what China will do. What Ballmer was concerned about was people. How many graduates can Ireland produce? If Ireland wants to remain as Microsoft's, Google's or Pfizer's European hub, we have to be able either to provide or host the brainpower. If we can, there should be no limit to the investment here. If we can't, then the US giants would have to go somewhere else and the Uruguay meltdown of the 1950s is staring us straight between the eyes.

During the World Cup of 2006, Microsoft in Sandyford had a sweepstake, with 40 different nationalities represented. (Of course it didn't include Ireland, because we didn't even qualify for the competition.) The company is already operating as a hub, with employees from every country playing at the World Cup. When you go into the canteen at Microsoft, you are as likely to hear Italian spoken as English. There are groups of Spaniards, French and the multilingual Scandinavians. It is then you realise that hosting is the key to the future. We are an incubator. We are hot-housing talented people from all over the world here and this is the way forward. The model is now not the cost of labour, but the ability of the company in a certain location to attract the right type of workers.

In Ireland, the local labour force is no longer enough. Microsoft locates in Europe to attract European, not just Irish, labour. The new model, where cheap flights allow an IT professional from Milan or Warsaw to work in Dublin, yet fly home twice a month, means that the key for Ireland is not necessarily to fall over ourselves to train our own graduates up to a certain level, but to make sure that there are enough talented people here at every level, and that the best and brightest come to work here. The Diaspora could provide those people, reinforcing Irishness and improving competitiveness at the same time.

This is what we could term the French Open economic model. This tennis tournament is held in France, the players are a combination of foreign and local, but the French rarely win it. So they provide the right environment, the right infrastructure, the right courts and host the best gig. After a while, they become such great hosts that the fixture becomes permanent. Then even if costs rise, they are still ahead of the pack. This is what the City of London has achieved. None of the big investment banks are British. They are American, German and Swiss, yet they all need to be in London because that is where the talent is. The City of London hosts the most successful financial market in the world.

Now think of Ireland, when the Diaspora comes home with their superior education and their 'go get 'em' entrepreneurial attitudes. The selling proposition of Ireland becomes irresistible for any global company. The company gets the best of Europe, in a tax-friendly environment with the crucial added bonus of the best of the Irish Diaspora, by which we mean the most successful exiles ever.

The Time is Now

It is often said that Ireland punches above its weight on the international stage. Others marvel at how such a small country can grab a disproportionate share of the global limelight. Well, it's not so much that the Irish punch above their weight, but that the Irish State lets us all down, all 70 million of us, by the paucity of its own ambition. The State is the custodian of the tribe. Ireland has a responsibility to the Irish. Without active guardianship from the home country, the tribe will not flourish and, in a few generations, this extraordinary opportunity will dissipate. For generations, Irish communities abroad have been replenished by new migrants, new exiles who constantly topped up the Diaspora, ensuring that the cycle of emigration, settling down, passing on and resuscitating the tribe repeated itself. This is no longer happening.

We appear to punch above our weight because up to now we have not told anyone, ourselves included, how substantial we actually are. Ireland doesn't realise how strong the Irish brand is. Irishness has been constructed inside the minds of, and propagated by, the Diaspora since the Famine. Today, it is the deepest resource any country could have. It is time for the Irish State to live up to its responsibility to be the dynamo behind an Irish Renaissance that transcends borders.

We can re-imagine Ireland and reposition ourselves for the 21st century. No other country is doing or can do this because no other small country has a bigger Diaspora, no other nation has fewer enemies, no other people have a stronger brand and no other tribe is as flexible.

Globalisation could be the golden era of the Irish. Our time has come. We can turn our historical defeat into a future victory. In the successful Republic of Ireland we have the platform, in the peaceful Northern Ireland we have the symbol and in the Diaspora we have the unique resource. For years, the exiled Irish reminded us of our economic failure back at home. They were traditionally the victims of a failed Ireland; in our globalised future they will be the saviours of a successful Ireland. The tribe is the catalyst which will power the Hibernian lift-off. All we need is the courage to imagine a Greater Ireland that transcends geography, where the country is the mother ship and the tribe is the nation.

There is nothing particularly new in this generational idea. The Irish Constitution aspires to it. As Article 2 states:

> ... *the Irish nation cherishes its special affinity with people of Irish ancestry living abroad who share its cultural identity and heritage.*

Let's make this 'special affinity' a reality by calling them home.

APPENDIX

The Impact of Proximity to Private Schools on House Prices in Dublin.*

South Dublin (City and County)		Semi-d			Detached			€ premium	% premium
		3-beds	4-beds	5-beds	3-beds	4-beds	5-beds	4-beds semi-d	All
All properties listed on Daft.ie, January 2006–March 2007									
Overall average		€625,014	€742,669	€963,925	€707,724	€843,625	€1,094,956		
Irish Times Ranking Top 10 Private School		€806,495	€961,389	€1,247,805	€916,126	€1,092,076	€1,417,426	€218,719	29.5%
Rank 10–20 Private School		€688,852	€824,152	€1,065,759	€782,492	€932,776	€1,210,667	€78,483	10.6%
Rank 20–50 Private School		€625,939	€746,155	€968,449	€711,026	€847,584	€1,100,096	€3,486	0.5%
Annual Fees Dearest (> €4000)		€685,480	€817,133	€1,060,572	€778,662	€928,210	€1,204,742	€74,463	10.0%
Middle (€3000–€4000)		€780,062	€929,879	€1,206,907	€886,100	€1,056,282	€1,370,969	€187,209	25.2%
Cheapest (€2000–€3000)		€662,964	€790,291	€1,025,734	€753,084	€897,720	€1,165,168	€47,622	6.4%
Fee-ranking combination Top Tier		€762,783	€909,282	€1,180,175	€866,473	€1,032,886	€1,340,602	€166,613	22.4%
Second Tier		€655,093	€780,909	€1,013,555	€744,143	€887,062	€1,151,335	€38,239	5.1%
Third Tier		€661,912	€789,338	€1,024,107	€751,890	€896,296	€1,163,320	€46,368	6.2%
Properties mapped to a building or estate on Daft.ie, January 2006–March 2007									
By Distance Top 10 Private School	Within 1km	€723,088	€861,963	€1,118,759	€821,382	€979,135	€1,270,838	€119,294	16.1%
	1–2km	€642,215	€765,558	€993,652	€729,515	€869,625	€1,128,702	€22,889	3.1%
Top 20 Private School	Within 1km	€639,563	€762,515	€989,683	€726,616	€866,168	€1,124,216	€19,846	2.7%
	1–2km	€630,463	€751,549	€975,450	€716,166	€853,711	€1,108,048	€8,879	1.2%
Top 50 Private School	Within 1km	€649,392	€774,709	€1,005,510	€738,235	€880,020	€1,142,195	€32,040	4.3%
	1–2km	€647,397	€772,330	€1,002,422	€735,969	€877,318	€1,138,687	€29,661	4.0%
Dearest (> €4000)	Within 1km	€717,729	€855,575	€1,110,467	€815,294	€971,878	€1,261,419	€112,906	15.2%
	1–2km	€634,724	€756,628	€982,045	€721,006	€859,481	€1,115,537	€13,959	1.9%
Middle (€3000–€4000)	Within 1km	€682,349	€813,399	€1,055,727	€775,104	€923,969	€1,199,238	€70,730	9.5%
	1–2km	€633,312	€755,540	€980,630	€719,969	€858,245	€1,113,933	€12,871	1.7%
Cheapest (€2000–€3000)	Within 1km	€646,560	€771,214	€1,000,974	€734,905	€876,050	€1,137,042	€28,545	3.8%
	1–2km	€655,201	€781,638	€1,013,724	€744,266	€887,208	€1,151,525	€38,368	5.2%
Top Tier	Within 1km	€725,932	€866,354	€1,123,159	€824,612	€982,986	€1,275,836	€122,684	16.5%
	1–2km	€636,729	€759,006	€985,129	€723,272	€862,182	€1,119,043	€16,337	2.2%
Second Tier	Within 1km	€675,648	€805,412	€1,045,360	€767,493	€914,896	€1,187,462	€52,743	8.4%
	1–2km	€620,097	€739,191	€959,411	€704,390	€839,674	€1,089,829	-€3,478	-0.5%
Third Tier	Within 1km	€645,697	€769,708	€999,019	€733,470	€874,338	€1,134,821	€27,038	3.6%
	1–2km	€654,429	€780,117	€1,012,529	€743,385	€886,163	€1,150,168	€27,448	5.0%
By Area Rank 1		€783,616	€934,116	€1,212,407	€890,137	€1,061,095	€1,377,216	€191,447	25.8%
Rank 2		€735,000	€876,162	€1,137,188	€834,512	€995,264	€1,291,772	€133,493	18.0%
Rank 3		€621,133	€740,427	€961,014	€705,567	€841,077	€1,091,650	-€2,243	-0.3%
Fee 1		€718,619	€856,636	€1,111,844	€816,305	€973,083	€1,262,984	€113,967	15.3%
Fee 2		€760,534	€906,661	€1,176,773	€863,975	€1,029,908	€1,336,738	€163,992	22.1%
Fee 3		€649,770	€774,564	€1,205,321	€728,037	€879,855	€1,141,980	€31,894	4.3%
Comb 1		€767,403	€914,754	€1,187,329	€871,726	€1,039,148	€1,348,730	€172,125	23.2%
Comb 2		€679,851	€810,458	€1,051,909	€772,321	€920,628	€1,194,901	€67,789	9.1%
Comb 3			€775,100	€1,006,017	€738,608	€880,464	€1,142,771	€32,431	4.4%

*(Source: *Daft.ie*)

NOTES AND REFERENCES

Chapter 1 Transit Nation 1 (pages 1–19)
1. Dublin Airport Authority statistics.
2. ibid.
3. MAC company sources.
4. Consulate General of Ireland, New York.
5. Dublin Airport Authority.
6. Author's calculation based on Dublin Airport Authority figures.
7. Population and Migration Estimates 2006, Central Statistics Office, *www.cso.ie.*
8. Dublin Airport Authority.
9. ibid.
10. ibid.
11. Passenger Movement by Air 2006, Central Statistics Office, *www.cso.ie.*
12. *Irish Independent*, 4 June 2007.
13. World Demographic Trends *www.nationmaster.com.*

Chapter 2 Vertigo (pages 20–28)
1. 2006 Census of Population: Volume 1—Population Classified by Area, *www.cso.ie.*
2. 2006 Census of Population, Principal Demographic Results, *www.cso.ie* and ESRI Quarterly Economic Bulletin, Spring 2007, *www.esri.ie.*
3. Kelly, John and Menton, Aisling: 'Residential Mortgages: Borrowing for Investments', Central Bank Quarterly Bulletin Q2, 2007.
4. Eurostat Regional Yearbook, 2006.
5. European Property Survey, Era Immobilier, 2005.

Chapter 3 The Jagger Generation (pages 29–45)
1. Principal Statistics: Migration Statistics, Central Statistics Office, *www.cso.ie.*
2. Principal Statistics: Marriages, Births and Deaths, Central Statistics Office, *www.cso.ie.*
3. Department of Justice, Equality and Law Reform.
4. Author's calculation using the population pyramid structure from the 2006 Census of Population.
5. Hannan, D. and Commins, P.: 'The Significance of Small-scale Landholders in Ireland's Socio-economic Transformation', ESRI 1994.

6. ibid.
7. Boyle G., McElligott R., and O' Leary J.: 'Public–Private Earning Differentials in Ireland', ESRI, 1 July 2004.
8. Hannan, D. and Commins, P., op. cit.
9. ibid.

Chapter 4 The Perfect Storm (pages 46–62)

1. Annual Demographia International Housing Affordability Survey 2006.
2. Irish Economic Commentary, Goodbody Stockbrokers, Q4 2006.
3. Irish Mortgage Broker Survey, Davy Stockbrokers, 26 February 2007.
4. Quarterly Survey of Construction, Central Statistics Office, Q1 2007, www.cso.ie.
5. 2006 Census of Population, Principal Demographic Results, Central Statistics Office, www.cso.ie.
6. ibid.
7. Construction and Housing in Ireland, Central Statistics Office, www.cso.ie.
8. www.finfacts.ie, March 2007.
9. Irish Economic Commentary, Goodbody Stockbrokers, Q4 2006.
10. ibid.
11. International Trade and Investment Report, Forfás, 2005.
12. ibid.
13. www.centralbank.ie.
14. ibid.
15. ibid.
16. 2006 Census of Population, www.cso.ie.
17. 'Profile of Lithuania', US Department of State, February 2007. The minimum wage in Lithuania is $225 per month.
18. Eurostat—www.ec.europa.eu.

Chapter 5 Botox Nation (pages 63–75)

1. Industry Profile Pharmaceuticals, Enterprise Ireland, 2005.
2. Statistics on Cosmetic Surgery, American Society for Aesthetic Plastic Surgery, 2006.
3. United States Census 2006, www.census.gov/pressrelease/www/releases/archive.
4. Irish Council for Science, Technology and Innovation.
5. Irish Pharmaceutical and Healthcare Association.
6. Pfizer Company Sources.
7. www.reductil.co.uk.
8. The Independent, 11 August 2006.

9. Department of Enterprise, Trade and Employment, press release, 29 April 2003.
10. Berkeley Clinic, Walkinstown, Dublin.

Chapter 6 The Bono Boomers (pages 76–85)

1. Fahey, Tony: 'Fertility in Ireland: Trends and Prospects', ESRI, 2002.
2. Delaney, Enda: 'Irish Emigration since 1921', Economic and Social History Society of Ireland, 2002.
3. *www.esri.ie.*
4. Bratman, Steven, *Health Food Junkies: Orthorexia Nervosa: Overcoming the Obsession with Healthful Eating,* Broadway, 2002.
5. 2006 Census of Population, Travel Statistics. *www.cso.ie.*

Chapter 7 The Hitchhiker's Guide to the Economy (pages 86–94)

1. Department of Transport and the Marine, Information on the Provisional Driving Licence, *www.transport.ie.*
2. IIB Bank, Irish Housing Market Outlook 2006.
3. Chancellor, Edward, *Devil Take the Hindmost—A History of Financial Speculation,* Penguin, 2000.
4. Annual Demographia International Housing Affordability Survey 2006.
5. ibid.
6. Central Bank of Ireland Quarterly Bulletin Spring 2007, *www.centralbank.ie.*
7. ibid.
8. 2006 Census of Population, Principal Demographic Results, *www.cso.ie.*
9. Central Bank of Ireland Quarterly Bulletin Winter 2006, *www.centralbank.ie.*
10. 2006 Census of Population, Ages and Marital Status, *www.cso.ie.*
11. 'First Time Buyers in the Housing Market', Permanent TSB and ESRI, 2005.
12. Bank of Ireland/MoneyMate: unpublished research.
13. 2006 Census of Population, Principal Demographic Results, *www.cso.ie.*
14. Bank of Ireland/MoneyMate, unpublished research.

Chapter 8 The Jugglers (pages 95–106)

1. Reagan, Ronald: Official Announcement of Intent to Run, New York, 13 November 1979.
2. de Tocqueville, Alexis: *Democracy in America*, Volume 1.
3. Quarterly National Household Survey, Educational Attainment 2002 to 2005, Central Statistics Office, *www.cso.ie.*
4. Unpublished work in progress, The Geary Institute, UCD.
5. Author's calculations adapted from sample costing from the National Children's Nursery Association.
6. National Children's Nursery Association.
7. *www.daft.ie.* For full survey results, see Appendix.

Chapter 9 Denial (pages 107–16)

1. Kelly, Morgan, 'On the likely Extent of Falls in House Prices', UCD Department of Economics, April 2007.
2. ibid.
3. ibid.
4. ibid.
5. ibid.
6. Honkapohja, Seppo, Koskela, Erkki, Gerlach, Stefan and Reichlin, Lucrezia: 'The Economic Crisis of the 1990s in Finland', Economic Policy, Vol 14, No 29, October 1999.

Chapter 10 Osama's Boom (pages 117–32)

1. *www.bloomberg.com.*
2. ibid.
3. ibid.
4. Balance of Trade Figures, International Monetary Fund, *www.imf.com.*
5. O'Sullivan Pat, 'The Wealth of the Nation', Bank of Ireland, July 2006.
6. ibid.
7. ibid.
8. ibid.
9. ibid.
10. ibid.
11. ibid.

Chapter 12 Transit Nation 2 (pages 145–58)

1. Borjas, George J., Grogger, Jeffrey and Hanson, Gordon H., 'Immigration and African-American Employment Opportunities', National Bureau of Economic Research. September 2006.
2. ibid.
3. *www.esri.ie.*
4. 2006 Census of Population, *www.cso.ie.*
5. An Post internal sources.

Chapter 13 Black Irish (pages 159–73)

1. Stott, Richard, *Workers in the Metropolis: Class, Ethnicity and Youth in Antebellum New York City*, Cornell University Press, 1990.
2. *www.cso.ie.*
3. Ignatiev, Noel, *How the Irish Became White*, Routledge, 1997.
4. *www.cso.ie.*
5. Stott, Richard, op cit.
6. *www.cso.ie.*
7. Stott, Richard, op cit.

8. ibid.
9. Anbinder, Tyler, *Nativism and Slavery: The Northern Know Nothings and the Politics of the 1850s,* Oxford University Press, 1992

Chapter 14 Reckless Trading (pages 174–89)

1. James Hanratty is a fictitious character but based on an amalgam of research and facts about Irish emigrants to Argentina and Uruguay. The *City of Dresden* did indeed leave Cobh in January 1889, bound for the River Plate. In particular, the author refers to research by Eduardo A. Coghlan (*El Aporte de los Irlandeses a la Formación de la Nación Argentina*, Buenos Aires, 1982) on the Irish in Argentina and Uruguay. The author also studied historical newspaper reports in the *Southern Cross* and travelled to Argentina and Uruguay to interview direct descendants of Irish emigrants who arrived from the 1880s onwards.
2. O'Rourke, Kevin H. and Williamson, Jeffrey G., *Globalization and History— An Evolution of a Nineteenth-Century Atlantic Economy*, Massachusetts Institute of Technology, 1999.
3. ibid.
4. Bulmer-Thomas, Victor, *An Economic History of Latin America Since Independence.* Cambridge University Press, 2nd ed 2003.
5. ibid.
6. ibid.
7. *www.irlandeses.org.*
8. Bulmer-Thomas, op cit.
9. Enterprise Ireland.
10. *www.grianan.com.uy.*

Chapter 15 Made in China (pages 190–201)

1. Irish Consulate General, Shanghai.
2. ibid.
3. ibid.
4. General Motors, China.
5 Irish Consulate General, Shanghai.
6. General Motors, China.
7. Irish Consulate General, Shanghai.
8. General Motors, China.

Chapter 16 Degeneration (pages 202–13)

1. O'Rourke, Kevin H. and Williamson, Jeffrey G., op cit.
2. Ferguson, Niall, 'Geopolitical Risk and the Markets', 29 May 2007, *www.schroders.com.*
3. ibid.

4. ibid.

Chapter 17 The Redhead Renaissance (pages 214–31)

1. *www.olivierblanchard.org.*
2. *www.esri.ie.*
3. ibid.
4. In September 2006, in Regensburg, Germany, Pope Benedict XVI, quoting a 1391 speech entitled 'Dialogue Held With A Certain Persian, the Worthy Mouterizes, in Anakara of Galatia' said: *'Show me just what Muhammad brought that was new and there you will find things only evil and inhuman, such as his command to spread by the sword the faith he preached.'* Muslims around the world reacted against this reference.
5. *www.asiantimes.com/spengler.*

Chapter 18 The Jack Charlton Theory of Economics (pages 232–43)

1. Principal Statistics: Migration, *www.cso.ie.*
2. Elmann, Richard, *James Joyce*, Penguin, 1984.
3. Florida, Richard, *The Rise of the Creative Class, and how it's Transforming Work, Leisure, Community and Everyday Life*, Basic Books, 2002.
4. Landes, David, *The Poverty and Wealth of Nations: Why Some are So Rich and Some So Poor*, W.W. Norton, 1998.

Chapter 19 The Global Tribe (pages 244–60)

1. US Census 2000, Ethnic Breakdown.
2. ibid.
3. ibid.
4. Canadian Census 2002, Australian Census 2001, Argentinian Census 2000.
5. Trade Figures, *www.cso.ie.*
6. Labour Market Statistics, *www.cso.ie.*
7. Italian Embassy, Dublin and *www.italiansinlondon.com.*
8. 2006 Census of Population.
9. Guinness/ICM survey: 'Be Irish, be counted', BBC, 16 March 2001.
10. ibid.
11. ibid.
12. Australian Census data 1986 and 2001.

BIBLIOGRAPHY

— Anbinder, Tyler, *Nativism and Slavery—The Northern Know Nothings and the Politics of the 1850s*, Oxford University Press, 1992.

— Bernstein, Peter L., *The Power of Gold: the History of an Obsession*, John Wiley & Sons, 2000.

— Brooks, David, *Bobos in Paradise: The New Upper Class and How they Got There*, Simon & Schuster, 2002.

— Brooks, David, *On Paradise Drive: How we Live Now (And Always Have) in the Future Tense*, Simon & Schuster, 2004.

— Bulmer-Thomas, Victor, *An Economic History of Latin America Since Independence*, Cambridge University Press, 2003.

— Bruck, Connie, *The Predator's Ball: the Inside Story of Drexel Burnham and the Junk Bond Raiders*, Penguin, 1989.

— Bywater, Michael, *Big Babies—Or: Why Can't We Just Grow Up?*, Granta, 2006.

— Chancellor, Edward, *Devil Take the Hindmost—A History of Financial Speculation*, Plume, 2000.

— Coogan, Tim Pat, *Wherever Green is Worn—The Story of the Irish Diaspora*, Arrow, 2002.

— Ellmann, Richard, *James Joyce*, Penguin, 1984.

— Emmott, Bill, *20:21 Vision—The Lessons of the 20th Century for the 21st*, Allen Lane, 2003.

— Ernst, Robert, *Immigrant Life in New York City 1825–1863*, Syracuse University Press, 1994.

— Fahey, Tony, Hayes, Bernadette C. and Sinnott, Richard, *Conflict and Consensus—A study of Values and Attitudes in the Republic of Ireland and Northern Ireland*, Brill Leiden, 2006.

— Fanning, John, *The Importance of Being Branded—An Irish Perspective*, The Liffey Press, 2006.

— Florida, Richard, *The Rise of the Creative Class, and how it's Transforming Work, Leisure, Community and Everyday Life*, Basic Books, 2002.

— Florida, Richard, *The Flight of the Creative Class: The New Global Competition for Class*, Harper Business, 2005.

— Fox, Kate, *Watching the English, The Hidden Rules of English Behaviour*, Hodder & Stoughton, 2004.

— Frank, Robert H., *Luxury Fever: Money and Happiness in an Era of Excess*, The Free Press, 1999.

— Friedman, Benjamin M., *The Moral Consequences of Economic Growth*, Vintage, 2005.
— Friedman, Thomas, *The World is Flat—A Brief History of the Globalized World in the 21st Century*, Allen Lane, 2005.
— Fussell, Paul, *Class: A Guide Through The American Status System*, Touchstone, 1992.
— Galbraith, John Kenneth, *The Affluent Society*, Mariner Books, 1998.
— Gave, Charles, Kaletsky, Anatole and Gave, Louis-Vincent, *Our Brave New World*, Gavecal Research, 2005.
— Gladwell, Malcolm, *The Tipping Point: How Little Things can Make a Big Difference*, Abacus, 2002.
— Gollub, James O., *The Decade Matrix*, Addison Wesley, 1991.
— Gribbin, John, *Science—A History: 1543–2001*, Allen Lane, 2002.
— Hutton, Will, *The Writing on the Wall: China and The West in the 21st Century*, Little, Brown, 2007.
— Ignatiev, Noel, *How the Irish Became White*, Routledge, 1997.
— Jacobs, Jane, *Cities and the Wealth of Nations: Principles of Economic Life*, Random House Inc., 1984.
— James, Oliver *Affluenza*, Vermillion, 2007.
— Kane, Michael A.C., *The Botox Book*, St Martin's Press, 2002.
— Kiberd, Declan *Inventing Ireland—The Literature of the Modern Nation*, Vintage, 1996.
— Kindleberger, Charles P., *Manias, Panics and Crashes: A History of Financial Crises*, John Wiley & Sons Inc., 2001.
— Kindleburger, Charles P. and Burns, Scott, *The Coming Generational Storm—What you Need to Know about America's Economic Future*, MIT Press, 2004.
— Krugman, Paul, *The Return of Depression Economics*, Allen Lane, 1999.
— Krugman, Paul, *The Great Unravelling: Losing Our Way in the New Century*, Allen Lane, 2003.
— Landes, David S., *The Wealth and Poverty of Nations: Why Some are so Rich and Some so Poor*, W.W. Norton, 1998.
— Leadbetter, Charles, *Up the Down Escalator, Why the Global Pessimists are Wrong*, Penguin, 2002.
— Lee, J.J. and Casey, Marion R. (eds), Glucksman Ireland House, *Making the Irish American—History and Heritage of the Irish in the United States*, New York University Press, 2006.
— Legrain, Philippe, *Immigrants—Your Country Needs Them*, Little, Brown, 2006.
— James Lovelock, *The Revenge of Gaia: Why the Earth is Fighting Back and How we can Still Save Humanity*, Allen Lane, 2006.
— Micklethwait, John and Wooldridge, Adrian, *The Company: A Short History of a Revolutionary Idea*, Weidenfeld and Nicholson, 2003.

— Micklethwait, John and Wooldridge, Adrian, *The Right Nation—Why America is Different*, Allen Lane, 2004.

— Nordau, Max, *Degeneration*, originally published New York, D. Appleton, 1895; University of Nebraska Press, 1993.

— Ó Gráda, Cormac, *Jewish Ireland in the Age of Joyce*, Princeton University Press, 2006.

— Ó Gráda, Cormac, *Ireland's Great Famine—Interdisciplinary Perspectives*, University College Dublin Press, 2006.

— O'Rourke, Kevin H. and Williamson, Jeffrey G., *Globalization and History— An Evolution of a Nineteenth-Century Atlantic Economy*, Massachusetts Institute of Technology, 1999.

— O'Sullivan, Michael J., *Ireland and the Global Question*, Cork University Press, 2006.

— Phelan, Angela A. (ed), *Who's Who in Ireland: The Influential Irish*, Madison Publications, 2006.

— Queenan, Joe, *Balsamic Dreams: a Short but Self-important History of the Baby Boomer Generation*, Picador, 2006.

— Quinn, Kevin, *Wealth Management: How Not to Throw Away your Riches*, Blackhall Publishing, 2007.

— Quinn, Peter, *Banished Children of Eve: A Novel of Civil War New York*, Penguin, 1995.

— Rees, Martin, *Our Cosmic Habitat*, Weidenfeld & Nicholson, 2002.

— Slezkine, Yuri, *The Jewish Century*, Princeton University Press, 2004.

— Stott, Richard B., *Workers in the Metropolis: Class, Ethnicity and Youth in Antebellum New York City*, Cornell University Press, 1990.

— Sullivan, Teresa A., Warren, Elizabeth and Westbrook, Jay Lawrence, *The Fragile Middle Class*, Yale University Press, 2000.

— Veblen, Thorstein, *The Theory of the Leisure Class*, Penguin, 1994.

— Warren, Elizabeth and Warren Tyagi, Amelia, *The Two-Income Trap: Why Middle-Class Mothers & Fathers are Going Broke*, Basic Books, 2003.

— Wolf, Martin, *Why Globalization Works*, Yale Nota Bene, 2005.

INDEX